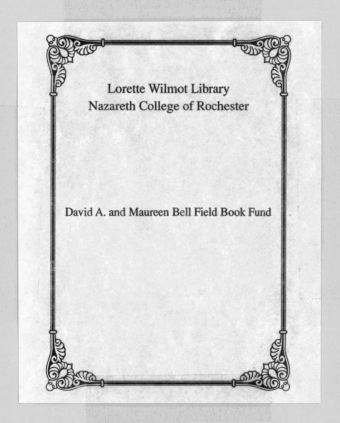

The Sacred Village

The Sacred Village

Social Change and Religious Life in Rural North China

 Thomas David DuBois

UNIVERSITY OF HAWAI'I PRESS · HONOLULU

© 2005 University of Hawai'i Press

Printed in

05 06 07 08 09 10   6 5 4 3 2 1

Library of Congress Cataloging-in-Publication Data

DuBois, Thomas David, 1969–
The sacred village : social change and religious life in rural north China /
Thomas DuBois.
p. cm.
Includes bibliographical references and index.
ISBN 0-8248-2837-2 (alk. paper)
1. Cangzhou (China)—Religious life and customs.
I. Title: Social change and religious life in rural north China.
II. Title.
BL1802.D83 2002
200'.951'152—dc22
2004006310

Designed by Chris Crochetière, BW&A Books, Inc.

Printed by The Maple-Vail Book Manufacturing Group

I should tell you, errant sir, that in these tiny places everything's discussed and everything's gossiped about; and you can be quite certain, just as I am, that a priest has to be a saint to make his flock speak well of him, especially in a village.

—Cervantes, *Don Quixote*, I, XII

Contents

Acknowledgments

To justly acknowledge all of the numerous individuals who have assisted me over the past few years would add at least one more chapter to an already lengthy book, but a few people do deserve special mention. First and foremost are Philip Huang and Kathryn Bernhardt, who provided me with years of professional guidance and personal example during my doctoral study at UCLA. Richard Gunde of the UCLA Center for Chinese Studies has been a great friend, providing me with encouragement, sound advice, and an extremely detailed critique of the text itself.

The longest period of fieldwork, from 1997 to 1998, was supported by a generous grant from the American Council of Learned Societies. During that time, I was the guest of the Tianjin Academy of Social Sciences, which was quite helpful to my work. Professor Li Shiyu, truly the great master of sectarian studies, gave me instruction, advice, and free access to his large store of materials. However great his role as an intellectual mentor, his personal example of integrity, generosity, and humility will always remain dearest to my heart. Pu Wenqi organized much of the initial stage of fieldwork, accompanied me to the villages of Cangzhou, and provided vital introductions and background. Dong Jiqun of the Tianjin Cultural Museum provided me with source materials on Cangzhou folk tales and on the Tianhou Temple of Tianjin, about which he has recently completed a monograph. In Japan, the Research Center on East Asian Culture (Tōyō Bunka Kenkyū Jō) at Tokyo University was especially helpful, introducing me to new colleagues and granting me full access to their library holdings.

Late in the dissertation phase, I was invited to participate in the conference "Religion and Chinese Society: The Transformation of a Field," organized by John Lagerwey and held at the Chinese University of Hong Kong, in which I was first introduced to the larger context of religious studies, along with an exciting new world of ideas, scholarship, and colleagues. Among the latter, my deepest thanks go to Paul Katz, who gave the rough manuscript an extremely close reading and not only saved me from making a number of embarrassing blunders, but also vastly expanded the intellectual scope and import of the final product. An earlier version of chapter 2 of this book will also appear in the conference volume of the same name, and I gratefully acknowledge the generosity of the volume editors and the Chinese University of Hong Kong Press for allowing me to reprint those materials here.

Over the years during which the dissertation was transformed into a book, I taught first in the Program in Religious Studies at Washington University, in St. Louis, and currently in the Department of History at the National University of Singapore. Each university provided me with time, funding, and facilities to work on the book, as well as opportunities to meet new friends, students, and colleagues, from whom I have benefited greatly. The maps and illustrations were drafted by Mrs. Chong Mui Gek, of the National University of Singapore Department of Geography. Finally, I would like to express my thanks and admiration to Patricia Crosby of the University of Hawai'i Press, who has been exceedingly patient throughout the publication process and has tangibly improved the text in a number of ways.

Naturally, my deepest and most heartfelt thanks go to my friends and family for their constant love and support. Tazuko Tanaka, Yao Hua, and, especially, Misako Suzuki have each given me years of friendship and have done more for me than I could ever hope to repay. My family carried me through the years of graduate school with their emotional and, all too often, financial assistance. My father, David DuBois, and sisters, Alicia and Jennifer, each of whom know the rigors of graduate education and academic life all too well, were wonderfully caring and supportive throughout the entire process.

I wish to thank my hosts in the villages of Cang County, most of whom must remain unnamed in this text. Throughout my stay, I was treated with honesty, respect, and compassion, all of which come quite naturally to these people. Their basic humanity to guests and to each other moved me deeply and imbued my scholarship with a very personal sense of mission. My task was to present the votive and organizational context that make up the religious lives of these peasants, not merely the surface accouterments as seen by the ethnographer, but also the religious experience as understood and lived by the believer. I leave it to the reader to judge my success in having done so.

Finally, this book is dedicated to my mother, Victoria, who died just as it was going to press. In many ways, she was the direct inspiration for this project. Her devotion to learning inspired each of her children to pursue a life of the mind, but, more important, it was her profound religious belief and love of mankind that led her son to recognize the same virtues in the villages of China.

Note on Conventions and Usage

This text uses pinyin romanization throughout, except in the case of direct quotations from earlier English sources. Personal names are rendered in romanized form rather than English translation.

Place names are rendered according to the following system:

1. When the final character of a village name denotes a place, the English translation is used. Most villages in the area encompassed by this study are named *cun, zhuang* (village), *ying, tun* (camp), or *si, miao* (temple). Thus, Wangzhuang is rendered as "Wang Village," rather than the redundant "Wangzhuang Village" (Wang Village Village). Similarly, certain very common conventions, such as adding the character *jia* (family) to the name of a village are translated literally. Wangjiatun is thus "Wang Family Camp." When the name of a village includes more than one surname, both names are capitalized and hyphenated. Quanwangzhuang is thus rendered as "Quan-Wang Village." To retain legibility, the names of most villages that fall outside this pattern are not translated. Thus, the village of Mumendian (Wood Door Shop) appears in pinyin.
2. The subcounty administrative unit, known variously as *zhen* and *xiang*, is translated as "township," regardless of changes in the Chinese usage.
3. *Cang* is at once the name of a city, county, and prefecture. To distinguish, I will use Cang County to denote the county, Cangzhou for the prefecture, and Cangzhou City for the city itself. A third designation, the pre-1949 Cang Township *(zhen)*, appears in the appendices, but not in the text.

Dates given according to the lunar calendar are written in the form "number of the month/day" (for example, 6/18). Dates written with the name of the month (June 18) correspond to the Western calendar.

Finally, for the safety and privacy of my informants, some personal and place names have been altered. Names of national figures, as well as those taken from published documents, are genuine and appear in the character glossary that follows the text. Other names, particularly those of persons still living, have been changed and do not appear in the character glossary.

◫ Introduction

Give or take a few days, it has been one year since the old woman was last here. At that time, she had been diagnosed with an incurable illness and been told to prepare for death. Instead, she came to the birthday celebration of a deified scholar, Dong Sihai, known and worshipped locally as the Great Teacher, to beg him to cure her illness. Now alive, healthy, and profoundly grateful, she is discharging her debt to the deity as she had promised a year ago, by draping herself in a saddle and bridle and crawling to the festival on her hands and knees. It is midwinter, and the ground is rocky and frozen; before she has even left her home village, the palms of her hands are already bloodied. Other villagers, who have heard about her miraculous recovery, line the road to witness this act of devotion, some attempting to soften her path by lining it with reed mats or corn stalks. When she reaches in the neighboring village where the birthday celebration is being held, the assembled crowd parts before her, awed by both her piety and the benevolence and power of the Great Teacher. Arriving at the festival tent where she had made her desperate plea the year before, she is overcome with emotion and unable to stand long enough even to place the incense in the burner before the tablet of the god.

This scene could be set in almost any village in late imperial China. Indeed, it seems to evoke the ahistorical quality that is often ascribed to religious belief in "traditional" societies. The fact that it occurred in February 1998 might suggest that the modern world simply had not yet caught up with this part of rural China and swept away the customs of the past. The apparent timelessness of this scene, however, also masks a great deal of change. Over the past century and a half, the village in the story and its neighboring communities have undergone constant structural, political, and social transformations. Every aspect of village life has been touched by change, not least of which is how villagers understand and relate to the sacred. Religion is hardly timeless, and numerous beliefs, customs, sacred sites, teachings, and rituals have come and gone.

1

What has remained constant is that religion continues to permeate all aspects of life in rural North China. People of all ages and stations engage the sacred in prayer and ritual, in a mentality of customary norms and mores, and in a diverse array of votive and charitable organizations. Religious groups and teachings give shape and direction to popular beliefs and concerns, and festival occasions provide both entertainment and an arena for the public expression of personal piety and commitment to the public good. Even after centuries of policy aimed at weakening, controlling, or eradicating it, local religion continues to remain as potent and vital a force in the village society of rural North China as it had been in that of early modern Europe or Tokugawa Japan.

This book will examine the varied expressions of religious life in rural North China as they intersected with the forces of historical change and evolution of local society over the course of 150 years, from the middle of the nineteenth century through the close of the twentieth. The geographic focus of this study is very limited, a small area of Cang, a county located in the southeast of Hebei Province. Over the course of 1997–1998, and again during the summers of 1999 and 2002, I conducted fieldwork in these villages, in the intervening periods collecting archival materials from libraries in Tianjin, Beijing, and Tokyo. My hope is thus to combine the anthropologist's understanding of local society with the historian's perspective on social change, the better to present the world of local religion on its own terms, and to show how an understanding of religion can shed light on aspects of the long-term evolution of rural North China.

Local Religion: The Issues

Scholarly understanding of local religion in rural North China has been based primarily on three types of source materials. The first are official records from the Qing and, to a lesser extent, those from the Republic and People's Republic. They would include central documents such as the *Veritable Records of the Qing (Qing shilu)*, as well as records of missionary affairs *(jiao'an)* and the depositions of captured religious rebels. To this category, we might add the semiofficial writings of the Confucian literati, such as the *Detailed Refutation of Heterodox Teachings (Poxie xiangbian)*, written by the mid-Qing magistrate Huang Yübian. Such records must be used with some caution, because they, like any official documents, present only the perspective of the state. Thus, when the records are interested in local religion at all, they tend to portray it as marginal or criminal, focusing primarily on instances of conflict, and by extension, on the use of religious belief as an arm of resistance or a tool of social control.[1] Other highly orthodox sources, such as county gazetteers, do provide information on significant events and landmarks, but are often so highly stylized as to reveal relatively little about local religious organization or custom.[2]

A second source is unofficial writings, both votive, such as scriptures and temple inscriptions, and descriptive accounts, such as literary portrayals of village life and reflections of folk belief in genres such as ghost stories and religious opera. Scriptures include both the official and apocryphal canons of Buddhism and Daoism and more significantly, those of the genre known as "precious scrolls" *(baojuan)*, the scriptural and historical record of the syncretic teachings known collectively as "sectarianism."[3] Temple inscriptions and other epigraphic materials from sacred sites reveal patterns in construction and patronage and reconstruct the miracle tales associated with temple cults. Literary sources, such as the genre of "strange stories," vividly depict stories of the gods and themes such as human profligacy and divine retribution.[4]

No more than official documents, however, can descriptive texts be taken as a direct expression of religious consciousness. As literature, their content was influenced by the conventions of genre, whereas the style of writing reflects a specific author and his perceived audience.[5] Thus, the prose of precious scrolls is often highly specialized, inscriptions in temples reflect the artistic and scholarly aspirations of the local literati who composed them, and the plot lines of plays or novels were altered to make them more entertaining. More fundamentally, those who actually penned these texts were quite often of a different class than the largely illiterate villagers for whom we hope the documents speak. In other words, although unofficial texts are free from direct government supervision and do suggest the sort of beliefs and ideas that may have circulated within local society, they rarely reflect the voice of the villagers themselves and cannot shed light on how ideas were manipulated or understood.[6]

Nor is the disjuncture between text and belief solely a function of class. Taking his cue from the school of microhistory, Paul Katz has shown that any religious text is a kind of public performance, whereas interpretation is a personal matter. As such, religious belief and devotion cannot simply be reduced to a function of class or any other system; the ultimate refuge of religious consciousness is in the heart and mind of the individual. Thus, although the detailed analysis of personal theology is usually reserved for religious thinkers, or at least those literary enough to have left a written record of their thoughts, it must have place in the study of popular theology as well. Outside of Chinese studies, microhistorical analysis of personal religious thought, the best known example being Carlo Ginzburg's landmark analysis of the belief system of a sixteenth-century Friulian miller, demonstrates the flexibility of individual belief, even within a highly dogmatic religious system. To paraphrase Ginzburg's own introductory statements, religion is as much personal "mentality" as mass "culture."[7]

Ethnography and fieldwork provide a third source of information on local religion and local society. Although the greatest concentration of fieldwork data in China still concerns Taiwan, Hong Kong, and increasingly, the southern provinces of Guangdong and Fujian, there is also a great deal of historical information available on North China. Many of the classic ethnographic studies of rural North China date from the Republican period, most notably those of Li Jinghan, Sidney Gamble, and the scholars of the Japanese South Manchuria Railway (Minami Mantetsu, hereafter referred to as the Mantetsu surveys). Such records are by far the most faithful representations of village society in Republican North China. Rich in data on a variety of topics, these sources often contain verbatim (although translated) records of interviews with peasants and have served as the empirical foundation for some of the most influential scholarship on rural North China.[8] Since the 1980s, the revival of opportunities to conduct research in China has resulted in an expanding number of field studies of the social history of the region. Recent works have examined the interaction between state and local society, the social dynamics of village society, and kinship structures. Fruitful cooperation between Chinese and Japanese scholars has resulted in extensive data collection projects rivaling those of the Republican period.[9] Fieldwork has also been the basis of recent work on topics related to religion, such as sectarianism, clan temples, and ritual theater.[10]

Each of these three types of materials—official, literary, and ethnographic—paints a different picture of local religion, which corresponds roughly to the disciplinary perspectives of history, humanistic religious studies, and anthropology, respectively. The difference among these pictures is often so great as to make them difficult to reconcile. Official attempts to suppress heterodox teachings focused on rooting out organizational structures, rather than policing or correcting the beliefs of ordinary individuals. Yet an analysis of Ming and Qing precious scrolls reveals the vibrancy of popular belief, the theological realm casually dismissed by the state as "wicked words" *(yao yan)*. Ethnographic studies, however, reveal that the battle between what the state would portray as its own orthodoxy and sectarian heterodoxy (for want of better terms) was not simply a tug-of-war between two poles. The ability of any religious institution, be it state or sect, to project its power and knowledge onto the real world of local society is, in reality, quite weak. Indeed, some would claim that such power is wholly illusory, existing only at the level of symbol and representation.[11]

The challenge is to combine these perspectives of policy, representation, and reception, and to demonstrate their interaction in local society. To be sure, scholars of Chinese religion have been keenly aware of the importance of both utilizing and transcending disciplinary boundaries and have produced work of extraordinary sophistication and conceptual breadth as a result.[12] Nevertheless, a great deal of territory remains unexplored, especially at the interstices. Indeed, many fundamental empirical and interpretive questions about daily religious life in rural North China remain subject to speculation. How did the successive waves of political and religious currents produced in Beijing and Tianjin actually reach the villages, and what sort of impact did they make? What sort of religious specialists lived in the village, what sort of extended networks did they represent, and how did their practice influence the everyday religiosity of the household? What role did organized teachings play in local religious life, and how did they fare under various political regimes? Perhaps most fundamentally, how did the numerous specialized layers of religious custom, performance, and knowledge interact to form a coherent whole? This study hopes to at least begin to answer some of these questions for one small part of North China.

This said, it should be emphasized that it does not intend to represent the entire North China Plain, much less to define a "North China type" of religious experience. Although ready contrasts can be made between the organization, ritual form, and social significance of religious life in rural Hebei and that in local studies of Guangdong or Fujian, it is a fundamental assumption of this book that local religion is precisely that—local. Although local society is part of a larger regional culture, it is not simply a product of that culture, but rather a discrete sphere of innovation, communication, and personal identification. Thus, rather than attempting to speak broadly for a North China (or any other) "type," this study will use the specific example of one part of Cang County to illuminate some of the larger themes of religion in the social history of rural China, which are briefly introduced below.

Local Religion and Political Change

The first question is how external changes affected local religion, how (to rephrase Charles Tilly's classic dictum of social history) ordinary villagers "lived the big changes" of policies and attitudes toward religion. From the Late Imperial period through the Republic and People's Republic, the practice of local religion became the object of increasingly ambitious programs of government control and regulation. During the Ming and Qing, central authorities attempted to infuse local and bureaucratic elites with Confucian values, but were less concerned with what Kung-chüan Hsiao called the "ideological molding" of the peasantry than in maintaining the appearance of orthodoxy around a set of common symbols and practices.[13] Especially among the lower classes, there was nothing akin to the inquisitions of Catholic Europe. Rather, the more pressing concern was the exertion of control over marginal religious figures, such as Buddhist monks, the eradication of heterodox sectarian organization, and the suppression of illicit cults.[14]

During the Republic and People's Republic, more ambitious policies were applied toward rural religion, facilitated by the ever-increasing access of central authorities to village life. Republican reformers attempted to free up local resources by tilling cemeteries into farmland, eradicating wasteful customs, such as elaborate funerals, and most notably, by continuing the late-Qing campaign to destroy temples and build schools (*hui-miao xingxue*), while at the same time promoting a politically charged Confucianism and "advanced" religions such as Christianity as a way of promoting a spiritual modernization of the masses.[15] The most sweeping policies came under the People's Republic, which envisioned a far more comprehensive reform of village society than had any of its predecessors. While asserting its authority over state-sponsored religious organizations in the cities, the government moved quickly to break the power of religious custom and organizations in the villages, a policy which reached fruition in the Cultural Revolution and softened significantly during the 1980s and 1990s. The 1999 campaign against Falungong, however, demonstrates that religion still occupies a special place in policy formation.[16]

The vicissitudes of policy aside, what impact did the sweeping political changes of this period actually have on local society? First, how were religious policies themselves implemented? How and when were local temples appropriated? Which religious groups were able to coexist with the state and what was the fate of those pushed underground? How did the cultural authority of religious figures fare under regimes that were overtly hostile to local religious organization? Of equal importance are the secondary effects of larger economic and social change on local religion. How did the insecurity brought about by all-too-frequent periods of war or famine reveal itself in the mentality of religious belief? Extreme duress often prompts a radicalization of belief, most notably toward millenarianism.[17] Although this particular reaction has occurred numerous times in the history of China, this fact alone should not lead us to believe that demographic insecurity automatically prompts peasants to begin planning for the apocalypse. Conversely, why did the relative security experienced under the People's Republic not erode religious belief, as so many observers of the 1950s and 1960s had predicted, but indeed lay the foundation for a revival of local religion in the 1980s?[18] Finally, beyond the simple rise or decline of religious fervor, how did the new political ideas (such as Maoism) that made their way into rural society shape the contours of popular belief?[19]

Local Religion and Local Society

In rural China, as in most local societies, religion both defines and expresses community. Within any territorially defined group, such as the village or neighborhood, as well as voluntary organizations, such as occupational or votive societies, participation in religious activities provides a public realm in which to exercise leadership.[20] The dual expression of civic concern and personal piety affords a very real customary power and stems from an understanding of the importance of religion to common welfare, in terms of both ensuring divine protection and fortifying the moral structure of the community.[21] Beyond simply representing the community, however, the power to define as well as associate with the greater moral good also suggests the ability of local elites to dominate it. This may be accomplished through personal association with the symbols of religious authority, including those promoted by the state, or through domination of the organs of spiritual efficacy, such as ritual functions. Nevertheless, just as perception of the religious good of the state is multivalenced, so too is the religious life of the community beyond the ability of any one group to dominate. Even public expressions of village hierarchy in highly structured rituals, such as processions, are necessarily contested in their interpretation.[22]

Beyond the constant redefinition of community in ritual practice, religious belief also retains a significant place in the local economy of knowledge. Despite the centralizing and standardizing influence of scriptural and liturgical traditions that have circulated around the North China Plain for centuries, as well as the ever-expanding network of mass communications and increasing mobility of peasants, rural China retains a dizzying number of local customs, cults, and rituals, leading anthropologists to once have questioned whether a "Chinese religion" existed at all.[23]

Indeed, the question of how local religious culture (and all culture, for that matter) fits into the larger context has engaged scholars of China for decades and turns to a large degree on the role of some form of political or social hierarchy in the propagation of culture. Such a hierarchy is implied in any model that proposes a binary division between the high culture of the elite and the expression of this culture by the masses. This division can be expressed variously as orthodoxy versus heterodoxy, great versus little traditions, or center versus periphery, but in each case assumes a unified cultural hub or network from which knowledge flows outward, often accompanied by some expression of authority or power.

This understanding of the flow of knowledge within local society is itself very much influenced by the Skinnerian model of the marketing of goods, which is based around a hierarchy of central places.[24] According to this model, not only goods, but also information and culture, are carried between villages and central market towns and cities, the latter serving as nodes of rural communication and effecting a certain standardization of the local; however, just as market exchange trades low-value raw materials from the periphery for finished goods from the core, the exchange of culture is not between equals. Whether the cities and towns were to be understood as bastions of standard, high, or orthodox culture, or simply of central control, it has always been assumed that they should exert a civilizing influence over village culture, keeping local deviation within a certain orbit.

Although this model has much to recommend it, an oversimplified model of a culturally orthodox semiurban core reigning in the rural periphery is certainly not the whole story. In light of the coincidence of the geography of imperial administrative authority and cultural expressions of geographic imagination, such as the "celestial bureaucracy" of spiritual forces, it is tempting to assume the existence of a single network along which all power, knowledge, and culture flowed. As Skinner himself was quick to point out, however, no single core-periphery model can stand alone, and the centers of trade, administration, and religion do not necessarily coincide. Particularly within local society, although the flow of knowledge and culture does rely heavily on nodes of communication, such as marketing centers, it also travels along routes exclusive of them.[25] Local expressions of culture are not merely a misunderstanding of high or official culture. Rather, the latter is itself a text, like a template, which local actors can interpret for their own ends. Rather than attempting to copy elite culture, local actors use it as a foundation upon which to "individuate," building consciously unique cults, rituals, and resources.[26] Such a perspective is particularly important in questions of religion, which must consider the interaction between strong cultural centers in terms of governmental and ecclesiastical orthodoxies, and the numerous layers of regional knowledge and tradition seen in local devotion.[27]

Fieldwork Methodology and Sources

The primary source for this study is fieldwork conducted in rural Cangzhou. Over the course of 1997–1998, and again during the summers of 1999 and 2002, I made eighteen trips to Cangzhou, in each visit remaining for three to six days. While in the villages, I stayed with peasant hosts, who were extremely hospitable and generally forthcoming about their histories, beliefs, and practices. On most occasions, I was accompanied by Pu Wenqi, of the Tianjin Academy of Social Sciences, who introduced me to the area and was of invaluable help in providing background information, introductions, and assistance with understanding the very thick Cangzhou dialect.

The interviews themselves were informal and only loosely structured. After our arrival in the village, friends would soon begin to gather in the home of our host and we would begin asking questions on a particular topic, such as the role of spirits in good fortune, the ritual activities of a particular sect, or the history of the village. After my first few visits, it became clear that prepared questions were of little use and that I would gain much more by letting conversation flow naturally. On returning to Tianjin, I would then review my notes to discover if any important points had been missed and make plans to address these points on my next visit.

Our closest interaction was with local religious leaders, particularly those of the two sectarian teachings introduced in chapter 7. In many of the villages that we visited, these sects remain the center of religious life: they provide ritual services for individuals within the community, are frequently touted as moral exemplars, and are by far the most knowledgeable about matters concerning the sacred and spirit worlds. Although this close association with sectarian leaders opened many doors with other villagers, it could also become a liability. When asked about their own beliefs, ordinary villagers would frequently defer to "experts," such as the sectarian leaders, scholars from Tianjin, and occasionally, even to me. Thus, to gain a more complete view of how different members of the community understood the same questions, we made a point of interviewing a range of people, men and women, young and old, in groups and individually. Again, the most successful interviews were ordinary conversations, and much of our work was conducted during the course of other activities, such as milling corn, pulling weeds, or repairing farm implements.

In addition to fieldwork, this study also relies upon a number of written sources. Two nineteenth-century surveys, the 1842 *Diagram of Household Registration in Tianjin (Jinmen baojia tushuo)* and *Diagram of Villages in Qing County (Qingxian cuntu)*, from roughly 1875, are an important complement to the interviews.[28] These sources provide detailed data on individual villages, such as size and structure, as well as numbers of temples and religious specialists in each community. Not only do these sources reach back to the early nineteenth century, but, because they cover every village in Tianjin and Qing Counties (the latter included my fieldwork area from what is now Cang County), they also provide far more breadth than interview data alone would allow. County gazetteers, generally of limited use as sources of local custom or religion, do provide important background on the history of Cang County, especially patterns of temple and monastic construction. Within Cang County, sources such as temple and grave stele (most of which are recorded in the gazetteers) provide further detail on individual events. Ethnographic studies of North China, such as those mentioned above, are cited to lend further context and corroboration to my findings in Cang County. The larger history of sectarian organization is recorded by sources in Tianjin. Within the Tianjin Municipal Library are personal reminiscences of members and leaders of the Li Sect and records of the 1951 campaign against the Way of Penetrating Unity *(yiguandao)*. The histories and teachings of the sects are recorded in sectarian scriptures, and I am grateful to Li Shiyu for allowing me to make photocopies of many of those in his collection. The question of how such scriptures were used and understood by the faithful is dealt with in the text itself.

Chapter Overview

The goal of this study is not to establish the hard rules that define the religious life of the typical North Chinese village, but rather to demonstrate the mosaic of forces that together have shaped it over time. After an introduction to the history and village society of Cang County in chapter 1, each subsequent chapter introduces a different facet of this picture: the role of the village, the circulation of knowledge, the inability of urban culture and sects to penetrate rural religiosity, the flashes of millenarianism, and the importance of everyday ritual and moral concerns to the long-term evolution of village society. Because the organization is thematic rather than chronological, each chapter will present a slightly different temporal focus, some reaching from the late Qing to the present, others presenting a closer examination of one or two decades.

Chapter 2 discusses the role played by the village in the organization and propagation of religion. Administrative reforms enacted in the late Qing and early Republic increasingly focused on the village as a unit of fiscal and social control. This strengthened the geographic and social boundaries of the village, further solidifying the criteria and responsibilities of membership, most notably in terms of an affective sense of collective religious welfare. Religious resources, such as temples and sectarian groups, were supported by the community and became closely identified with the religious life and interests of the village as a whole, although this rarely was reflected in a collective ritual regimen. The administrative and affective importance of the village as an organizational unit of secular and sacred life was seen again beginning in the late 1970s, when the infrastructure of rural religion was reconstructed in the wake of Collectivization and the Cultural Revolution. Although village boundaries had been frequently erased and redrawn over the previous two decades, these newly formed villages quickly recreated a sense of religious community and identity during the post-1979 reform era.

Chapter 3 addresses the economy of religious belief as seen in the case of *xiangtou,* villagers who heal through the power of fox spirits. Literature and scripture abound with stories of the ability of spirits to sicken and heal. Yet in Cang County, knowledge of the power and motivation of fox spirits, as well as the specific healing arts of *xiangtou,* are products of an intensely immediate and local culture. Most Cang County peasants know of fox spirits through stories of cures enacted by them through local *xiangtou.* Reflecting the immediacy of the sacred, such stories take place in neighboring villages, and in the present day. Local beliefs concerning sickness, spirits, and the efficacy and arts of *xiangtou* reflect the influence of written culture, but this is far from doctrine. Rather, because religious knowledge is transmitted and shaped through an evolving oral tradition, it is constantly reincarnated as a meaningful part of a living local culture.

In the case of *xiangtou,* knowledge of spirits and healing reflected in literature indirectly inspires a living, oral culture of belief, but does not dominate it as would a fundamentalist reading of scripture. A similar role could be attributed to other religious institutions, such as sects, which did not dictate local belief, but rather engaged it in a dialectic exchange. Over the course of the late nineteenth and twentieth centuries, a number of religious teachings were active in rural Cang County, each gaining ascendancy as they appealed to social realities and needs. Chapter 4 examines the state of monastic Buddhism, demonstrating that the teaching as a self-consciously distinct tradition had all but disappeared by the late Qing. During the Republican period, the few Buddhist institutions that did remain in Cang County were not connected to a larger Buddhist tradition or network, despite the Buddhist revival that was taking place in Jiangnan. In rural Cang County, Buddhism had become entirely incorporated into local religious life. Monks were recruited and trained locally, lived in village temples, knew little of Buddhist scripture or ritual, and were virtually indistinguishable from popular specialists.

A similar phenomenon characterized the numerous sectarian teachings that flourished among the villagers themselves. Best known to historians for their millenarian tendencies, such teachings actually represented a wide range of beliefs and organizational styles. Chapter 5 introduces the Li Sect, which was immensely popular in the city and suburbs of Tianjin but could not develop a significant following in rural Cang County. Like monastic Buddhism, the pseudomonastic Li Sect relied upon highly trained, celibate specialists, a prospect that was more economically viable in urban neighborhoods than villages. Thus, while the teaching developed independent soteriological and social significance in Tianjin or the nearby town of Duliu, in rural Cang County, it was reduced to a mere shadow of its most characteristic doctrines, most notably the admonition to refrain from alcohol, tobacco, and opium.

Chapter 6 examines the explosive rise and precipitous decline of the Way of Penetrating Unity. This teaching, with its high degree of mysticism and predictions of an immanent apocalypse, found a ready audience in the troubled first half of the twentieth century, particularly in the war-ravaged villages of Republican North China. By 1950, the teaching had a nationwide following, including large numbers of devotees in the Communist Party and People's Liberation Army, yet had all but disappeared by the end of 1951. This was partially due to the concerted campaign to eradicate the sect, but more fundamentally to the return of a degree of stability and prosperity to rural society.

Finally, chapter 7 presents yet another view of sectarianism with an introduction to two more teachings, the Teaching of the Most Supreme (*taishangmen*) and the Heaven and Earth Sect (*tiandimen*). In contrast to the Li Sect and Way of Penetrating Unity, neither of which was able to establish a significant foothold in village religious life, the Heaven and Earth Sect and Teaching of the Most Supreme have been active in rural Cang County since the early Qing dynasty and continue to flourish at the outset of the twenty-first century. These teachings are integral to village life and identity, a source of ritual power, and an outlet for the sincere devotion of the villagers who train to become ritual specialists. As such, it is not surprising to see the longevity of these organizations, even during the darkest days of the Cultural Revolution, or their energetic revival since the late 1970s.

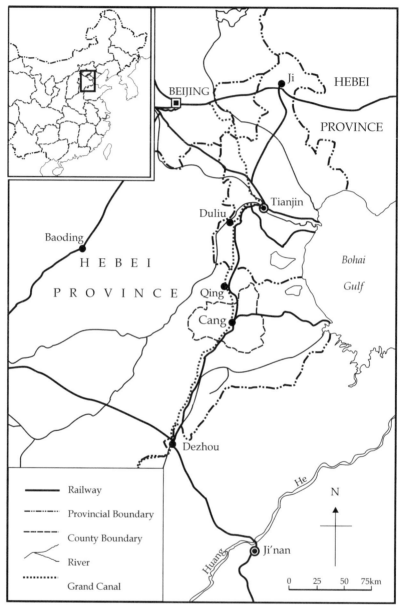

Map 1.1   The location of Cang County in North China.

1. Background

Rural Cang County

Cang County is located in the southeast of Hebei Province, roughly midway between Tianjin and Ji'nan. At the center lies Cangzhou City, with a population of 315,000. Cangzhou City is the site of the majority of industrial development in the county, including a state-supported chemical industry, and is the administrative and commercial center of the fourteen-county Cang Prefecture *(zhou).* Outside these urban precincts, Cang County is primarily rural and agricultural. Exclusive of Cangzhou City, in 1985 the county recorded a population of 563,180, of whom 548,986—just over 97 percent—were classified as farmers. Rural Cang County is today divided into thirty township-level districts, six *zhen* and twenty-four *xiang,* ranging in size from 10,000 to 30,000.[1]

History

Situated near the geographic center of the North China Plain, Cang County has always been somewhat of a crossroads. Since at least the fourth century A.D., the county has been traversed by numerous long-distance roads, which connect the area around modern Beijing with the heartland of the country further south. This was the route taken by the most famous sojourner to pass through Cang County, the martial hero Lin Chong from the novel *Heroes of the Water Margin,* who fled the penal colonies here for haven in the mountains of Shandong. Cangzhou City was also an important port on the Grand Canal, which passes through the center of the modern city. Villages along its banks, with names like Hai Family Dock or Third Li Bridge, bear witness to the former importance of the waterway. In 1910, the county was bisected by the Tianjin–Pukou line, one of the first extended railways in China.[2]

Unfortunately, lying at a communications hub also exposed Cang County to ill forces, including a succession of marauding armies that ravaged the area on their way to more important destinations. Like most

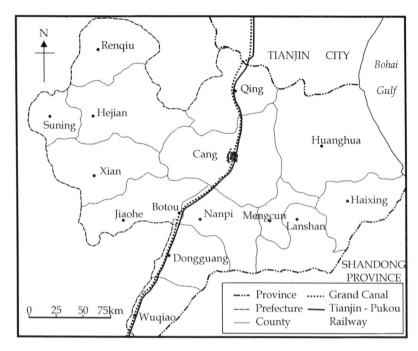

Map 1.2   The counties of Canzhou, showing current boundaries.

places on the North China Plain, the Cang County area was decimated during the wars that ended the Yuan dynasty and ushered in the Ming. The 1933 Cang County gazetteer briefly but effectively describes the effect of these wars on the area. "In three years, for thousands of *li* in every direction, the slaughter left nobody behind. It was like nothing that had ever occurred before."[3] A new era in the history of Cang County opened in the second year of the Yongle reign (1404), when the area was resettled with immigrants, primarily from Shanxi and Shandong provinces. Throughout much of the Ming dynasty, Hebei remained relatively underpopulated, with peasant manpower in shorter supply than arable land. Two centuries later, the wars of the Ming–Qing transition again revisited a similar hardship, but this trauma was less severe and shorter lived. Neither local histories nor oral traditions within villages record a second repopulation effort similar to that carried out in the early Ming.[4]

Years of relative stability and the introduction of new food and commercial crops during the Qing dynasty allowed the population of Cang County to rise, but the intensification of agriculture also increased its vulnerability to natural disaster. Between 1820 and 1883, for example, the population of Tianjin Prefecture *(fu)*, which included the counties of Cangzhou, grew by 23 percent. During the same period, that of adjacent Hejian Prefecture grew by 35 percent.[5] Even without the threat of war, however, life in rural Cang County was precarious. With no local source of stone and little forest cover, houses and structures were generally made of unfired straw and mud bricks. These structures are particularly vulnerable to flood, such as the one in 1891, which destroyed tens of thousands of peasant homes.[6] Agriculture remained a similarly risky venture. During the Qing dynasty, Cang County was struck by droughts, floods, hail, early frost, and other disasters no less than sixty-four times, an average of once every four years. In the worst cases, the human toll could be staggering. Droughts in 1832 and 1877, for instance, reportedly left the ground "scattered with dead."[7]

Rising population density during the late nineteenth century further exacerbated this already difficult situation. According to the late Qing *Diagram of Villages in Qing County*, the sixty-seven villages of what was then designated as Dulin Township (the current boundary demarcates a smaller area) held a population of 5,399 households, with 18,749 adults. The latter figure reveals a highly disproportionate number of males, 10,042, compared to only 8,707 females. This is most likely a result of female infanticide, suggesting the strains of overpopulation. The excess of males, known as "bare sticks" *(gu gun)*, accounted for roughly 13.3 percent of the total population and, having no local prospects for marriage, often proved to be a destabilizing influence on local society.[8]

During the nineteenth and early twentieth centuries, Cang County again saw more than its share of war and military occupation. Late in 1853, the Taiping army entered Cangzhou City and killed the magistrate, Shen Ruchao, before moving north.[9] Local uprisings, fed by recruits from among the "bare sticks," broke out in 1868 and 1871, but each was quickly put down. During the summer of 1900, Cang County became engulfed in the Boxer Uprising. When the local magistrate refused to support the Boxers, the latter besieged the city for twenty-nine days, before being brutally dispersed by Muslim troops and a small German force. In February 1925, troops from Fengtian and Shandong took the rural areas of Cang County from their Guomindang defenders, and the two armies continued to fight over the walled city for another month.[10]

Evidence suggests continued demographic hardship throughout the Republican period (1911–1949). Rural population figures from 1928 and 1937 record a sharp decline, from 451,644 to 374,817, just over 17 percent.[11] Although villagers have no memory of such a dramatic depopulation, all agree that the basic needs of survival were uncertain during this period. During the early twentieth century, Cang County villagers planted a combination of maize and sweet potatoes, a crop portfolio that reliably produces a high number of calories in limited space and is characteristic of privation.[12] Even these hearty crops, however, did not always produce a large surplus. Peasants from Quan-Wang Village report that the common bride price of seven to eight *dan* (one *dan* being equivalent to roughly fifty kilograms) of unground corn was very difficult for most families to produce, further compounding the difficulties of unmarried males. Annual taxes, to the tune of three to four *diao* of cash per *mu* of farmland in 1937, (later changed to one *dan* of grain per *mu* under the Japanese) added yet another layer of hardship.[13] With so little agrarian surplus, a series of poor harvests could literally spell starvation for a peasant family.

The greatest hardship of this period came under the Japanese occupation, which the 1995 gazetteer estimates to have directly caused the deaths more than 7,000 people and prompted the emigration of many more.[14] Because of its position on the Tianjin–Shanghai railway, Cang County was an important strategic priority for the Japanese military, which decimated local defense forces in a brief but devastating artillery and bombing campaign of the walled city of Cangzhou in September 1937. While the majority of the occupation forces were stationed in the city of Cangzhou itself, small towns, such as Dulin, each had garrisons of ten to twenty Japanese soldiers, in addition to a vast network of Chinese informers, which reached almost every village. Despite this presence, Communist Eighth Route Army guerrillas operated in the area, making constant raids against Japanese installations throughout the course of the war.

Unable to locate the Red Army itself, particularly in the rural areas, Japanese forces instead chose civilian targets for brutal public reprisals. The case of Zhang-Xing Village, which was suspected of harboring guerillas, provides an instructive example. Late in 1937, Japanese troops suddenly surrounded the village, slaughtered the occupants, and burned every standing structure to the ground. The only residents spared were small children, who were sent off in separate directions to spread word of the price of resistance to neighboring communities. While relatively few villages in the area were subjected to such extreme brutality, the reality of the Japanese occupation was known to all and remains deeply etched in local memory.[15]

The population of Cang County grew dramatically under the relative prosperity of the People's Republic. In 1949, the population of rural Cang County was 378,787. By 1964, this figure had grown to 425,414, with 166,447

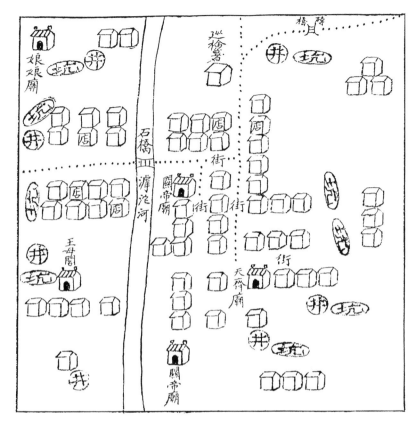

Figure 1.1   Dunlin Town during the 1880s.

(just over 40 percent) under the age of fifteen. By 1985, the population had risen to 563,160, an increase of nearly 49 percent over the 1949 figure.[16] Much of this change can be attributed to an improvement in rural living conditions, including nutrition. A healthy adult caloric intake requires roughly 285 kilograms of grain per year. With the notable exception of the years surrounding the Great Leap Forward, when per capita production in Cang County fell far below this figure (with a low of 124.5 kilograms per capita in 1960), these needs have been consistently met. Per capita production of grain in Cang County for 1985 was a comfortable 386 kilograms, leaving a surplus for livestock production or sale. Since the mid-1980s, peasants have begun to supplement their diet with eggs and fresh vegetables, and older peasants are quick to point out that they currently eat better than at any point in their lives.[17]

Village Structure and Economy

It is difficult to generalize about the structure of the villages themselves, particularly before 1949. Even within a very small area, individual communities differed considerably, a point that must be remembered when trying to relate village studies to larger social or regional trends. Data from the *Diagram of Villages in Qing County* demonstrate a wide range of village size during the nineteenth century. A survey of the sixty-eight villages in Dulin Township revealed an average of just over eighty households and 280 residents per community. Of these villages, the smallest, Zhao Family Camp, had only four households and twenty-three adult residents, while the largest, Shanhu, had 306 households and 1,026 adults. The standard deviation of village households was 68 and of population, 213. In other words, the size of villages in late Qing Dulin Township varied significantly, with nearly half of the sixty-eight villages being 50 percent larger or smaller than the average. Although these data represent a period before increasingly strict regulation, such as the Rural Reorganization Act *(xian zuzhi fa),* of 1929, began to standardize the size and structure of peasant village, they do clearly demonstrate the diversity among communities within a small area, and limited utility of understanding rural society through the lens of "typical" or "model" communities, even when regional variation is taken into consideration.[18]

By the late Qing dynasty, Cang County had few single-surname communities and a limited role for lineage organization within the village. The preponderance of villages named after one or two families demonstrates the role that individual surname groups had played in founding villages during the Ming repopulation.[19] At least by the late nineteenth century, however, most villages were a collection of surnames. Although the *Diagram of Villages in Qing County* does not list the surnames present in each village, it did record the names of scholars and the village head *(cun dong),* along with the oldest *(qilao)* and poorest *(qiong min)* villagers, revealing a multiplicity of surnames even in those villages that appear to have been founded by a single clan.[20]

Field research has demonstrated that, in contrast to the canonical view of southern lineages (which has recently been challenged by Michael Szonyi), those in the North China Plain rarely owned significant corporate property, a characterization borne out by evidence from late Qing Hebei Province.[21] Late-nineteenth-century surveys of Tianjin and Qing counties list village temples in detail, but reveal very few ancestral temples.[22] Cang County villagers confirmed this to have been the case during the Republican period, as well. A few of the more notable extended common descent groups, such as the wealthy Wang family of Wang Family Village (later combined with Quan Camp to form the current Quan-Wang Village), did maintain an ancestral shrine, as well as a small amount of corporate property; however, such cases were memorable precisely because they were so exceptional.[23]

One area in which the influence of the surname group was felt was in the ability of certain rural families to produce candidates for imperial civil service examinations. Although this area was by no means wealthy, it did produce a significant number of degreed scholars. During the late nineteenth century, rural Dulin Township boasted no less than fifty-four *shengyuan*, approximately one per 100 households, a figure almost identical to that seen in rural Tianjin County a generation earlier. What is most significant about these *shengyuan* holders, however, is the number who came from rural households and the concentration of degree holders and positions of village authority within particular surname groups.[24] The 152-household village of Dadukou, for example, had four *shengyuan*, three of whom were surnamed Su, as was the village head. In Zhang Family Village, the three *shengyuan*, the village head, and the teacher were all surnamed Zhang. In such cases, it is only by looking at the identity of the oldest or poorest villagers that the presence of other surname groups becomes evident.[25]

Outside of the examination system, certain families and individuals were able to amass significant wealth and influence. The Xu family of Lit-

Table 1.1   *Shengyuan* in Nineteenth-Century Tianjin and Qing Counties

	Urban Tianjin Area, 1842	Tianjin County, Including Urban Area, 1842	Tianjin County, Excluding Urban Area, 1842	Rural Dulin Township, circa 1875
Number of *shengyuan*	597	1,082	485	54
Number of households	32,857	83,991	51,134	5,399
Households : *shengyuan*	55 : 1	77.6 : 1	105.4 : 1	100 : 1
Adult population	105,097	265,043	159,946	18,749
Adults : *shengyuan*	176 : 1	245 : 1	329.8 : 1	347.2 : 1

Source: *Jinmen baojia tushuo, Qingxian cuntu, juan* 12

tle Terrace Village, for example, not only was wealthy, but also descended from former bannermen who had been related by marriage to Zhang Zhidong. In Feng-Guan Village lived a former imperial eunuch, who had accumulated a vast personal fortune and donated large sums of money to village and charitable projects. One landlord family near Rear Camp Village was said to have had holdings of more than 6,000 *mu*. During the mid-Qing, the Wangs of Wang Family Village purchased landholdings of 1,800 *mu* in six villages, reportedly using their Manchu ancestry to leverage financing from local officials.

In spite of these colorful examples, it seems that most communities evinced far less economic striation. Most were composed primarily of small owner-cultivators, with very few wealthy peasants; however, despite the general poverty of the area, few people lived in absolute destitution. When investigators for the late-nineteenth-century *Diagram of Villages in Qing County* canvassed each village for "poor people," many communities had no one to place in that category, and few had more than three.[26] This was still generally the case during the Republican period. For example, during the 1940s, Yang Camp had no resident landlords, most of the land having had been owned by the Wang family in neighboring Wang Family Village for generations. Within Yang Camp, however, the market for usage rights was stable and most families had long-term rights to sufficient crop land. In the large village of Rear Camp, one family had holdings of more than 400 *mu*, and two others held about 100 *mu* each, but most farmed their own land, and the village had neither *dian* tenants nor extremely poor families. As villagers describe it, most families had a small, but sufficient, piece of land to farm, and only in cases of famine or severe mismanagement would a family be reduced to begging.

During the late Qing, Hebei villages maintained semiofficial status and de facto administrative significance. Although the county magistrate was officially the lowest rung of the Qing bureaucracy, various strata of subcounty officials were responsible for the day-to-day affairs of government. Despite the fact that peasant villages had no official legal status, each village was represented by a single responsible individual.[27] In Cang County, this was the village head, who was himself often a *shengyuan* scholar, demonstrating that, at least in this period, the position of village head was prestigious and sought after.[28]

The semiofficial status of the village and its representatives is demonstrated in the mediation between village and state over payment of taxes. Although from 1726 through 1900, peasants were theoretically charged with remitting taxes in person to the county government, most areas of

Hebei developed systems of mediated remittance through a single responsible villager. As Li Huaiyin has demonstrated in the southern Hebei
county of Huailu, this mediated interaction was independent of state law
but was more formal and open to official arbitration than a simple customary arrangement. The nomination and responsibilities of this middle-
man were policed by clearly articulated village regulations *(cun gui)*. Dis-
putes occasionally resulted in formal adjudication, in which the magistrate
often based his decisions on these village regulations.[29]

Over the course of the twentieth century, administrative and economic
changes increasingly bound the villages of Cang County to the state, first
by local agents and later through direct administration. Throughout Hebei
and Shandong, increasing demands for provincial revenue throughout the
early twentieth century prompted expansion of the land tax and especially
of irregular levies. This fiscal need, plus a desire to reform and modernize
rural society, powered an expansion and formalization of the subcounty
administrative apparatus at two tiers, the larger corresponding roughly
to the township and the smaller to the administrative village *(xiang)*.[30] In
Cang County, these two tiers were called *bao* and *jia,* respectively. Before
1937, the *bao* of Dulin Township was headed by a wealthy peasant named
Yang Hongbin, who lived in Little Terrace Village, rather than Dulin itself.
Yang performed basic administrative functions, such as recording births
and deaths, in addition to his primary job of collecting taxes, and was re-
munerated by a salary from the county government, as well as a portion
of the tax revenue from the thriving Dulin market. Each village (by the
1930s, the number of villages was counted at seventy-two) corresponded
to a *jia* and interacted with Yang through a *jia* headman *(jiazhang)*.[31]

Nominally, this structure remained in place during the Japanese occupation, although it came to operate rather differently. During this period,
a *jia* was redefined as ten households, with roughly ten *jia* constituting a
bao.[32] In practice, the *bao* took the place of the idealized hundred-household
administrative village envisioned by Republican reformers, as smaller rural
communities voluntarily combined to put up a united effort to meet increased grain and labor exactions.[33] Under the Japanese occupation, positions in local administration not only grew more numerous, but also presented greater fiscal demands and opportunities for personal gain. Few
peasants were willing to serve as the conduit between the community and
the occupation, and these positions were increasingly filled by what Prasenjit Duara has termed "entrepreneurial brokers," who took up these positions for the promise of monetary rather than social capital.[34] The head
of the *bao* that included the two villages of Ni Camp and Yang Camp had

been chosen by the occupation government and was apparently just such a type. He is remembered as a local tough *(tu gun)*, who extorted money from village households by such schemes as selling New Year firecrackers at ten times the normal price and threatening any who refused to purchase them with a beating.

After 1949, the internal composition of Cang County villages continued to change as their administrative and political significance increased. During Land Reform and Collectivization, which were carried out on an increasingly ambitious scale beginning in 1953 and culminated in the formation of People's Communes in 1958, the village remained an important social and administrative unit, here reincarnated as the "production brigade" *(shengchan dui)*.[35] As the rural population rose, small villages were further combined into larger entities. As a result of these two processes, village size increased significantly, the average growing threefold, from eighty households in the late nineteenth century to 243 in 1985. Even those villages that retained similar physical boundaries had changed internally. Three decades of social revolution stripped once-powerful families of wealth and prestige, and the economic and social basis of the community and its leadership were redefined. By the late 1970s, the villages of Cang County were very different places than they had been a generation earlier.

The Sphere of Local Culture

Although Cang County sat at a crossroads of land and water travel, most peasants had very limited means of transportation. Before 1949, horse or mule carts were a luxury of the rich; the great majority of peasants would conduct their business on foot, usually venturing no farther than the periodic market to do so. Rare occasions or circumstances might take them farther from home. Adult males occasionally hired out as seasonal laborers, usually in porting or construction, which might take them to the city of Cangzhou, whereas a career as an itinerant trader or in the military might take them even farther. During the first few decades following the Revolution, transportation improved little, while the reorganization of rural society and attenuation of local marketing networks provided new pressures to remain close to home. As late as the 1970s, few Cang County peasants had ever traveled more than a day's walk from their home village.[36] Even within the city of Cangzhou, streets were generally no more than dirt tracks, which became impassable in inclement weather, and rural roads were even worse. Until the late 1980s, the world of most peasants was restricted to the distance that could be traveled on foot in the morning so as to return in the afternoon. For practical purposes, that distance was roughly thirty *li*, or fifteen kilometers.

As such, almost all of the resources of daily life could be found within walking distance of any given village. The geography of periodic markets provides a good illustration. Such markets *(ji)* were the primary site not only to buy and sell goods, but also to seek employment and services such as dental care and veterinary services. Beyond this, the periodic market was the most exciting event in the daily lives of most peasants, who attended as a social occasion, to see itinerant performers, and to catch up on local news. Most villages had such a regular market within walking distance, and transportation, employment, and social networks were all oriented toward that center. The gazetteers of Jiaohe, Nanpi, and Qing Counties—all adjacent to Cang—each list large markets, scattered more or less evenly throughout the countryside, with most villages easily within ten *li* of at least one major market and even closer to minor ones.

From the perspective of Yang Camp, in Dulin Township, one can easily appreciate the central role of local markets in the lives of villagers. During the 1870s, markets in Dulin and Qian-Hai Village, each held once every five days, were the only two in the area.[37] By the 1930s, however, a number of smaller markets had proliferated, and a peasant from Yang Camp could attend a market within easy walking distance from his home any day of the year. Of these, Dulin was by far the largest, and almost any good or service could be obtained there. During the 1930s, Dulin had a labor and animal market, smithing and repair of farm implements, professional animal slaughterers and butchers (including a distinct group of Muslim butchers), seed and fertilizer vendors, and peasants from roughly seventy nearby villages. Although the market did fall into decline during late 1950s, it saw a quick resurgence during the late 1970s and remains very active today. Even during the winter months, the Dulin market will attract tens of thousands of peasants, who arrive to conduct business or simply watch the crowds. As during the 1930s, peasants from Yang Camp can still satisfy all of their daily needs without traveling more than half a day's journey from home.[38]

Another illustration of the geographic boundaries of peasant life is marriage patterns. As in most of rural China, peasant marriages in Cang County were most often arranged by a go-between *(meipo)*, who would introduce two families who had children of marriageable age. Until the 1990s, marriage within the same village was extremely rare, if not unheard of, the ideal having been to find a bride from a distant village to encourage her to make a complete break with her natal family; however, because both

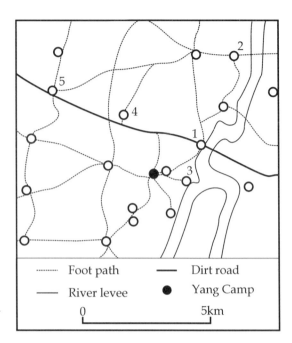

Map 1.3
Periodic markets
near Yang Camp
during the Republi-
can era.

┄┄┄ Foot path		⎯⎯ Dirt road	
⎯⎯ River levee		● Yang Camp	
0		5km	

families were generally personal acquaintances of the go-between, they were rarely separated by a significant physical distance. Using Mantetsu survey data from the early 1940s, Ishida Hiroshi has discussed the geography of marriage in rural North China, demonstrating that the great majority of marriages were arranged within a radius of ten *li*.[39] My own interviews further confirm this pattern in Cang County over a longer period of time. Of seventy-four marriages dating from the late Qing to the late 1990s, sixty-nine had been arranged within a thirty-*li* radius.[40] The few that did exceed this distance were generally the result of special economic circumstances. One large landlord family (the Wang family of Wang Fam-

Table 1.2   Periodic Markets Near Yang Camp during Republican Era

Town	Held on Days Ending in
Dulin	2, 7
Zhao-Guan Camp	1, 6
Little Terrace	4, 9
Chapeng	5, 0
Chenwu	3, 8

ily Camp) had arranged a marriage with an equally wealthy family in neighboring Shandong, approximately 100 *li* away. Since the late 1980s, a number of peasant men working as laborers in the city of Cangzhou have contracted to purchase brides from an impoverished area of western Sichuan.[41]

Inspired by Skinner's conception of culturally endogamous marketing communities, scholars in Japan and Taiwan have emphasized the geographic boundaries of these networks as marketing and marriage *spheres*.[42] As the case of marriage networks suggests, however, the limited geography of peasant society is also a broader cultural boundary, one to which I will refer as the "sphere of local culture." At some levels, this sphere would appear to correspond with the marketing structure, which suggests that cultural dialogue and the exchange of information runs parallel to the flow of goods. They could also, however, be quite independent of the marketing center itself and often extended beyond the geographically limited marketing communities envisioned by Skinner, particularly in densely populated areas that could support more than one large market within walking distance of a village.

The sphere of local culture in Dulin was not only larger than the marketing area, it was also largely independent of the marketing center itself. In contrast to the data discussed by Prasenjit Duara, villagers in this area indicated that the marriage go-between was more likely to come from a neighboring village than from the market town of Dulin, and an examination of the geographic dispersal of brides reveals that the town did not exert an overwhelming influence.[43] Not only did economic exchange rely on a proliferation of smaller markets, even if a villager did most often frequent the largest market town for economic exchange, human interaction within the sphere of local culture was not channeled through this central place. Rather, villages and individuals were also linked directly to each other linked in relationships of kinship, commerce, cooperation, and belief, many of which extended beyond the marketing community. As we shall see, one example of this interaction is religious, such as votive travel and sectarian networks, many of which traversed numerous marketing communities and none of which centered on the market town of Dulin, which at least by the twentieth century had little religious significance.[44]

Beyond these specific networks, upon which Duara bases his "cultural nexus" formulation, the flow of information about local places and events defines the sphere of local culture as a decentered, abstract space, the realm within which a peasant would actively interact, either physically or cognitively. This sphere is thus a realm of personal knowledge and cultural reference, the world of significance to a peasant with a great deal of local mobility but very limited experience of the world beyond. The significance of these borders as cognitive landmarks is immediately evident in the detailed knowledge that most villagers have of the immediate area, in contrast to their limited understanding of or interest in the world beyond. Most peasants interviewed could easily name all of the villages in Dulin Township but had far less knowledge of national or world geography.[45] The same holds true for historical knowledge, which is remembered less from an imagined national perspective than from the very local view of the villages themselves. Older peasants have only a vague memory of the national politics of the Republican era but immediate recall of events of local significance such as droughts, floods, or the deaths of important personages. Similarly, historical memory of landmarks such as the Boxer Uprising and Japanese occupation does not concern events on the national scale or those in distant cities of Tianjin or Beijing as much as the experience of neighboring communities. Thus, the oral culture of stories and rumors that often served as news about the outside world was filtered through and elaborated within local society. Even when information originated elsewhere, it came to take on a distinctly local flavor and significance as it traveled from village to village. Folk tales, the likes of which are heard throughout China, were incarnated as part of local culture by locating the stories within local geography.[46] As discussed in detail in chapter 3, this also holds true for knowledge of the immanent sacred realm.

The role of oral culture is best appreciated in light of the low level of education and literacy. As mentioned previously, rural Dulin Township produced a significant number of *shengyuan* holders during the 1880s. At this time, thirty-four of the sixty-seven Dulin villages supported charitable or village schools *(yi xue, xiang shu),* with a total of fifty-two teachers and 321 students.[47] Outside of the study of the Confucian classics, it can be assumed that others within the village had some degree of functional literacy that might be highly specific to the circumstances of use. A Dulin merchant would need to understand the written language of commerce and accounting, a village functionary (such as the *jiazhang*) enough to keep accurate statistics of population and tax payments. Even illiterate peasants would be likely to at least recognize the characters of their own names, as well as those of many of the ancestors on the family genealogy *(zupu),* even if they could not write them from memory.[48]

During the early Republican period, the government of Cang County embarked upon a nationally mandated program of educational reform, and by 1933 had built 280 elementary schools, with just over 40,000 students officially enrolled.[49] The most significant advances were made under the People's Republic, particularly with regard to giving large numbers of peasants some form of rudimentary education. The general picture is best illustrated by local cadres. In 1952, more than 70 percent (4,700 of 6,564) of rural cadres were illiterate, and another 26 percent (1,700) had only a primary education. In 1985, the picture was vastly improved but still reveals the limits of a half century of educational reform. Out of 19,910 local cadres, 13 percent (2,673) were illiterate, and more than half (10,005) had only a primary school education. In contrast, only 214 (1 percent) had a college education.[50] Nevertheless, by 1990, most villages had access to primary schools, and the proportion of peasants with basic literacy was certainly higher than at any point in local history.

Religious Life: Vows and Morality

As in much of the world, the most fundamental religious practice in Cang County is individual prayer and supplication for divine assistance. Religious faithful visit shrines and temples to pray for any and all needs of daily life, promising a repayment of action or devotion when the wish comes true. The sort of vows commonly made reveals a clear morality consistent with the religious and social values of village society. Acceptable requests, made with sincerity, are likely to be answered. These include prayers for children, for the health of parents, or for wealth, all of which are all ultimately based on Confucian values of filial piety as well as the importance of the family as a social and economic unit. Agrarian and occupational vows hint at an unspoken moral contract between the human and sacred realms and an implicit belief that people should be allowed to engage in good and useful trades for their own sustenance, as well as for the good of society at large.[51]

Crossing this unwritten moral boundary may actually bring misfortune upon the supplicant. When one peasant in the village of White North Pagoda greedily (and unsuccessfully) asked Caishen, the God of Wealth, for 100,000 *yuan*, promising only 1,000 *yuan* of votive donation in return, he found himself a laughingstock of the village. Not content to learn his lesson the easy way, he publicly cursed Caishen for having ignored his request. The next week, his face was covered in pustules, causing his wife to turn him out of the house for fear of infecting their children. Only after he had apologized to Caishen did the pustules disappear. Similarly, during the early 1980s, Meng Village asked specialists of the Heaven and Earth Sect in nearby Yang Camp to perform a ceremony to ward off hail, which the specialists did for free. The village leaders, however, used the ceremony as an opportunity to earn a profit, charging peasants ten times the usual price for the incense and steamed bread *(mantou)* commonly used as sacrifices. As a result, the village was struck by hail for five years in a row, while neighboring villages were unharmed.[52]

Most strikingly, none of my interviewees ever mentioned the use of a vow to inflict harm. When asked if one could request a deity to make a neighbor ill, informants universally replied that such a request was not only impossible, but might even bring misfortune upon the supplicant himself. While such malevolent magic does certainly exist, it is considered the purview of the more capricious and dangerous spirits, such as foxes and ghosts, and their human specialists. Ordinary faithful generally seek to avoid contact with such dangerous deities and therefore restrict their requests to the morally defensible.[53]

Tales of vows made and answered circulate freely from village to village, representing a vehicle by which religious knowledge is reincarnated within the sphere of local culture. Peasants learn the identity, power, and personalities of different deities through stories, scriptures, iconography, and, increasingly, mass media.[54] Yet, knowing is not the whole story; the ordinary concerns that peasants address in vows demonstrate the immanence of the gods and the importance of the sacred in everyday life. Stories concerning the efficacy and mercy of a god are developed through stories of successful prayers, not in the distant past or faraway lands, but in the present day and in neighboring villages. Just as historical memory takes as its point of reference the immediate area, stories of the sacred dwell upon areas of personal significance to the listener, such as the benevolence of divine actors and efficacy of techniques.

Religious Life: Temples and Temple Cults

Throughout China, local religious life has long been centered around temples and shrines, construction of which came in a number of distinct waves. Using data from gazetteers of four southern Chinese provinces, the historian Wolfram Eberhardt demonstrated a peak in temple construction during the waning years of the Tang, another small rise in the first fifty years of the Ming, and sustained growth during throughout the Qing, rising sharply during the second half of the nineteenth century. Although these data cannot account for numerous variables, such as settlement patterns, and disparities in reporting, they do confirm the general characterization that temple construction rose during periods of prosperity and that construction continued apace throughout the Qing dynasty.[55]

Republican-era gazetteers of Cang (1933) and Qing (1931) Counties (Appendix A-2, Temple Construction and Repair Led by Buddhist Monks) give dates for 133 instances of temple construction and 242 of temple repair (again, this figure includes Buddhist institutions) and confirm both the importance of village temples and this general chronology of building activity. As was the case in Eberhardt's study, temple construction was brisk during both the high Ming and Qing. In each of the counties, the high point of temple construction during the Ming was slightly later than that in the South, reflecting the greater scale of devastation of the North China Plain during the Yuan–Ming transition. As in the South, the pace of construction continued unabated throughout the Qing, increasing slightly during the final half of the nineteenth century. Even more striking is the record of temple repair, which follows a similar temporal pattern as construction, with an especially dramatic increase in activity during the late nineteenth century.

This last burst of temple repair, which continued into the twentieth century, is especially significant in light of the religious iconoclasm of the late Qing and Republic, which targeted those bastions of polytheistic superstition, popular temples. Nevertheless, although campaigns against popular religion during this period took shape in a concerted campaign to destroy or occupy temples of all sorts, popular sentiment was clearly otherwise. According to late Qing survey data of Tianjin and Qing counties, most temples were clearly located within the precincts of a village, and most villages maintained at least one temple. Even during the Republic, temple repair remained a frequent votive activity, and temples that were torn down or defaced by outsiders were often rebuilt soon thereafter by the villagers themselves.

The deities represented in the temples of late Qing Dulin Township reflected a thematic similarity to those seen elsewhere in Hebei. In his detailed surveys of more than 1,200 temples and shrines in the northern Hebei counties of Wanquan and Xuanhua, Willem Grootares discovered that four deities—Wudao, the Dragon King (*Longwang*), Guanyin, and Guandi—accounted for over half. Together, these four deities represent the basic elements of temple worship. Here, small shrines to Wudao served as bureaucratic outposts, similar to those of the tutelary deity (*tudi*) elsewhere in China. The Dragon King was associated with rainfall, and his temples were the sites for Prayers for Rain, a vital concern in the dry fields of Hebei. Guanyin and Guandi represented the complementary forces of the kindly bodhisattva, who showers the community with motherly mercy, and the male martial deity, who protects it from evil forces. In rural Tianjin and Dulin Township, as well, a preponderance of temples were dedicated to a handful of deities. Moreover, although the tutelary deity here takes the place of Wudao as the celestial administrator, and the cult of the three matron deities *(Niangniang shen)* has replaced that of the Dragon King, the overall picture represents the same balance of concerns (if not the precise proportions) and remains quite similar to that seen in other parts of the province.

In the temples of Cang County, individual and organized worship was generally restricted to the first and fifteenth of the lunar month, and especially on days of temple festivals *(miao hui)*. Individuals would visit village temples to report a birth or death (*bao miao*, usually performed at the shrine of the tutelary deity), to pray for general protection, or to make a specific vow. Larger ceremonies were performed regularly at the New Year, or episodically in case of need. The birthday of the main deity was often the occasion for a temple festival. The largest of these, such as the annual festival at the Balang Temple in Zhao-Guan Camp, were comparable in scope to the Dulin market, attracting peasants from dozens of surrounding villages. This three-day festival, which continued until the late 1930s, combined religious worship with trade and entertainment and is remembered as one of the most exciting events in the area.[56]

Most of the twentieth century saw a decline in the physical maintenance of village temples and an attendant weakening of temple networks and culture. During the early Republic and the Japanese occupation, gen-

Table 1.3   Popular Temples in Nineteenth-Century Tianjin County and Dulin Township, Qing County

| Primary Deity | Rural Tianjin County, 1842 | | Dulin Township, circa 1875 | |
	Number of Temples	Percent of Total (326)	Number of Temples	Percent of Total (52)
Tutelary *(tudi)*	80	25	8	15
Guandi	46	14	16	31
Guanyin[a]	38	12	13	25
Niangniang	18	6	9	17
Total	182	57	46	88

[a] Including temples listed as being dedicated to "bodhisattva," a reference to Guanyin.

eral economic hardship and the pressures of warfare, not to mention repeated campaigns to destroy or appropriate village temples, saw many temples abandoned or allowed to fall into decay.[57] Like the Balang Temple festivals, which died out near the eve of the Japanese invasion, most large ceremonial activities were scaled back or discontinued during this time as well. This process came to fruition after 1949, when any remaining village temples were pulled down, often accompanied by the public destruction of the temple statuary. Not surprisingly, the destruction of temples was especially intense during political campaigns, such as Land Reform, and the 1966 campaign to "Destroy the Four Olds" *(po si jiu)*. As all public religious activities, temple worship and festivals had completely ceased by the opening of the Cultural Revolution.

The resurgence in public religious activity since the late 1970s has seen the limited reconstruction of village temples and, more frequently, the reformulation of earlier practices to account for their absence. Although some villages, such as Hai Dock, have engaged in significant and costly temple construction, the most common project is far less ambitious: a modest shrine to the tutelary deity. Such shrines cost from a few hundred to more than a thousand *yuan* to build and serve both to protect the village from roving spirits and as a site for simple, individual devotion, such as burning incense and paper money in payment of a vow or as a sacrifice for a dead ancestor. In those villages without such a shrine, villagers often conduct individual worship at makeshift locations, such as the village crossroads, as in Little Terrace Village, or the site of the old temple, as in Yang Camp.

Larger ceremonies that had once centered on temples, such as the Balang Temple festival, have been slower to revive in the absence of new votive construction; however, new solutions solve old problems. During the mid-1990s, one peasant from Yang Camp invested in a large cloth tent, which has been painted to resemble a temple, complete with a red tiled roof and an entrance flanked by the Eighteen Arhats. The tent is used primarily for funerals and is rented out along with mourning clothes for 500 *yuan* per day, a reminder that public religion is as often motivated by profit as by devotion.[58]

Religious Life: Sectarians

Since the Ming dynasty, the North China Plain has been a center of lay religious teachings, known to scholars as "sectarians."[59] These teachings descend from Song-dynasty popular Buddhism, but came under attack as a result of the aggressive assertion of religious orthodoxy during the Ming and Qing. Official sources characterized these teachings as heterodox, millenarian, and subversive and plastered them with the already anachronistic label of "White Lotus."[60] Nor was the pressure against these teachings purely discursive; an often quoted statute from the Ming and Qing codes demanded a penalty of strangulation for White Lotus teachers and banishment to a distance of 3,000 *li* (1,500 kilometers) for followers.[61]

Ming-dynasty sectarian teachings were especially active in the Shandong peninsula and northern mountains of Hebei, and communication between these two points of genesis exposed Cang County to this tradition from its earliest days.[62] Despite consistent pressure against sectarian organization, particularly following the rise of religiously inspired violence during the mid-Qing, these organizations continued to thrive, particularly in the rural areas.[63] Evidence for early nineteenth-century sectarian teachings in Cang County comes from an unlikely source, the 1834 antisectarian treatise *A Detailed Refutation of Heterodox Teachings (Poxie xiangbian)*, which was written by Huang Yübian, the former magistrate of Cang County, using dozens of sectarian scriptures collected there and in his earlier posting of Julu County, also in Hebei. These scriptures include the canonical works of the sectarian tradition, such as the highly influential *Five Books in Six Volumes (Wubu liuce)*, as well as a number of works attributable to more specifically linked to the Vast Yang *(hongyang jiao)*, Western Great Vehicle *(xi dacheng jiao)*, and Primordial Chaos *(hunyuan jiao)* teachings.[64] Although the existence of these scriptures alone cannot necessarily demonstrate the organizational history of the Vast Yang or any other teaching in the area, it does confirm that sectarian tradition in early nineteenth-century Cang County was both well established and highly sophisticated.

From the mid-nineteenth through the mid-twentieth century, a number of sectarian teachings thrived in the villages of Cang County. Four of the most important—the Li Sect, the Way of Penetrating Unity, the Heaven and Earth Teaching, and the Teaching of the Most Supreme—are described in detail below. The coexistence of these teachings is due to the fact that each organized along very different lines, responded to diverse social needs, and sought a distinct sort of devotee. Local manifestations of the Li Sect and the Way of Penetrating Unity were products of expansive recruitment networks, which were centered largely in Tianjin. Each of these teachings tended to recruit individuals according to specific circumstances, and neither played a large role in public religious life. In contrast, networks of both the Heaven and Earth and Most Supreme teachings were centered in rural Cang County, were more generally appealing to ordinary peasants, and were more active in village religious life. Although these teachings recruited individuals as ritual specialists, they also served the ritual needs of unaffiliated villagers and maintained a visible presence in the community at large.

After 1949, sectarian teachings in Cang County came under intense pressure to disband. The early 1950s saw a series of campaigns against local sectarians, the most successful of which was an energetic and well-coordinated movement in 1951 to eradicate the Way of Penetrating Unity. Although lower-profile teachings such as the Heaven and Earth and Most Supreme escaped such campaigns, they were forced to scale back their public religious activities during the 1950s. By the mid-1960s, even the most devoted of these groups had altogether ceased conducting public rituals.

The 1980s and 1990s saw the open revival of many local sectarian groups and practices. Although very specific teachings such as the Li Sect and the Way of Penetrating Unity were unable to revive, branches of the Most Supreme and the Heaven and Earth teachings began to conduct small rituals as early as the late 1970s. Often with the technical assistance of sectarians from neighboring villages, or financial assistance from within the village, many sectarian groups have revived to their pre-Revolutionary strength and importance.

Much of this activity has been conducted quite openly and is common knowledge within neighboring villages. Local cadres are loathe to interfere, either because they remember the excesses of the previous decades—as one informant put it, "After the Cultural Revolution, nobody has the stomach to try to control religion"—because they personally believe in the efficacy of the group or ritual, or because they do not want to alienate themselves from the peasants by attacking an extremely popular institution. To avoid overtly condoning these activities while still retaining their place in local society, however, village cadres and officials might make a conspicuous donation but not personally attend, or else attempt to paint local religious activity in a more acceptable light as "folk culture" (*minjian wenhua*).

At the same time, to retain this tacit acceptance, sectarian activity must remain within certain boundaries. The first is that it can in no way constitute a political threat, either real or symbolic. The Way of Penetrating Unity, which was so thoroughly painted by decades of propaganda as a reactionary threat to the Communist state, will not likely ever be granted the legal status it gained in Taiwan, nor would it be allowed to quietly exist locally, simply because the name carries too strong a political connotation. Of course, the degree of control is highly dependent upon the proclivities of local authorities. In some areas of Hebei and in Shandong, including Cang County, large religious festivals are organized with little government interference, while other areas are policed with draconian efficiency.[65]

Islam and Christianity

In addition to what are typically thought of as Chinese religious traditions, Cang County also has strong Muslim and Christian communities.[66] Although neither of these groups is discussed explicitly in this study, they deserve mention for their impact on local religion and local society. Of the two religions, the larger in Cang County is Islam, which was brought to the area by migrants from Jiangsu and Shandong during the early Ming dynasty. Since that time, Cang has had one of the largest concentrations of Muslim Hui in Hebei province. The 1933 gazetteer estimated the Muslim population of Cang County at around 5,000 persons and listed forty-seven mosques, including the Great North Mosque *(Qingzhen beida si)*, one of the largest in North China.[67] Today, the Muslim population is just under 15,000, or about 2.8 percent of the total population.[68] For the most part, this population is concentrated within the city of Cangzhou and, to a lesser extent, a small number of wholly or largely Muslim villages. Since the late 1970s, many of these rural communities have become more integrated into the Muslim population in and beyond the city and have experienced an upsurge in votive construction. Late nineteenth-century Dulin Township only had one mosque, located in the large village of Huichu (currently Dachu). Even the town of Dulin, which has a sizable Muslim minority (enough to support a distinct group of Muslim butchers and food vendors at the Dulin market), did not have an operational mosque during the late nineteenth century. In the 1990s, however, the Muslim population of Dulin raised funds, both within its own community and among faithful in Cangzhou City, to construct two small mosques and engage an imam *(ahong)* from western Ningxia province.[69]

Unlike some of its neighboring counties, Cang never had a large Christian presence. Although adjacent Xian County was one of the earliest centers of Catholic missionary work, with hospitals, schools, and twenty-five churches, Cang had very few Catholics and very little Catholic organization. Even during the Republican period, Cang County had no Catholic churches. Various Protestant denominations had more impact within Cang County itself, the most notable contribution being the hospital in Cangzhou City built just before the Boxer Uprising and rebuilt soon thereafter. A group of British missionaries under the Christian Society of China based their local operations within Cangzhou City and provided the most sustained missionary contact, but their stay lasted only until the Japanese invasion.[70]

Like the Muslims, the small Christian population of Cang County is located primarily within the city of Cangzhou itself, with very few Christians being found even in the larger towns. Christianity is not carried by brides to their new homes because city women rarely marry into the rural areas. None of the peasants interviewed in villages of Dulin knew of any rural Christians, although they did know of the teaching itself and many had heard of the large Catholic cathedral in Xian County. Perhaps because of its historical weakness in the area, Christianity does not seem to carry any particular negative connotations among Cang County peasants. Even at the time of the Boxer Uprising, when the recently completed Christian hospital in Cangzhou City was besieged for nearly a month, missionaries inside noted that most of the Boxers themselves were not local and that the groups generally did not have much success recruiting in the area.[71]

In general, both Muslims and Christians in Cang County can be characterized as relatively closed communities. In terms of religious doctrine, certain syncretic teachings in Cang County, such as the Way of Penetrating Unity, emphasized that Islam and Christianity were part of a divinely inspired greater truth. This, however, originates in the doctrine of the sect itself, which was formulated elsewhere and brought into the area. Although many unaffiliated peasants do know the basic elements of Islam and Christianity, few have enough understanding of or interest in these teachings to influence their own religious lives.

Conclusion

In many ways, Cang County is typical of much of the North China Plain. It has experienced all of the forces that shaped the modern history of the region: warfare, invasion, extension of state power during the late nineteenth and first half of the twentieth centuries, structural transformation under the first few decades of socialism, and limited prosperity since the late 1970s. In terms of religious life, there is little in Cang County that is unusual or remarkable. Peasants maintain regimens of personal prayer and devotion, whereas village temples and local sectarian networks both inspire and express the full range of emotions and needs with which individuals and votive bodies approach the sacred. Ethnographic and episodic accounts reveal similar tendencies and expressions in village society and religious life in communities throughout Hebei and into neighboring provinces.

Nevertheless, this apparent degree of uniformity and typicality masks the significance of the local in the formulation and expression of religious knowledge and devotion. As both Skinner and Duara have discussed, Chinese local societies can be defined as bounded, culturally endogamous spheres. Although the two would seem to define the parameters of these spheres according to slightly different criteria, as the community based around the market town, or as a "cultural nexus" of human networks, both emphasize the radial extension of power, culture, and communication from central points.[72] Such characterizations hold true for certain, but not all, aspects of religious life. In the context of the village, centrally construed networks do find expression in the allocation of resources and various elaborated regimens of ritual life. Yet other aspects of religious knowledge, particularly that of direct encounters with the immanent sacred realm, do not depend on religious, marketing, or other networks, but rather are geographically determined by an imagined sphere of relevance, specifically the necessity of taking place in a setting with which the hearer is personally acquainted.

2. Religious Life and the Village Community

Assuming, as did Maurice Freedman, that a "Chinese religion" exists, scholars are faced with the daunting task of giving shape to its many centers and boundaries, from the vague "paradigmatic unity" that Freedman saw as binding the entire tradition together, to the intensely local world of belief and practice that make up the religious lives of the majority of its adherents.[1] Any model of hierarchical organization of religion—such as the conceptual structuring of divine power into a celestial bureaucracy and the role of nested central places in culturally endogamous communities—is eventually based on an ordering of space, specifically of territorial units.

As discussed briefly in the introduction, recent scholarship has demonstrated the limitations of any hierarchical understanding of local religion, in terms of both structured religious affiliation and the transmission of religious beliefs, practices, and cults from center to periphery. In response to earlier characterizations of the Chinese religious universe as a conceptual corollary to the secular bureaucracy, propagated by state-sponsored networks and supportive of official power, these scholars have emphasized the transmission of religious knowledge through iconography and vernacular literature and the extrapolitical, even subversive, nature of nonelite religious networks. Even such a reevaluation, however, still assumes the central importance of hierarchies of knowledge and organization in the territorial structuring of local religious belief and networks. This chapter will revisit the question of the structuring of territoriality by focusing the role of the village in the organization of local religious life and the propagation of religious knowledge.

In late Qing and Republican Cang County, public religious life was centered on and definitive of the village community. The village was the site in which religious resources, influences, and organizations were concentrated and elaborated, allowing individual villages to develop idiosyncratic religious resources and activities. This, in turn, shaped the unique identity of each village with regard to neighboring communities. The administrative necessity of supporting communal resources, religious and otherwise, fostered a sense of shared welfare within the village, a point made by Japanese scholars during the 1970s, while the corporate ownership and care of religious resources further fostered a sense of common welfare vis-à-vis the sacred.[2] In addition to their importance to the community as a whole, religious resources concentrated within the village also served as the physical and human infrastructure for the votive life of the individual household. This did not, however, necessarily draw these households into a ritual or votive regimen of the village as a whole. In most cases, the household gave social and financial support to the religious resources of the village, but its ritual obligation was owed primarily to itself.

Both village society and local religious life underwent substantive changes after the founding of the People's Republic in 1949. Beginning with the 1951 campaign to "suppress counterrevolutionaries" (zhenya fangeming), the government of the People's Republic employed its unprecedented administrative presence in rural areas to embark upon successive movements against local religion. This pressure gradually increased throughout the 1950s and 1960s, culminating in the well-known excesses of the Cultural Revolution. Campaigns against religion were waged as part of a larger program of rural transformation, one aimed at the wholesale reorganization of village society. During the 1950s and 1960s, once-powerful families were brought low, while small, formerly independent villages were combined into larger communities, particularly during the early years of Collectivization. Thus, as rural religious life was being gradually dismantled, the internal social structure and physical boundaries of villages themselves were being redrawn.

In Cang County, the internal cohesion of these newly reformed villages was put to the test beginning in the late 1970s, when a loosening of policy allowed for the reconstitution of the human and material infrastructure of local religion. In some cases, villagers attempted to reconstruct specific resources that had been destroyed, but at least as often they built from scratch, according to new needs and realities. Most significantly, religious reconstruction since the 1970s has generally followed the contours of the current, reformed villages, rather than those of pre-1949 communities.

As had been the case during the late Qing and the Republic, individual villages are marked by distinct variation in their religious institutions.

Since the late 1970s, some villages have been remarkably successful at rebuilding their religious resources and, as of the early twenty-first century, maintain vibrant and active public religious lives. Others have almost none. Of those villages that have reconstructed previous religious resources or built new ones, some support a local sectarian group and others a village temple. The marked diversity among villages prevents one from making any blanket statements about the religious life of post–Cultural Revolution Cang County, except for the fact that such diversity continues to occur primarily at the level of the village itself.

Village and Religious Community in Late Qing and Republican North China

Although the principles of rural organization differ greatly from one part of China to another, the village remains a socially significant unit of organization and personal identification. Local and village communities throughout China can be characterized as having some sort of ascriptive value and sense of mutual welfare, which generally include some degree of common religious identity. As such, individual communities are often locally distinguishable from each other in some aspect of their religious life, which in turn reinforces the importance of the village as the site of religious elaboration. Nevertheless, the difference between communities is very much a matter local perception, rather than ideal types defined in normative terms. For example, in one area of northern Taiwan, Donald DeGlopper noted that ritual organization was relatively permeable but that each neighborhood worshipped a different deity.[3] In a neighboring district, Stephen Sangren studied villages that all worship local tutelary deities (*tudi gong*), but do so in clearly defined and delineated ritual communities.[4] Even within this small area of Taiwan, villages are united and divided by very different sorts of religious bonds. At first glance, the precise nature of the distinction between villages might not seem as significant as the fact of this distinction itself as a subjective marker of community.

The actual bonds that shape a village as a self-consciously distinct religious entity, however, do deserve closer examination, not only because they subjectively distinguish the village from its neighbors, but also because they define the place of the individual within the community itself. The examples from northern Taiwan present villages that are defined by characteristic religious devotion and adherence to a common ritual regimen, respectively, and both differ from the type of community seen in the villages of Cang County, which is based around particularistic use of common resources. The first two factors are similar in that they actively draw the individual into the village as a body and are thus sources of ascriptive identification, but with the potential to serve as a basis for the exercise of coercion.[5] In contrast, the use of common religious resources assumes that, even if the village does share a sense of common welfare, the individual or household approaches its own religious needs as a free agent. In this case, the individual may be accountable to the community in the administration and use of these resources, but this relationship lacks the implications of individual compliance being necessary to guarantee the welfare of the community.

Village as Community of Devotion

In his study of local religion in sixteenth-century Spain, William Christian demonstrated how villages maintained a special votive relationship with patron saints, who themselves held a special affection for the community, as revealed through divine portents. Similarly, villages in Qing and Republican Cang County did exhibit particularistic devotion to deities and spirits, and this was to a large degree a function of local religious knowledge. Deities represented in the iconography of shrines and temples and in religious performance evolved within village folklore to develop individual personalities and affection for the community. As such, village cults of even the more common deities could become quite idiosyncratic.

Before the decline of temple culture during and after the 1930s, iconography in temples acted as local repositories of knowledge about the sacred realm, visibly representing who the deities were, what they looked like, and even their areas of expertise. Many village temples retained physical representations of quite obscure deities, such as the Spotted Pox Matron or the Fire-Eating Monkey, both of whom graced the Empress of Heaven Temple in Republican Tianjin.[6] More than maintaining the cults of obscure deities, however, village temples provided the platform by which the common deities were given local significance. Individual statues or shrines developed a local reputation for benevolence or efficacy. For example, the Sanguan temple of Little Terrace Village once held a statue of Guandi that was known to be especially powerful, particularly in the service of Prayers for Rain. The fame of this statue was such that neighboring communities would occasionally steal it for their own ceremonies, to the annoyance of villagers of Little Terrace, who were then forced to ritually reinstate the statue in the temple at their own expense. Eventually, the fame of the statue proved to be its undoing. In 1947, a lower-level Communist cadre arrived in the village and smashed the statue, daring Guandi to take what punitive action he liked. As villagers remember, this challenge was ill advised. Soon after the incident, an irrigation well caved in, killing several villagers, although the cadre himself remained unharmed.[7]

Folklore surrounding temple iconography not only attested to the power of a statue; it also personalized the relationship between the deity and the village, transforming universal cults into icons of local identification.[8] For example, the Guandi temple of Ni Camp, located in the suburbs of Tianjin, houses a small wooden statue of a tutelary deity that is known to be especially powerful. Normally the tutelary deity of a village is seen as an impersonal bureaucrat and is thus rarely the object of devotion. Over the past hundred years, however, this particular statue has survived numerous mishaps, always to return unscathed to Ni Camp. Peasants take this as a sign of the fondness the deity has for the village and treat it as a local patron.[9] The festival held on the birthday of the god is packed with villagers, who burn incense, make offerings, and fight to tear off a piece of the red cloth in which the statue has been wrapped. In Ni Camp, the lore surrounding this one statue has thus tangibly affected religious practice, changing a rarely noticed functionary into a much sought-after personal patron with a well-known affection for that particular village. Moreover, villagers understand their practice to be distinct from that of surrounding communities and attribute it specifically to the unusual power and benevolence of their own tutelary deity, of which they are justifiably proud.

Public performance also shaped local religious knowledge. Ritual performance, such as Mulian operas, depicted mysteries of the afterlife in vivid and terrifying detail, and the gods and heroes portrayed in recited fiction and opera made their way into popular religious consciousness and worship.[10] Similarly, the public ritual activities of sectarian groups, although not necessarily a function of the village as such, still exerted a strong influence on the religious understanding of the community as a whole. The Heaven and Earth Teaching, for example, maintained ritual devotion to their founder, Patriarch Dong Sihai. In communities with an active Heaven and Earth contingent, the presence of Patriarch Dong loomed large in popular religious consciousness, in part, at least, because of the frequency in which villagers would encounter him in a ritual setting. Within these villages, it was common for most families to maintain a spirit tablet of Dong Sihai, even if they had no formal affiliated with the teaching.

In each of these examples, religious representation within the village was incorporated into local folklore and thus transformed from particu-laristic cults transformed into village patrons. These gods were felt to have an affection or affinity for the community, although the theft of village statuary demonstrates that these boundaries were also somewhat mal-leable; however, although gratitude toward a divine patron demonstrates the affective importance of the village, the structure of the community is seen in the regimen of active worship—that is, the life of the village as a ritual community.[11]

Village as Ritual Community

The notion of the village as a ritual community has been discussed ex-tensively, particularly in the context of southern China.[12] Though by no means a universal phenomenon, there exist numerous examples from Tai-wan and the southeast coast of villages that assemble for rituals in order to secure the welfare of the community as a whole. Participation in village ritual can define the boundaries of the community, as demonstrated by David Faure in the New Territories of Hong Kong.[13] Within the commu-nity, such participation in ritual activities is both right and responsibility. Stephen Sangren's study presents a particularly clear example of villages in which ritual participation in territorially defined cults, such as those of local tutelary deities, is clearly delineated by place of residence, with universal attendance by village households. At the same time, the hierar-chical organization of ritual action demonstrates gradations of member-ship and authority. Aspects of communal ritual, such as processions, are rigidly ordered and immediately tangible expressions of the structure of the village.[14]

Ethnographic evidence from Republican North China suggests that some villages there acted as ritual communities as well. In one example from southeastern Shanxi, ritual and theatrical performance of religious operas *(sai)* was formally divided among four "societies" *(she)*, which to-gether represented the village as a whole.[15] Chinese ethnographers work-ing in the same area have documented communities in which each house-hold had a hereditary responsibility for particular roles in village ritual dramas.[16] As for the North China Plain, Japanese ethnographic materials occasionally speak of rituals characterized as "village festivals" *(cun hui)*, which could be taken to imply participation of the collective in a ritual ca-pacity. Prasenjit Duara notes that, in the northern Hebei village of Shajing, "all village members were in theory expected to participate" in village reli-gious functions. Whether this participation was strictly the case or not, the fact that certain members of the community felt the need to emphasize the universality of their ritual functions does speak for the *idea* of village as a community organized around and bound by a schedule of collective ritual practice.[17]

In Republican Cang County, however, villages rarely came together for mass rituals, nor was the individual required to participate in the ritual affairs of the community. To be sure, each village maintained its regimen of public rituals, the most important of which was the Upper Primordial (*shangyuan*) festival celebrated at the New Year. Nevertheless, peasants insisted that even ritual activities called "village festivals" were performed for, rather than by the community, and did not demand the attendance or participation of ordinary villagers. In fact, most of my respondents found the idea of mandatory attendance (either by the individual or representative of the household) in village religious activities to be extremely odd. Rather, they felt that mandatory ritual participation was a hallmark only of the votive life of the family or, to a lesser extent, the lineage group.[18] Thus, most could conceive of such activities only in the context of single surname villages, which by the Republican period were extremely rare in this area. None of my respondents in rural Cang County had ever heard of a non-Muslim village that had held religious activities at which participation was in any way policed by the community or required as a function of community membership.[19]

The Prayer for Rain ceremony illustrates the relationship between an understanding of common welfare and mass participation in ritual practice. This ritual, which can last from one to three days, addresses the most basic need of the dry farming regions of North China. Rainfall being a universal necessity, and, moreover, one that generally does not distinguish among individual households, Prayers for Rain are the epitome of a common concern and a common good. Ethnographic accounts from various locations in Republican North China suggest that village Prayers for Rain were often not only a collective effort, but also a recreation of the village in ritual form. In most cases, the ritual began with a formal procession around the village, which delineated the boundaries of the community. According to village leaders in Shajing and Houxiazhai villages (in northern Hebei and northern Shandong, respectively), one adult male from each household would participate in the procession, although ordinary villagers questioned on the topic were less emphatic about the universality of this custom. In Wudian Village, near Beijing, the procession stopped in front of each household so that the residents could burn incense to the statue of Guandi carried at its head. In the large village of Lengshuigou, near Ji'nan, nearly a quarter of the 400 households participated in the prayer, each in a specific ritual capacity. Even those who did not perform a ritual function maintained the purity of the sacrifice by abstaining from certain foods (such as meat and onions) and sexual intercourse during the three days of the ceremony.[20]

In contrast, other ethnographic work in the same area suggests that, although this ritual was conducted on behalf of the village, most ordinary villagers were not actively involved. When asked whether the gods would hear a Prayer for Rain that was not attended by the entire community, peasants in Gangzili Village in northern Shandong responded that very few villagers actually attended the ritual. There, the community was symbolically represented by the attendance of the village head and a few of the older peasants, but even this arrangement was very informal. Similarly, although the ceremony in Cao Village, located in southwestern Shandong, sounds quite exciting, with villagers waving knives and spears in the air to gain the attention of Sun Wukong (the Monkey King from the novel *Journey to the West*), who would carry the prayer to heaven, attendance was entirely voluntary. Peasants in Xiao Village, near Beijing, emphasized that, because everyone needs rain, most villagers would visit the ceremony, but did not mention the necessity of attendance for the ceremony to be efficacious or any attempt by village leaders to encourage or require attendance.[21]

Religious activities in Republican Cang County generally conformed to the latter characterization. In these drought-plagued villages, where the Prayer for Rain was among the most important ritual occasions, attendance was entirely voluntary for most villagers. Moreover, many of those who did attended the ritual did so for the sake of entertainment, out of a sense of community solidarity, or to satisfy specific ancillary religious needs such as making or repaying a private vow. This latter concern was especially common in villages such as Ni-Yang and Rear Camp, in which local Heaven and Earth sectarians performed the ceremony. Although the ceremony was ostensibly dedicated to the performance of one specific prayer, peasants still used it as an occasion to pray for healing, wealth, and general good fortune.

This is not to say that village ritual activities, such as Prayers for Rain, did not involve the entire community. At the most basic level, the village itself was understood to be the patron of the ceremony, and this was re-enacted in ritual acts such as pacing the borders of the village in procession or asking for rain in the name of the community. It is clear that the votive relationship was understood to flow between a particular deity and the village as a whole; however, in contrast to Christian's characterization

Figure 2.1   Sectarian procession around the village of Rear Camp. Note the relative absence of onlookers. During this particular procession, only a few village children were in attendance.

of Spanish villages, which presented a "united front" of ritual action and required the active participation of all members, the villages in Cang County engaged in a kind of representative devotion.[22] The welfare of the community was secured by the ritual action of a sectarian group or village elders, or the prophylactic presence of religious architecture. In terms of active participation of individual households, however, the criterion was not ritual but financial, specifically a donation to defray the costs of the ceremony. In this sense, ritual activities were similar to any other concerns of the village, such as road repair or self-defense, which required financial contributions from all but the poorest members of the community. In these and other communal projects, the contributions of each family were posted prominently in the village (in the same way that more weighty fund-raising activities might be recorded on stele) and represented a tangible display of village solidarity. Refusal to contribute to such an effort was an unthinkable breach of this solidarity, as seen in the often-violent rifts created when Christian villagers refused to fund village religious activities in late nineteenth-century Zhili.[23]

The importance of these financial contributions to village solidarity is especially evident considering the disparity of funds collected. During the

1930s, the most significant contributions to village-level rituals were usually made by one or a few wealthy families, who were often designated as "association heads" *(huishou)* for their efforts. This authority was parallel to, but distinct from, the religious authority of the ritual specialist *(dangjia)*. Although the role of the *huishou* was generally administrative, rather than ritualistic, association with and willingness to take partial responsibility for village religious projects afforded these individuals significant prestige within the community.[24] At the other extreme, even the poorest villagers tried to make some sort of visible contribution to these projects, preferably in cash, but occasionally in kind. In the more economically striated villages of Republican Cang County, the contributions of one or two very wealthy families might equal those of half of the poorer families in the village combined.

This was the case in the small community of Wang Family Village, which had only forty households in the late nineteenth century. During the 1930s, the position of *huishou* had been held by the wealthy Wang family for at least three generations, roughly to the 1880s. At this time, this single family held more land than the rest of the villagers combined and usually put up most of the money for village religious undertakings. Nevertheless, other households in the village were held equally responsible for whatever contribution their means would allow. Although conspicuous contributions to village religious activities did afford certain individuals and families significant prestige, I think that it would be an exaggeration to say that doing so represented an attempt to hijack the public ritual face of the community so as to exclude the very poor, as appears to have been the case in more commercialized areas of Hebei.[25] Even in the highly striated community of Wang Family Village, the significance of such donations was not in the amount of the given, but rather the positive expression of village solidarity that they represented.[26]

Village as a Shared Resource Community

Although many villages in late Qing and Republican-era Cang County maintained special devotion to a patron deity, this was rarely expressed in a common ritual life. Rather, active worship was the purview of both votive groups within the village, who acted on behalf of the community and, especially, the individual household, which engaged the sacred to secure its own welfare. The physical and human resources built and maintained by the community enhanced the religious identity of the village and served as the vehicle by which the individual brought his or her needs and concerns to the sacred. Tendencies of idiosyncratic belief and practice, however, were functions of proximity, convenience, and local identification within the village rather than a monolithic view of the sacred, which was forced upon the community by its leaders. With this in mind, let us examine in more detail the types of religious resources.

Village Religious Resources: Temples

The prevalence and importance of temples in the villages of Republican-era North China are borne out by contemporary ethnographic studies. Sidney Gamble considered one or more temples to be a necessary feature of most North China villages. In his surveys of northern Hebei, Willem Grootaers found an average of 6.8 temples per village in Wanquan County and 4.5 per village in neighboring Xuanhua.[27] In these and many other areas, the well-known Republican campaigns to convert popular temples into village schools *(hui miao xing xue)* appear to have had relatively little effect. Even the "model" Ding County, Hebei, where the policy was enforced with unusual vigor, still had fewer than two temples per village, with new temples being built as late as the 1940s.[28] In many of the Mantetsu villages, such as Lengshuigou and Shajing, temple cults were the center of village religious life.

In and around Cang County, village temples were certainly common, but not quite so universal as the evidence above would suggest. Mid-nineteenth-century surveys of Tianjin County show a relatively small number of village temples. Excluding the city of Tianjin, this county had a total of 332 temples in 485 villages and towns, an average of just over two temples for every three villages.[29] Within Cang County itself, the sixty-seven villages of Dulin Township had only sixty-eight temples during the late Qing. Of them, seven were no more than simple shrines to the tutelary deity. Moreover, temples were not apportioned evenly. Seventeen of these villages, roughly one quarter of the total, had no temple at all.

As mentioned in the preceding chapter, village temples represented a duality of purpose. For the village at large, temples had a general prophylactic influence, protecting the community and everyone in it, but the relationship of the individual, particularly the nonspecialist, to this function was primarily passive. In addition, village temples were centers of numerous individual regimens of devotion and supplication. Thus, when a temple housed a Buddhist monk, Daoist priest, or other resident religious specialist, as was the case in twenty-three of the sixty-seven villages, this individual acted as a ritual resource for hire rather than a spiritual and

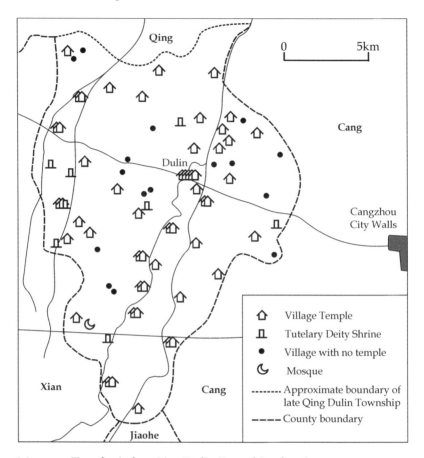

Map 2.1   Temples in late Qing Dulin Township, showing contemporary boundaries of Cang and Qing Counties.

moral leader of the community. The crowd of patrons who came to the temple on important days came as individuals, bringing with them private needs, concerns, and prayers. When the asked about votive use of village temples, my respondents in Cang County echoed the sentiments of Shandong peasants interviewed in the late 1980s, who stated matter-of-factly that one only visits a temple "only when someone gets sick."[30] Peasants in Cang County universally responded that during the late Republic, as now, they would visit the temple only for a specific reason, such as praying to be healed, for a good harvest, or for safety during a hazardous undertaking. Certainly, many considered the security of the village (as well as the region and even the nation, for that matter) to fall within their general prayers for "peace and safety" but emphasized that the focus of their devotion remained on their own families.

The small village of Quan Family Camp demonstrates both the limited role of temples in public religious life and their importance to private devotion. Late Qing surveys record a population of ninety-seven adults in Quan Family Camp, although villagers report that, by the outbreak of the Japanese invasion, the total population was just above forty. Despite its size, this village had two temples, a Guandi Temple on the eastern road and a temple to the tutelary deity on the western. Both were small, single-room shrines, although the location of the Guandi temple on the right-hand side of the village signified its superior status. Both temples were kept locked, except on the first and fifteenth of the month, and neither was the site of regular rituals or temple festivals. The Guandi temple had two statues, each about one meter tall, of Guandi himself and the Dragon King, both of which were brought out during Prayers for Rain. This was the only large ritual occasion involving the temple and was conducted only in times of drought. The ceremony itself was organized by the village head but was performed by the Heaven and Earth sectarians from neighboring Yang Camp. Although technically of lesser importance, the more significant of the two temples in the eyes of villagers was the shrine of the tutelary deity. This shrine had no public ceremonial but was the site to which peasants would take individual religious needs and occasional reports.[31]

Village Religious Resources: Sectarians and Specialists

Resident ritual specialists, particularly those belonging to sectarian groups, served as important religious resources within the village, and sectarian festivals had a similar place in the religious life of the community as village temples. At the most basic level, the presence of a sectarian contingent within the village exerted a general prophylactic influence over the community. Peasants in Yang Camp attributed the high moral character of their community, as well as their good harvests, to the presence of Heaven and Earth sectarians. Public sectarian rituals, like temple worship, were held on the important days of the religious calendar, such as the Three Primordials (sanyuan), as well as in cases of episodic need. As with temple patronage, however, the few who attended sectarian rituals did so not as a function of village unity but for specific, personal needs.[32]

Donation records from sectarian festivals give an indication of the importance of the community in funding such rituals during the late Qing and early Republic (discussed in chapter 7). Since that time, the festival of

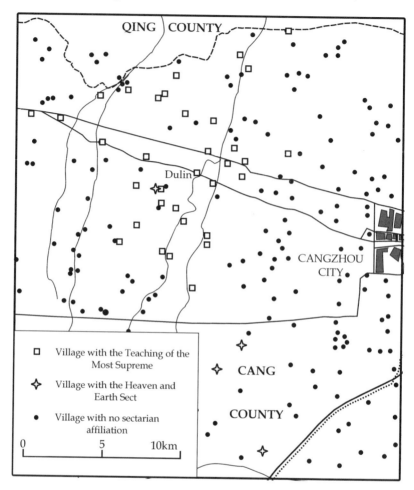

Map 2.2   Sectarian villages in late Republican Dulin Township.

the Heaven and Earth Sect has alternated between the two villages of Rear Camp and White Yang Bridge, receiving a large number of donations from each community. This broad base of support from within the two host villages demonstrates the process by which a particularistic sectarian festival could become a function of local community. Other donations came from a large geographic area, but were concentrated within a small number of villages, further demonstrating that devotion to Dong Sihai, the founder of the sect, did not radiate out evenly across the landscape but, rather, was localized within particular communities. Thus, although the festival itself was performed by members of a strong and discrete sectarian network, devotees that came from outside of this network still tended to be concentrated within particular villages.

As with temple construction and temple festivals, the concrete expression of village solidarity in sectarian functions was financial support, rather than ritual participation. Although the above example refers to a sectarian festival that alternated between two communities, most were conducted by the sectarians of a single village. Like temples, sectarian rituals were vital to the welfare of the village and provided a common resource for individual devotion. As a common good, festivals of sects such as the Heaven and Earth and Most Supreme Teachings were financial responsibility of the village as a whole. Within the living memory of the oldest villagers—that is, from the 1930s—all families in which these sects were active were socially obliged to make at least some token show of support for their activities. In the sectarian villages of Cang County, it was common practice to record donations of each household to public sectarian functions and post the results in the center of the community.[33]

Not all sectarian groups or specialists were suited to serve as the foundation for village religious life. The importance of groups such as the Heaven and Earth Sect and the Teaching of the Most Supreme to the larger village community resulted from a combination of their broad religious appeal and reputation of their specialists. Groups such as the Li Sect and the Way of Pervading Unity appealed to very specific moral and eschatological needs but did not have much to offer the generalist. Moreover, in contrast to professional religious specialists, lay teachings such as Heaven and Earth Sect and the Teaching of the Most Supreme were composed of ordinary villagers who had trained as ritual specialists of the teaching but were still engaged in agriculture and otherwise members of the village community. Professional Buddhist monks or Daoist priests might be granted a small piece of land to farm but generally depended on the paid performance of ritual services for their livelihood. In contrast, sectarians performed their ritual services for free, incurring only the costs of materials used in the rituals themselves. Not only were sectarian rituals less costly to perform, but the specialists themselves were respected for their piety, devotion, and selfless honesty. Like other aspects of local culture, the respect and affection shown toward the local sectarian contingent was particularly strong within the village itself, in part because these groups gave preferential treatment to fellow villagers when arranging ritual functions.

Finally, although both temple communities and sectarian groups were important to the religious life of the community, neither held a monopoly on village religiosity nor were their activities exclusive to or mandatory for the village. Even when closely identified with the village community, these resources were by no means the only access to the sacred. Villagers employed communal religious resources for the sake of convenience, because they were used to doing so and because they had a special affinity for their own resources, if for no other reason than that they had in the past paid to support them; however, they could easily take their religious needs elsewhere, either to other sacred sites or ritual specialists in their own village or to similar resources in adjacent communities. Thus, even as they shaped the public religious persona of the village, neither those villagers most active in caring for the temple (often formally designated as a "temple committee," *miao hui*) nor the administrative or religious leadership of a sectarian group could be said to have controlled access to the sacred or dictated the practice of the community.[34]

Reorganization of the Village and Reconstruction of Religious Resources

Throughout China, the 1950s and especially the period of and immediately following the Cultural Revolution (1966–1976) were marked by exhaustive efforts to destroy local religious tradition. Extant temples were destroyed, statues and holy objects were smashed, and scriptures and votive prints were burned. In Cang County, at least, ritual specialists were generally not subjected to "struggle" (except in the case of sects branded as "reactionary," such as the Way of Pervading Unity), although they were unable to continue to practice publicly, and much of their practical and oral traditions were lost. Beginning in the late 1970s, the changing political climate allowed for a limited resurgence of rural religious life, and rural areas were anxious to begin rebuilding their religious culture. Despite the renascent interest in religion, the physical, intellectual, and practical foundations of this culture lay in ruins.

As mentioned in chapter 1, the size and structure of Cang County villages underwent dramatic change throughout the course of the twentieth century. In the last decades of the Qing, villages varied in size and structure and interacted with the state through semiofficial agents. In the first decades of the Republic, attempts were made to standardize village size and rationalize rural administration, but, ironically, these policies only succeeded when villages banded together to face warlord and Japanese exactions. Not surprisingly, the greatest changes in village society came after 1949, particularly during the first three decades of the People's Republic, when the state expanded its unprecedented presence into rural society, while the villages themselves were thrown into internal revolution.

Despite these profound changes in the nature and composition of the villages themselves, when peasants sought to rebuild their religious culture, the impetus of organization came primarily from the village level. Some pre-Revolutionary villages that had been incorporated into larger communities continued to maintain a degree of independent identity. During the 1930s, the two villages of Yang Camp and Ni Camp had each supported a contingent of village sectarians, the former of the Heaven and Earth Sect and the latter of the Teaching of the Most Supreme. After the two villages combined during the Japanese occupation, they continued to maintain a degree of independent identity, and the two sectarian groups continued to exist separately. During the early 1980s, both groups revived, and now continue to perform independent rituals, occasionally providing moral or material support to each other. For individual ritual needs, such as funerals, peasants from the former Yang Camp still tend to rely on the Heaven and Earth Sect, whereas those from what had been Ni Camp employ the Teaching of the Most Supreme. In general, however, the coexistence of sectarian traditions is a rarity, simply because the weaker group became seen as superfluous. This process hints at the sense of community within the newly combined villages. Although these villages only vaguely resemble those of a half century earlier, many having been created by administrative fiat, the necessity of operating as a single entity for three or more decades had served to foster a sense of identity and patterns of cooperation, begging the question of whether these new communities are now "natural" or "administrative" villages.[35] Despite the difference in size and structure, and the fact that many had been formed by external authorities, these villages continue to behave very much like their Republican counterparts.

In the reconstruction of religious resources, however, some communities have been more successful than others, and the village level currently exhibits the greatest degree of differentiation. Whereas before 1949, most communities had some sort of religious resources, in present-day Cang County this reconstruction has not occurred evenly, and thus villages can thus be divided into three types: temple, sectarian, or dependent communities. In the first two, the village temple or sectarian group—in most cases, one that had existed before the 1950s—was recreated by the village, usually at the prompting of one or a few especially devout individuals. The third type is characterized by a relatively new phenomenon, the *absence* of significant religious resources within the village. Peasants from these communities must travel elsewhere to satisfy their ritual needs. Just as before 1949, all of these villages belong to the same regional religious culture and, in terms of basic religious beliefs and needs, remain very similar to their neighbors. The difference among them often lies in the simple fact that, in the latter sort, no individual has stepped forward to take charge of a village campaign to rebuild religious resources within the community.

Temple Village: The Guanyin Hall in Hai Dock

Since the Ming dynasty, religious life in Hai Dock Village has been dominated by various reincarnations of its Guanyin Hall *(Guanyin tang).*[36] According to villagers, the temple was once part of a large Buddhist monastery, supported through the lavish patronage of court eunuchs originally from the Cang County area. It fell into gradual decline during the Qing, and by the end of the dynasty in 1911 the only remnant of its earlier splendor was a handful of scattered stelae, a dilapidated three-room temple, and, most significantly, three stone statues of Guanyin and her two attendants, each standing roughly two and a half meters tall. In 1956, the temple building was finally pulled down at the insistence of cadres from the local town of Dulin, but the statues, each weighing well over a ton, were spirited away by villagers at night and secretly buried in the corner of a field, where they would remain for the next two decades. In the early 1980s, the statues were disinterred and returned to the former site of the temple, protected from the elements only by a plastic tarp.

Throughout the 1980s, villagers had discussed rebuilding their temple, both because it was felt that the village had been generally better off during the days that it had had the temple and because villagers wanted a "place to go and burn incense." No specific action was taken until 1994, when Wang Chunting, a peasant and old soldier from Mudanjiang who had married a woman from the village, took up the campaign to have the temple rebuilt. This plan, however, presented two problems. First, authorities in Dulin and Cangzhou City had flatly refused permission to build a temple in the village. In response, Wang took his request to the county Bureau for the Preservation of Cultural Relics *(baohu wenwu ju)*, claiming that the village wished only to build a structure to protect the three Ming dynasty statues. The bureau at first suggested that the statues be turned over to the county or provincial museums. When Wang rejected the idea, the bureau grudgingly gave permission to build a simple shed to cover the statues. This was taken as (and may have been) implicit permission to rebuild the temple.

Figure 2.2
The Guanyin Hall
of Hai Dock Village.

Figure 2.3   Bodhisattva statues inside the Guanyin Hall.

Here Wang faced the second problem: how to fund his construction project. As might be expected, he went first to the villagers of Hai Dock itself. He was not disappointed. In all, 293 households, nearly every one in the village, made a contribution to the temple, ranging from 1 to 1,000 *yuan*, for a total of nearly 15,000 *yuan*. What is most notable is the value placed on the participation, no matter how nominal, of each household in the village. For example, it is common knowledge that one wealthy peasant secretly gave one *yuan* to each of the poorest households so that these families would have some funds to donate and could go on record as having made their contribution to the construction effort. Villagers who recounted this story regarded this act as a tactful way of sparing these families the shame of being unable to make their proper contribution to a village project.

A significant portion of the money collected came from outside the village. The two neighboring villages of Liu Dock and Qian-Hai Village also accounted for 231 donations, but they were smaller and together brought less than 2,000 *yuan*. Still lacking funding, Wang began to canvass neighboring villages, occasionally divining *fengshui* and asking for donations in return. The most generous of these came from Hai Dock women who had married out of the village or else were repaying a vow to Guanyin. Together, these came to a rough total of 3,900 *yuan*, only a fraction of what had been collected in Hai Dock itself.

After the funds had been collected, a small, one-room building was constructed to house the three statues, which has since become the center of village religious practice in Hai Dock and the site of two annual temple festivals. As was usually the case during and before the Republic, the temple is not the site of daily devotions and is open only on the first and fifteenth of the lunar month. Even on those days, only a relatively small number of villagers will visit the temple. There, they burn incense, make various requests to Guanyin, and leave—possibly waiting around the outside of the temple to chat or enjoy the weather. The annual temple festivals (held on the Upper and Lower Primordials, corresponding to the birthday of Guanyin, and the festival of Dizang, Bodhisattva Kshitigharbhpa, respectively) are the only occasions likely to attract large crowds to the temple.[37] The former coincides with similar religious or popular festivities in almost every village and is thus attended primarily by peasants from Hai Dock itself. In contrast, the latter has been touted as a local attraction by village authorities, who hire entertainers and musicians as well as religious specialists. These festivals draw faithful from as far as fifteen kilometers (thirty *li*) away but relatively sparse attendance from Hai Dock itself. Regardless of attendance, the funding of temple festivals in Hai Dock closely resembles the pattern seen in the construction: donations come from both within and without the village. Within the village, though, every family will make some token show of support, regardless of whether they have any interest in or plan to attend the festival.[38]

Sectarian Village: The Heaven and Earth Sect in White Yang Bridge

White Yang Bridge is one of a relatively small number of Cang County villages that supports the Heaven and Earth Sect. This tightly knit sect has been present in rural Cang County since the early Qing dynasty, largely continuous within the same villages, including White Yang Bridge. The group in White Yang Bridge has historically acted as a part of a local sectarian network, including the village of Rear Camp, which is commonly recognized as the center of the teaching in the area. Donation records (see table 7.1) confirm the fact that these few villages have supported the sect and cooperated closely since at least the middle of the nineteenth century. The oral history of the teaching, formally recorded in memorized scriptures, further confirms the presence of the teaching in this village another fifty years earlier.

In White Yang Bridge, as elsewhere, pressure against sectarians began to increase during the 1950s. The 1951 movement against the Way of Pervading Unity was the first indication of the importance that the new government would place on the control of religion and religious groups. Throughout the 1950s and early 1960s, sectarian groups of all sorts gradually withdrew from public life, curtailing their largest activities in the hope of avoiding criticism. By the dawn of the Cultural Revolution, village sectarians were all but invisible; rituals were small and secret, and some had already taken the prudent measure of hiding or destroying sectarian ritual objects and scriptures. The ten-year hiatus of activities during the Cultural Revolution itself severely diminished the place of sectarians in the village and, more important, made it impossible to train young devotees the rituals and scriptures of the teaching for an entire decade. By the end of the Cultural Revolution, many villages that had once housed large, flourishing sectarian groups found themselves unable to revive the teaching, simply because the oldest specialists, with the greatest store of ritual and scriptural knowledge, had died and could not be replaced.

This was the situation in which the Heaven and Earth group in White

Yang Bridge found itself in the late 1970s. Although many of the older members of the sect were still alive, they had neither the critical number of specialists nor a sufficiently knowledgeable leader to rejuvenate the ritual life of the teaching. As had been the case in Hai Dock, this was solved by the efforts of one villager, who stepped forward to lead a drive to reconstruct the religious life of the community. In White Yang Bridge, that person was Zheng Hong, then in his thirties, who walked the fifteen kilometers to Rear Camp and formally acknowledged the head of the Heaven and Earth Sect there as his teacher. From 1978 to 1985, he spent each winter (the agricultural slack season) in Rear Camp, relearning the tradition that had been lost in his community. With this base, he returned to White Yang Bridge and trained a new coterie of Heaven and Earth Sect specialists. Since the late 1980s, the sect has remained at the center of individual religious life and village identity in White Yang Bridge.

Just as with temple festivals in Hai Dock, the activities of the Heaven and Earth Sect in White Yang Bridge are financially supported by the entire village. The Upper and Lower Primordial festivals, each three days of scripture chanting, generate considerable expenses, such as food and alcohol for sacrifices, incense, firecrackers, and the cost of feeding the sectarians themselves. This cost is borne by the families, with the amount donated by each family recorded on a large sheet of red paper and posted in the center of the village and, occasionally, even read over the village public address system.[39] Again, outsiders, particularly those who have come to make or repay a vow, are certainly welcome to make donations and often do so. For villagers in White Yang Bridge, however, some token show of support is socially required.[40]

Although villagers in White Yang Bridge enjoy a sense of spiritual protection because of the presence of the sect and most feel a special devotion to local sectarian deities, such as Dong Sihai, ordinary villagers are not formally affiliated with the sect as much as they receive services from it. Unlike the Way of Pervading Unity or the Li Sect, there is no formal process by which households enter the Heaven and Earth Sect or the Teaching of the Most Supreme.[41] No demands are placed on ordinary villagers to participate in or even understand the functions of the sect. Instead, the sect is a resource made available to fellow villagers. The Heaven and Earth Sect in White Yang Bridge performs all important individual ritual functions, such as healing, blessings, and, especially, funerals, in the village. Because these rituals are uncompensated, fellow villagers, who financially support the large activities of the sect on a regular basis, feel comfortable asking for them, but outsiders often do not. In general, only those with some tie to the sect will approach them for ritual services. Although this includes sectarians from outside the village, it also includes all White Yang Bridge households.[42]

Dependent Village: Little Terrace

The two villages of Hai Dock and White Yang Bridge are not remarkable for their piety as much as for their organization. In each, the religious needs and financial resources of individual villagers have been channeled toward a communal goal, usually under the direction of a particularly devout villager, who takes on the onus of managing the project. Should such a person not step forward, however, these resources simply do not materialize: the temple never gets rebuilt, and the remains of the sectarian group fall further into decay. This is seen in the village of Little Terrace, which had once had two temples—a large Sanguan temple and a small Bodhisattva shrine—as well as a contingent of specialists of the Teaching of the Most Supreme.[43] In the years before the Cultural Revolution, both temples were destroyed and the sect was forced to cease its ritual activities. In subsequent decades, neither the physical nor the human religious resources of this village have been reconstructed. Instead, Little Terrace villagers are forced to rely on the resources of neighboring communities.

Villagers in Little Terrace share the same basic religious needs as their neighbors. They still pray, make vows, and require the presence of the sacred to mark and bless the great life events, especially the passage into death. With few religious resources in the village, peasants are forced to be less discriminating in how these needs are met. The complete dearth of religious resources in Little Terrace, however, now forces peasants to take their religious needs outside the village, most often to the sectarian groups in Ni-Yang Camp and Quan-Wang Village. Little Terrace villagers not only attend and financially support the sectarian functions of neighboring villages, but, occasionally, the entire village will hire in sectarian groups to perform a ritual on their behalf. During the unusually dry summer of 1997, representatives from Little Terrace asked sectarians from each of these two villages to come and perform the Prayer for Rain. Unfortunately, they were not alone—sectarian groups in Ni-Yang Camp and Quan-Wang Village were also inundated by similar requests from neighboring villages, and Little Terrace was unable to have the ceremony performed. In the end, the rain did not come. Months later, many Little Terrace villagers attributed their poor harvest to the fact that, with neither a resident sectarian group nor a village temple, they had been unable to pray for rain.[44]

Finally, the dearth of religious resources in Little Terrace has diluted the public religious life of the community as a whole, particularly the expectations of ritual propriety placed on the individual. This is most tangibly expressed in funerals, which, although a private ritual function, are still very much matters of public display. It has often been noted that lavish funerals are also displays of family wealth, meant as much to enhance the prestige of the living as to appease the soul of the dead. In the poorer villages of Cang County, however, they are equally displays of filial piety. Proper performance of the rituals surrounding death and burial, especially of a parent, are one of the few instances in which communal norms are brought to bear on the religious practice of the individual. Without exception, villagers in sectarian communities such as White Yang Bridge emphasized that it would be unthinkable to bury a relative without a proper funeral, which here usually means a sectarian ritual. In many villages, those who had died during the Cultural Revolution and been buried (there having been no crematorium in the area during this time) without the benefit of this ritual were later disinterred (literally or symbolically) and reburied with a proper funeral. Nor is poverty necessarily an impediment. The Teaching of the Most Supreme performs its funerals without charge to fellow villagers, and Heaven and Earth Sect rituals are free even to outsiders. In cases of extreme poverty, villagers will often pitch in to defray expenses. In villages with a developed public religious life, even individual religious practice thus remains subject to certain standards.

The weakening of public religious life has, however, also inhibited the ability and interest of the community to impose ritual norms upon its members. Villagers in Little Terrace confirmed that some sort of religious ceremony always accompanied funerals during the Republican period, but noted that the general atmosphere of religiosity within the community has declined since then. Although many still employ neighboring sectarian groups to perform funeral rituals, others will simply burn paper money and light firecrackers. A significant minority will simply transport the body to Dulin for cremation. Certain aspects of the funeral, in particular the banquet for relatives and neighbors, are still socially required, but the ritual element has become optional.[45]

Conclusion: Rural Religion and Village Society

It remains generally accepted that the pressures of the twentieth century worked to rework the social fabric of rural North China, in which the peasant village was a primary casualty. Philip Huang and Prasenjit Duara

each attribute the deterioration of village society during the early twentieth century to different combinations of internal change and external
pressure. In Huang's analysis, villages of the late Qing tended to be stable,
insular communities composed primarily of independent cultivators. Under the economic stratification that accompanied rural commercialization
of the early twentieth century, these communities could fragment along
lines of land ownership, undermining the social fabric of the village and
exposing it to exploitation. For Duara, the development of the village as a
fiscal and administrative unit by the expanding Republican state pushed
traditional elites out of positions of leadership, leaving these positions to
be farmed by "entrepreneurial brokers." In both cases, the decline of public religious life during the Republican period is taken as an indication of
the weakening of village structure.[46] The differences between the two are
significant. Reflecting his conception of the Qing village as a "community
of cultivators," Huang emphasizes the integrative function of ritual, the
expression of community that would "cloak the gap between the more
well-to-do members from the poorest members of the community."[47] In
contrast, Duara focuses on the village as a hierarchy of cultural authority
and on religion as "the public domain through which the village elite was
able to express its leadership responsibilities."[48]

Despite their differences, each of these characterizations resonates with
the data from Republican-era Cang County. As discussed in the previous
chapter, villages in this area exhibited relatively stable patterns of land-
holding and long-term tenancy and were less prone to the sort of social
disintegration that affected more heavily commercialized communities
closer to Beijing. The primary unit of economic, social, and votive welfare
was the independent household, and when peasants participated in village
religious functions the household was the ultimate beneficiary. Nevertheless, the village did retain a collective identification with its religious identity, meaning its resources, customs, and spiritual patrons and the coordination of this public religious face were very much a reflection of the
internal structure of the village, what Stephen Sangren characterized as an
"assertion of differentiation within encompassing identity"; however, although Sangren had been speaking of public participation in ritual, in
Cang County the criterion was financial support.[49] Reflecting the structure of the community, larger contributions came from wealthy families,
but all village households were expected to make some show of financial
support for the upkeep of religious resources.

Although the first few decades of the People's Republic saw the attenuation of religious life and restructuring of village communities, the recon-

struction of religious infrastructure since the late 1970s demonstrates both the profound changes undergone within the villages themselves and the affective significance of newly formed villages. With a loosening of religious policy, villages that had been created by administrative fiat during the previous three decades still banded together to rebuild temples and reform sectarian groups for the general welfare of the community and as a resource for individual households. This mobilization of village solidarity in the service of newly formed communities reveals that even administrative structures such as the village are less determined by normative criteria than evolving products of rhetorical and ritual practice.[50]

3. Spirits, Sectarians, and Xiangtou

Religious Knowledge in Local Culture

Among the most important achievements of the People's Republic has been to bring at least the rudiments of modern medicine to all but the most remote areas. Since the late 1960s, most peasant villages have had access to some sort of medical care (such as the famous "barefoot doctors"), and many now have basic clinical facilities.[1] Yet even in more developed areas, the services of *xiangtou*, practitioners who heal through the power of fox spirits, remain very much in demand.[2] *Xiangtou* employ the power of the supernatural in order to cure illnesses caused by forces, such as malevolent ghosts, that are out of the reach of modern medicine.

Even within this relatively small area, the number of *xiangtou* in any one village, their specific practices, their social role and relationship to organized religion are all beyond easy characterization. Most villages in this area have at least one *xiangtou*—as many peasants put it, "there is no such thing as a village without a *xiangtou*"—and some have as many as ten. In some villages, this number has increased over the past fifty years, while in others it has declined. Within a single village, a number of *xiangtou* may practice similar arts, but each will have his or her own characteristic style and area of expertise. Moreover, the place of the *xiangtou* within the village and his or her relationship to other religious specialists and organizations are shaped primarily by individual circumstances and can vary significantly from one village to the next, or even among *xiangtou* within the same village.

Xiangtou grow out of a tradition of belief that has existed across China for thousands of years, yet they remain an extremely local phenomenon. The belief that animal and human spirits can cause and cure sickness and that certain individuals have power to interact with and engage these forces is amply documented in religious texts and literary sources reaching back to the dawn of Chinese civilization. In the world of the peasant village, however, it is the local culture of tales about *xiangtou* that incarnates this vast tradition of belief and gives it significance to daily life. The fame of individual *xiangtou* or stories concerning the role of the spirits in the physical health of the individual generally remain within a very small area, the limit usually being about thirty *li* (identified earlier as the "sphere of local culture"), and are most often drawn from recent memory. The customary knowledge that most villagers have of sickness and healing and *xiangtou* arts and powers, as well as the practices of the *xiangtou* themselves, grow directly out of this local culture.

Causes of Sickness

In his classic 1939 study of rural society in the Yangzi valley, Fei Xiaotong divided peasant responses to crises into "science" and "magic." In solving their agricultural problems, peasants clearly discriminated between those that could be solved by technological ingenuity and those for which one must remain dependent upon the will of heaven, employing science for the former and magic for the latter. These two systems were not adversarial, but complementary. Magic is not a disavowal of science, but rather recognition of its limitations, and the two are employed "hand-in-hand to attain a practical end."[3]

The problems of relying on concepts such as science and magic aside, peasants in Cang County distinguish between ordinary sicknesses of the body *(shi)* and those of supernatural origin *(xu)*.[4] *Shi* sicknesses can be thought of as clearly defined and evident maladies, such as cancer or infection, which should be treated by a physician, of either Western or traditional Chinese medicine. In contrast, *xu* sickness is a general weakness of the body, which can easily give rise to *shi* sickness and require the services of a *xiangtou*. *Xu* illness can be caused by fatigue or poor conditions, but is most often attributed to one of a number of supernatural causes.

A basic cause of sickness is the burden of an evil act or immoral lifestyle. Popular belief in China, as in many societies, makes a connection between individual morality and material well-being, including physical health.[5] This fundamental aspect of Chinese folk belief can be seen as early as the second century A.D. in the Five Pecks of Rice *(wu dou mi)* Teaching, which treated sickness through personal examination of one's conscience *(zishou suoguo)* and became an integral theme to Daoist thought on healing.[6]

Two traditions of thought explain why an evil deed can lead to physical sickness. The first is simply that a bad conscience debilitates the spirit and thus physically weakens the body. This thinking is particularly characteristic of the Heaven and Earth Teaching.[7] According to Yao, the head of the Heaven and Earth Teaching in Yang Camp, one who has committed an evil act will become sick because that person's conscience will not allow him or her to sleep or eat properly.[8] The more common view among interviewees (which included both specialists and ordinary peasants), however, was that an evil deed will be punished by supernatural powers, such as human or animal spirits, and that this punishment often takes the form of physical sickness. Some expressed that this can occur in conjunction with the general weakness caused by a poor conscience, but not all drew a direct connection between the two.

Belief in the ability of human ghosts and animal spirits to cause physical harm is deeply rooted in Chinese tradition and remains common throughout China. As early as the Shang dynasty (1766–1154 B.C.), nobles afflicted with illness consulted oracles to determine which ancestor was responsible. The *Fifty-Four Prescriptions,* a recently unearthed medical text from the Han, outlines a number of ghosts and spirits who were known to cause disease.[9] The writings of Song literati include detailed descriptions of spirit-induced illness and of the different classes of priests and shamans recruited to face this threat.[10] The popularity of such healers was unabated by the Qing, when such customs were recorded in local gazetteers throughout China. One such source from Hunan states that the local people "believe in spirits and trust *wu* (witches), and when someone becomes sick, they say that it is caused by a spirit."[11] Another from the same period laments that "Southerners often get sick. . . . They forsake medicine and instead all sacrifice to spirits."[12] From the far northern province of Heilongjiang comes a similar description, "*Wu* are everywhere, and when a person becomes sick, his family do not understand medicine, and instead enlist a *wu* to come and read sacred books."[13]

Although any number of demonic forces can cause illness, among the most common are the disaffected spirits of human dead, particularly one's own ancestors *(jia xian)*. Human spirits are usually angered by specific causes, such as the desecration of graves or a lack of filial piety on the part of their living descendants. In the villages of Cang County, most peasants knew of specific cases from their own or nearby communities in which ancestors were known to have caused sickness or even death. For example, Yao, the head of the Heaven and Earth Sect in Yang Camp, related the following account: "In Ni Bridge Village, there was a circus performer who was particularly unfilial. When his mother died, he did not return home for her funeral. Months later, he finally returned to the village, but neither went to visit his mother's grave nor burned paper money for her, and instead treated himself to a lavish dinner. The next morning, he was found dead, and nobody had any doubt that it was because his mother's spirit had come during the night and taken his life as punishment."

Spirits of the dead can sometimes cause people to become ill to attract their attention to a certain need. For example, a girl in Rear Camp began to experience debilitating headaches and consulted *xiangtou* in her own and three other villages. They all agreed that the headaches were caused by a spirit, but none could discern what sort. Finally, she visited a *xiangtou* in Ni Bridge Village, who identified the problem to have been caused by a lonely male spirit who needed a wife.

A second group of spirits able to cause sickness are the Five Animal Spirits (*wu da xian*, specifically the fox, mouse, snake, hedgehog, and weasel). Belief in these spirits is prevalent throughout China, Korea, and Japan, and they are mentioned in association with the magic arts (*wushu*) as early as the second-century B.C. *Classic of Mountains and Seas (Shanhai jing)* and early fourth-century A.D. *Investigations into the Divine (Soushen ji).*[14] The most elaborate collections of animal tales derive from literature, such as Tang dynasty ghost stories, and later compilations of strange stories such as the Song dynasty *Extensive Record of the Taiping Period (Taiping guangji)* and the *Strange Stories from a Chinese Studio (Liaozhai zhiyi),* written in early Qing dynasty Shandong. Many of these tales center on the antics of fox spirits, who reward or punish their human acquaintances by affecting their wealth, romantic affairs, or physical health.[15]

Animal spirits are believed to be mischievous and temperamental, but not necessarily evil. Both literary accounts and local belief in Cang County portray animal spirits as protecting good people, particularly those who sacrifice and speak kindly to them, but punishing those who offend them.[16] Thus, people try very hard to placate these spirits, particularly foxes, who are considered to be the most powerful and capricious of the five. A fox den, for example, is under no circumstances to be disturbed, and the sight of a mother fox taking her young and moving to a new home is considered an extremely bad omen.

The connection between animal spirits and illness is mentioned specifically in the 1933 Cang County gazetteer, which laments that peasants "worship the fox, hedgehog, snake and weasel. When someone has a sickness, these foolish people prolong it because they attribute it to a snake or weasel spirit."[17] Indeed, a number of conditions, including physical and mental illness, as well as inexplicable changes in fortune or personality are commonly attributed to these spirits. Note both the diversity and underlying similarities among the following cases.

Xu, a sixty-year-old woman in Yang Camp, was preparing food for a religious festival in the village, when she suddenly became afflicted with large, painful swellings on her right arm and the side of her face. A *xiangtou* who was attending the festival looked at the swellings and immediately knew that they had been caused by a fox spirit.

In nearby Lai Village, a thirty-year-old man began to become increasingly belligerent over the space of a few weeks. One day he got into a fight in another village and was taken by his father to a *xiangtou*, who decided that the man was possessed by a fox spirit.

A girl in Tianjin had a mental problem that progressed to the point where one day she soaked herself in gasoline and set herself on fire. The girl was taken to a hospital and treated for her burns, but her sores would not heal properly. Her parents contacted Wang, a healer from this area, who came to Tianjin to see the girl. Wang decided that both the mental problem and the inability of the sores to heal were caused by not one, but many fox spirits who were fighting inside the girl.

A home in Tianjin was plagued by fighting and strange occurrences. In addition, anyone who passed through the front room would immediately contract an intense headache. Wang came to the House and immediately recognized the problem to be that the Guanyin statue in the front room was possessed with a fox spirit.

A final cause of illness, particularly such conditions as a generally weak constitution or lingering malady in children, is that the child is being called to the spirit realm. This is either because a spirit has taken a special interest in the child or, more commonly, that the child is in reality not human, but a "heavenly child" (*tongzi* for boys, *huazi* for girls).[18] In the latter case, the afflicted individual need not be a child, chronologically speaking. Such children are themselves the progeny of celestial beings and are living temporarily in the Mortal World either as a prank or to escape punishment for some minor offense incurred in the spirit realm. Naturally, the true parents of these children wish to call them home by shortening their mortal lives.

Although anyone, including adults, can be "heavenly children," the majority are actually children, particularly unusually beautiful or intelligent ones. Similarly, children who exhibit strange or otherworldly qualities are diagnosed as having come from the spirit realm. In two recent cases, local *xiangtou* found both a teenage girl who "suddenly went crazy, would laugh, cry and sing for no reason and ate bowls and bowls of food at a time" and another seven-year-old child who would cry incessantly, often until she fainted, to be "heavenly children."

These stories of foxes and spirits demonstrate first that the sacred realm as a source of good or harm is by no means a single voice but, rather, numerous actors, representing as many interests and motivations. One can, however, also discern certain trends. For all of their diversity, these stories all demonstrate a popular perception of spirits as not only capricious and powerful, but also mysterious. The *xu* sicknesses that the spirits bring about share an inscrutability, in that the condition defies both explanation and treatment by conventional means. Similarly, the maladies themselves tend to fall into the realm of the strange and inexplicable. Changes in behavior, the extreme case being the self-immolation of the young girl in Tianjin, strange sores, and swellings are all phenomena that fall outside the realm of normal experience and are thus taken as being beyond the explanation and reach of conventional medicine. Because such phenomena are not attributed to medical—that is, *shi*—causes but are rather brought about by *xu* forces, they are the work of the *xiangtou* to purge.

Diagnosis

Considering the numerous different forces which can cause illness, the first task of the *xiangtou* is to determine exactly which one or ones could be responsible. Each *xiangtou* has his or her own method of divining if an illness is *shi* or *xu*, or possibly a combination of both, and, if *xu*, what sort of force is causing the problem. The method related below was related by Chen of Yang Camp and is very common among *xiangtou* in this area:

> First the *xiangtou* burns three sticks of incense. On the right is the "spirit incense" (*shen xiang*, also called the "ghost" *guiling* or "ancestor" *jiaxian* incense). On the left is the "animal spirit" incense (also called the "misfortune" incense, *zai xiang*). Finally, the stick of incense in the center is called the "life incense" *(ming xiang)*. This stick signifies the life force and natural life span of the patient.
>
> The *xiangtou* watches these three sticks of incense to see which burns "brightest." If it is the right or the left stick, the person is being affected by a ghost or animal spirit, respectively. If the stick in the center burns alternately bright and dark, the person has simply reached the end of his or her life and will die within a few days. On the other hand, you can tell from the center stick if the person sim-

ply has a physical *(shi)* illness *(shibing)* or is possibly a Heavenly Child.

Although this basic diagnostic method is common throughout most of North China, the arts of local *xiangtou* evince numerous variations on this theme, as well as other techniques that are completely unrelated to it.[19] One *xiangtou* in nearby Ni Bridge Village burns three sticks of incense in each of four burners. Two *xiangtou* in Quan-Wang Village and Xu Village burn a single cigarette and watch the way that the ashes take shape. Some, such as Xu of Yang Camp, combine folk medicine with divination similar to that introduced above. Wang of Rear Camp burns only one stick of incense, and then not as a divining tool, but out of respect to the Heaven and Earth Sect tablet. The actual diagnosis comes from an instinctive feeling in his hands.

Finally, the arts of at least one *xiangtou* demonstrate a link with a shamanistic tradition that actively survives only weakly in this area. Unlike the methods outlined above, in which the spirits communicate with a conscious *xiangtou* through signs, this tradition relies on the direct possession of the *xiangtou* to be possessed by the spirit. As Edward Davis demonstrates, spirit mediums were a common feature of village religion during the Song dynasty, despite official attempts to suppress such practices, as well as competition from other sorts of religious specialists.[20] Nevertheless, the use of direct possession by village healers continued well into the twentieth century. Li Jinghan saw such methods employed in his 1933 study of nearby Ding County, where the family of a sick peasant would invite a female medium *(ding daxian de furen)* to effect a cure. The visit would take place at night, and no lamps were allowed to be lit. The medium sat on the *kang* (a large brick platform, which serves as both bed and seating), surrounded by sacrifices of boiled eggs and wine, and would call out, "What sickness does this person have?" The spirit answered directly in a weak, singsong voice, "this person has _____ sickness," while the family, no doubt in great terror, continuously kowtowed to the spirit.[21] This shamanistic tradition of healing was strongest in Manchuria, where such activities were often the center of large temple cults.[22]

One of the few *xiangtou* in the Cang County area who maintains a link with this shamanistic tradition (and the only one I was able to interview) is Wu, of Quan-Wang Village. In conversation, Wu is quick to emphasize that she is not a *xiangtou*, but rather a "doctor" *(daifu)* and that she diagnoses by taking the pulse *(haomai)* of the afflicted person. Her method, however, is quite different from the traditional Chinese medical technique of the same name. When diagnosing a patient, Wu sits alone on the *kang*, closes her eyes, and enters a trance. In order to "take the pulse," she pinches the cloth on her own pants, while the patient sits out of reach on a nearby chair. During the time she is in the trance, Wu communicates directly with fox and other spirits.[23]

Despite the wide range of techniques employed by each individual *xiangtou*, there remain certain important similarities. The first is that only the *xiangtou* can understand the results of the divination. All *xiangtou* who diagnose by burning incense stressed that the "brightness" they look for is a light that ordinary people cannot see. This figures even more prominently for those *xiangtou*, such as Wang, the Heaven and Earth Sect *xiangtou* in Rear Camp, who do not read the incense at all, but rather rely on a combination of intuition and direct communication from a particular supernatural being. All of these forces are inaccessible to ordinary people. The second is that all of the *xiangtou* share the same fundamental set of beliefs concerning the causes of sickness. Each recognizes the various spiritual forces, such as those mentioned above, that can cause a person to become ill. Diagnostic technique thus consists primarily of determining which is responsible.

Healing

The healing powers of *xiangtou* are limited to *xu* sicknesses, or *shi* sicknesses that are brought about by a *xu* condition. Each of the elements that can bring about a *xu* sickness, such as an evil deed, human ghosts, animal spirits, or celestial beings calling their Heavenly Child home, has its own particular remedy. These remedies are often applied in conjunction with each other and with basic folk remedies for comforting minor physical ailments. Just as the commonly recognized causes of illness can be divided into basic elements, the cures of the *xiangtou* that address each of these conditions.

The simplest cure is moral examination, but this method is practiced primarily by members of the Heaven and Earth Sect. Although all *xiangtou* seem to recognize a causal connection between evil deeds and sickness, most attribute the physical manifestation to the influence of ghosts or animal spirits. The Heaven and Earth Sect is relatively unique in treating a guilty conscience itself as a cause of sickness, and thus focusing the cure on the psychological well-being of the afflicted. Yao, the head of the Heaven and Earth Sect in Yang Camp, is not a *xiangtou*. He will reluctantly see sick villagers, but emphasizes that he personally has no power to heal.

Figure 3.1
Xiangtou giving
instructions to a
patient.

Rather, he instructs the patient to kneel before the Heaven and Earth Sect tablet and silently "admit his mistake" *(ren cuowu)*. Often this is the only effective remedy.

Liu is sixty-seven years old and has been a *huitou* (responsible for organizing *hui*, the religious rituals and festivals of the village) of the Heaven and Earth Sect for more than twenty years. Recently, his wife became sick and he was forced to borrow 3,000 *yuan* of the sect's funds in order to pay her medical bills. As the time for the New Year *hui*, the most significant religious event of the year, approached, he found himself unable to repay the money and was forced to admit to the other members that he had mishandled the money. Soon after this, he became seriously ill and was unable to move his legs. He was taken to the village doctor and to numerous *xiangtou*, none of whom could cure him. Finally, he went to Yao and admitted his misdeed before the Heaven and Earth Sect altar *(paiwei)*. Within a few days he recovered.

But even within the Heaven and Earth Sect, the merging of tradition can lead to significant variation. Wang, the healer from Rear Camp Village, is a member of the Heaven and Earth Sect and refuses to be called a *xiangtou*, but, in fact, represents a merging of sectarian healing practices with those of *xiangtou*. Like Yao, Wang emphasizes the role of personal morality in physical well-being. He advises moral self-examination and says that he can immediately sense whether a disease has been brought about by a misdeed. In such cases, he instructs the person to return home, burn incense, and examine his or her conscience. His purpose, however, is not merely to pacify the soul of the afflicted, but also to address any external forces, such as fox spirits, that might be causing the illness as punishment for a moral offense.[24]

In some cases, sickness is caused by the misdeed of another. A forty-year-old woman in Yang Camp was told by a *xiangtou* in nearby Ni Bridge village that her affliction was caused by a spirit that her husband had offended. Similarly, Wang related a case in which a six-year-old girl from Zhao Family Grave Village, fifteen kilometers away, inexplicably became sick, often having particularly bad nosebleeds. She was taken to a number of doctors and *xiangtou,* none of whom could cure her. Finally, she was brought to a healer in Rear Camp, who immediately recognized the problem to have been a past transgression on the part of the girl's father. Upon further examination, it was revealed that the father had, in fact, once beaten two dogs to death. The father was instructed to admit his mistake as the first step in his daughter's recovery.

Sickness effected by restless spirits is most commonly healed by placating these forces, and in this the *xiangtou* serves as a bridge. Should the illness have been brought about by a misdeed, the individual is instructed to admit his or her mistake and ask the forgiveness of the spirit, usually accompanied by sacrifices of wine and *mantou*. Placating the spirits is relatively straightforward in cases in which these spirits make a person ill for a specific reason. For example, the girl in Rear Camp who had been made ill by a lonely male spirit was cured by giving that spirit a wife. This consisted of the *xiangtou* making a paper doll of a woman wearing red bridal clothes, which was burned to send it to the spirit world. Thus satisfied, the spirit no longer bothered the woman, and she soon recovered.

More malicious spirits, however, will cause illness simply out of mischief and malice, and toward these spirits *xiangtou* take a more aggressive tone. In most cases, Wang of Rear Camp sees animal spirits as renegade forces that should be controlled, rather than appeased. Wang thus relies heavily on exorcism through chanting the scriptures of the Heaven and

Earth Sect. He recounted numerous instances in which capricious spirits, particularly those of foxes, caused mental and physical ailments; in each of these cases, he solved the problem by immediately reciting a scripture.[25]

Other *xiangtou* exorcise spirits by other means, sometimes with tragic results. When the *xiangtou* in Lai Village diagnosed a certain belligerent peasant as being possessed by a fox spirit, he decided to exorcise the spirit by "burning it out." The peasant was chained inside a wooden box throughout the day and to a radiator pipe at night and was given neither food nor water. As this occurred during a particularly hot summer, it was not long before the peasant died of exposure.[26]

Another veiled show of power directed at potentially troublesome spirits is the custom of formally promising sickly children to a religious order to convince roving spirits that the child is both needed in this world and protected by higher powers. This is seen in a Republican-era custom from the Tianjin area, called "jumping over the wall" *(tiao qiang)*, in which the child was taken to a temple, dressed in Buddhist robes, and made to symbolically perform some of the duties of a monk (followed by the assembled crowd shouting, "He's a monk all right!" *[ta jiu shi heshang!]* to trick the spirits into thinking that the child had entered monastic orders).[27] Peasants recalled that a similar ceremony, in which the child was promised to a monastery and given a Buddhist name, was practiced in Cang County as late as the 1930s by the monks of Stone Buddha Temple. More recently, peasants have revived the Republican-era practice of bringing children to leaders of the Most Supreme and Heaven and Earth Sects in so that the children will formally recognize a sectarian teacher *(ren shifu)*, that is, to give the appearance that these children have "crossed the threshold," *(guo menkang)* and promised themselves to become disciples of the teaching.[28]

Those found to be "heavenly children" are treated by "exchanging children" *(huan tongzi)*. This ceremony is performed by some but not all *xiangtou* and uses a paper doll, which is burned to take the place of the child in heaven. It is imperative that the ceremony be performed relatively quickly; most local villagers know the case of a family in Qian-Hai Camp whose only son died when they did not have the ceremony performed in time. Although there is some variation among practitioners, the basic content of the ceremony is similar to the following description given by Chen of Yang Camp:

When it has been determined that one is a "heavenly child," the first task is to determine exactly which spirits are his or her true parents. This is done by burning incense while chanting a secret incantation *(zhouyu)* and reciting a sacred text *(jing)*. During this time the spirit will tell the *xiangtou* the spirit to whom the child belongs, how much paper money to burn and what sort of sacrifices to prepare. The *xiangtou* prepares a two-foot-tall paper doll *(tongzi)*, which will be burned to take the place of the child. If the child does not have a specific illness to be cured, the doll (also called a *tongzi)* can be burned at any time. Otherwise, it is burned only *after* the child has recovered. The *xiangtou* performs 180 *ketou* (kowtow) to Heaven to ensure that the bargain is enforced.

Xiangtou and the Worship of Fox Spirits

Quite often, however, the precise reason for the sickness is clear to neither the patient nor the *xiangtou*. In such an event, the *xiangtou* enlists the general aid of supernatural forces. In the great majority of cases, this means animal spirits, especially foxes. Although both human ghosts and fox spirits can cause sickness, only the latter can heal. In his work on fox spirits, itself based on years of experience as a doctor in rural Shandong, Shan Min asserts that this association with healing is one of the most important reasons that the popular worship of fox spirits has continued unabated for thousands of years.[29] In modern Cang County, the worship of these spirits remains strong for the same reason.

If they are to heal, though, animal spirits and *xiangtou* enter into a cooperative relationship. Rather than affecting humans directly, such spirits prefer to use the *xiangtou* as a vehicle by channeling their power through them. In turn, the *xiangtou* maintains a *paiwei* to a particular animal spirit, which it takes as a patron. Some *xiangtou* keep this altar hidden, but most display it prominently in the front room of the home. These altars can be inscribed with pseudonyms such as "Spirit Teacher" or "Spirit Aunt" *(shenshi, shenyi)* or ordinary human names with the surname Hu or Huang, an oblique but common reference to foxes *(huli)* or weasels *(huang shulang)*, respectively.[30] Although most peasants fear and respect these spirits, their active worship is generally restricted to *xiangtou*, and the presence of such an altar is thus a sort of advertisement of *xiangtou* powers.[31]

Like diagnostic technique, the particular arts used in healing general ailments vary among individual practitioners, although all share the trait of being relatively simple procedures that are effective only when applied by that *xiangtou*. Xu of Yang Camp, for example, reads an incantation over ordinary sugar, divides it into nine portions and instructs the patient to drink the sugar in water three times a day over the course of three days. If there is any improvement during this time, the patient should return for more medicine. If there is no improvement, the patient should try the services of another *xiangtou*. Chen of Yang Camp also follows this basic pattern, using tea leaves in place of sugar.[32]

Many *xiangtou* also employ a number of folk remedies *(pianfang)*, producing what appears to be an eclectic mix of medicine and magic. For example, Xu of Yang Camp has raised nine children and numerous grandchildren and has decades of experience with the home remedies that she now employs in her practice as a *xiangtou*. Most other *xiangtou* know of some herbal remedies and can give basic acupuncture and massage. One *xiangtou* from Quan-Wang Village and another from Xu-Zhang Village both employ cupping *(huoguan)*, a technique of both traditional Chinese and folk medicine, in which heated glass jars are applied to skin in order to create a vacuum and draw toxins to the surface. It is worth noting, though, that even when the *xiangtou* employs medical techniques the power to heal ultimately comes from the spirits, which is channeled through the person of the *xiangtou*. To employ again the terminology of Fei Xiaotong regardless of the nature of the practice employed, the *xiangtou* performs magic, not science.[33]

Repaying the Spirits

Healing is a business that relies upon a specific result, and neither the *xiangtou* nor the spirits are paid until the cure is effected. The *xiangtou* is paid relatively little when the treatment is given, usually only a few *yuan* or small gifts of food and alcohol. Similarly, no sacrifices are given to the spirits at that time; at most, some *xiangtou* may burn a few sticks of incense to gain the attention and cooperation of the spirit. Once the cure has proven itself, however, both parties are paid through gifts of gratitude to the *xiangtou* and sacrifices to the spirit.

Payment, both to the *xiangtou* and to the spirits, consists of the patient returning to the home of the *xiangtou* with sacrifices of food and alcohol of a value and nature determined by the *xiangtou*. This is known as "repaying the wish" *(huan yuan)*, a custom that extends beyond curing sickness to the more general practice of making vows. The sacrifices are placed overnight in front of the altar of the spirit and later eaten by the *xiangtou* himself.

The value of sacrifices varies widely among *xiangtou*, depending upon their fame and their own moral preference. Xu of Yang Camp only requires a few bowls of *mantou* and fruit, or possibly a few bags of prepared snacks, usually not in excess of thirty *yuan*, and even then returns half of the sacrifice for the patient to take home. At the other extreme is one old *xiangtou* in Rear Camp who earns 8,000–9,000 *yuan* per year in sacrifices and gifts. These sacrifices are, in effect, the fee charged by the *xiangtou* and usually range between 100 and 200 *yuan* for an average sickness. In addition, many are given gifts of inscribed pictures or mirrors, which are inscribed with congratulatory messages and prominently displayed to attest to the power of the *xiangtou*.

The most notable exception is Wang, who does not accept any gifts or sacrifices for healing for his services. The custom of the Heaven and Earth Sect, which is followed quite strictly in the sectarian villages of Cang County, is for wishes to be repaid directly to the spirit of Dong Sihai himself. To do so, the leaders of the Heaven and Earth Sect arrange a special ceremony *(hui)*—alternately, the person can attend another scheduled Heaven and Earth Sect function—for the cured individual to thank Dong Sihai for his benevolence. At this *hui*, the person should make some donation of money, although this is a personal expression of sincerity and the amount is be kept secret. As with other functions of the teaching, the donation is to be used in the ceremonial life of the group as a whole; the individual practitioner remains uncompensated.

Profile of *Xiangtou* and the Source of their Power

As the variation in the above descriptions of *xiangtou* arts suggests, such healers are beyond easy characterization. In these villages, we encountered nearly two dozen *xiangtou*, both male and female, of ages ranging from forty to eighty. One village may support a number of *xiangtou*, each of whom has his or her own mixture of healing arts, area of expertise, specialized clientele, and reputation—both personal and professional. In terms of personality, *xiangtou* can span a wide range, from kindly to intimidating to otherworldly. The three outlined below come from the neighboring communities of Yang Camp and Quan-Wang Village and represent the diversity among these practitioners.

- Chen is sixty-six years old and learned the arts of the *xiangtou* from his mother thirty-five years ago. He is a physically large man with a loud voice and an intimidating demeanor and carries around a large hawk, which he recently purchased in Shanxi for 1,000 *yuan*. He practices some acupuncture, but relies primarily on incantations and sacrifices to cure sickness. He was quick to emphasize that he has seen patients from as far away as Heilongjiang and Beijing, but reluctantly admitted that the majority of his patients come from nearby villages. In addition to *xiangtou* arts, Chen also practices *fengshui*. Chen demands that the sacrifices be of a certain quality; commonly, the cost is around 200 *yuan*.

- Xu is seventy years old and has been a *xiangtou* for just over ten years. She is a soft-spoken woman with a kindly face and pleasant manner. She has had nine children and is usually seen being followed around by one or more grandchildren. She practices the same arts as Chen, but relies more heavily on folk medicine *(pianfang)* than he. Although the majority of her clients are children, Xu does not perform the *huan tongzi* ritual. Most of her clients come from Yang Camp itself, although some also come from neighboring villages—usually at the suggestion of a friend or relative. Xu also does not accept money for her services and utilizes inexpensive sacrifices of *mantou* and fruit—usually amounting to a total of less than thirty *yuan*.

- Wu is a woman in her forties. She lives in a relatively nice house in Quan-Wang Village, where she displays three pictures and mirrors donated by grateful clients. Unlike the other *xiangtou* with whom we spoke, she did not wish to be interviewed. Wu has a generally disturbing manner and four times during our interview, she rolled her eyes back into her head and made a growling noise that we were told was the sign a she was entering a trance. For the author this was an unnerving enough sight, but for our host, an illiterate peasant wife, it was absolutely frightening. Wu insisted that she practices only basic Chinese and folk medicine and that she diagnoses by "taking pulse," although it was later revealed that this is in reality communication with a fox spirit and has nothing to do with the traditional Chinese medicine technique of the same name. She cures using many thus altered folk remedies such as medicine and cupping. As mentioned earlier, she took offense at being called a *xiangtou* (much less a "witch" [*wupo*]) but rather, considered herself a "doctor."

These three individuals all live within a few minutes' walk of each other and together demonstrate of the range of personalities that could become *xiangtou*. Naturally, each of the three enjoys a very different relationship with his or her fellow villagers. Whereas Chen is considered the most effective *(ling)* healer, he also has a reputation for being greedy and rather pushy. Xu, on the other hand, maintains close ties with the Heaven and Earth Sect, which is very well respected in the village, and is herself known to be honest and straightforward. Finally, villagers are clearly intimidated by and uncomfortable around Wu of Quan-Wang Village and maintain a distance from her. Despite these differences, each is noticeably different from other villagers. Whether kindly or intimidating, *xiangtou* are recognized by others as having a particular power that makes them extraordinary. This difference is precisely the source of *xiangtou* power—and this link to the spirit world, particularly to fox spirits, is innate to that person.

The source of *xiangtou* power is evident in the following two accounts of how Chen and Xu were chosen by fox spirits to become *xiangtou:*

Chen: My mother was a *xiangtou* in this village. Originally I did not believe in the art but was influenced by two events involving fox spirits and my mother. The first occurred when I was in Manchuria working as a traveling street martial arts performer. While practicing, I seriously injured my hand with a knife and that evening had a very high fever, causing me to soak my clothes with sweat. That night, when I went out to the bathroom, I saw a large fox who stared at me for a long time. By the next morning the fever had passed and I soon recovered. When I returned home, my mother somehow knew of the entire episode and asked me, "So you just cheated death—do you know that someone [the fox spirit] helped you?" The second case was when I lost a money pouch that was in a pocket under many layers of clothing. When I returned home, my mother knew that the pouch had been lost (in fact, stolen by a fox spirit) and where I should go and find it. From this time I believed and began to practice the *xiangtou* arts. I was thirty-one years old.

Xu: Originally I did not believe. When I was already near sixty, I suddenly developed large, extremely painful swellings on my arm and cheek. I saw a *xiangtou* named Liu, who was also a member of the Heaven and Earth Sect, who said that the swelling was caused by a fox spirit who was trying to get my attention. He rubbed my tooth and arm and the swelling went down immediately. He told me that if the swellings still hurt after three days, I should "set up an incense burner" (i.e., begin healing). I did not really have to learn, the talent came naturally.

In each account, both Chen and Xu were anxious to emphasize that they were originally skeptical of *xiangtou* and certainly had no desire to become one themselves—or, in Xu's own words, "Aya! Witches and sorcerers, doesn't it sound terrible!" *(Aya! Wupo shenhan, zhenma nanting!).* In both cases, the individual was made to believe through an extraordinary event involving both a fox spirit, who for some reason took a special interest in that person, and a practicing *xiangtou,* who interpreted these signs. The fox spirit that healed Chen was also in communication with his mother back in Yang Camp, and the spirit that healed Xu (also the one that had afflicted her in the first place) spoke through a Heaven and Earth Sect *xiangtou.* Regardless of whether these stories are meant to be taken as strictly true or have been stylized to fit the expectations of other villagers, in both cases an otherwise unwilling or uninterested person was clearly chosen by the fox spirit to act as *xiangtou.*

Similarly, all of the *xiangtou* to whom we spoke emphasized that they did not have to study, or only did so for a very short time, and that the talents for curing sickness and interpreting the incense came quite naturally. In other words, the burgeoning *xiangtou* did not learn an art, but rather simply channeled and refined forces *(ling)* that already existed within him or her. The presence of this power is what first attracts the attention of the fox spirit. If it is not extant, no amount of study can replace or create it.

Even Wang, the Heaven and Earth Sect healer, is considered to possess extraordinary personal powers. A tradition of healing arts based on message and *qi* circulation figured quite prominently in earlier manifestations of the teaching.[34] In this case, however, the ability to heal is not a product of sectarian arts, but rather the personal power of one of its members. Within the sectarian villages in Cang County, Wang is well known as a healer but otherwise does not have a particularly high place in the teaching. More striking is the fact that the head of the Heaven and Earth Sect in Wang's village, who is generally regarded as the most pious and knowledgeable Heaven and Earth Sect leader in the area, does not have the ability to heal and refers sick peasants to Wang. Apart from the fact that Wang incorporates certain ideals and rituals of the Heaven and Earth Sect into his own arts, his healing power is very much like that of other *xiangtou* and is innate rather than a function of his sectarian ties.

Similarly, although both Chen and Xu relied on a practicing *xiangtou* to interpret the intentions of the fox spirit, both were left to their own devices to learn how to heal. Whereas Wang was able to seek inspiration for his healing arts from the tradition of the Heaven and Earth Sect—such as the custom of moral examination, power of the Heaven and Earth Sect scriptures, and devotion to Dong Sihai—most *xiangtou* draw from the rich body of folk beliefs. Returning to the diversity of diagnostic and healing arts employed by *xiangtou* in this area, it is easily evident how different *xiangtou* each created an eclectic mix of arts drawn from his or her own experience. Most have visited or seen the basic elements of *xiangtou* arts, such as the burning of three sticks of incense as a diagnostic technique and reading incantations over sugar to dispense as medicine, and these rituals form the practical foundation for most new practitioners. Beyond this, Wu of Quan-Wang Village uses techniques taken from traditional Chinese medicine in name only; the content harkens back to a locally weak but important shamanistic tradition in healing. Xu of Yang Camp continues to employ basically the same home remedies that she perfected during the course of raising nine children, and Chen uses techniques, such as massage, that he learned from his mother.

The Place of *Xiangtou* in Village Society

The final question we must ask concerns the place of *xiangtou* in village society. As the stories told here show, people are very willing to travel to other villages in to employ the services of a *xiangtou*, particularly for serious or long-term conditions. Why then do most peasants in this area agree that "there is no such thing as a village without a *xiangtou*"?

Again, the answer is found by looking not at one *xiangtou* but at all of the *xiangtou* within this area. Depending on his or her reputation, each *xiangtou* draws clients from within a particular area. The smallest scale is that of a village *xiangtou*, such as Xu, who sees patients primarily from her own community. At the other end is Wang, the Heaven and Earth Sect *xiangtou*, who routinely travels as far as Cangzhou City and even Tianjin to see patients. Although the majority of Wang's clients do come from within the area, his fame is still wide enough to consider him an extralocal phenomenon. The majority of other *xiangtou* fall somewhere in the middle of these two. Their fame is spread by word of mouth through friends and relatives of former clients, but the range of this interaction is geographically limited. Most *xiangtou*, like the beliefs and stories upon which their arts are based, are an intensely local phenomenon.

As for any service, the local market for spirit healing includes a range of large and small players, with varying degrees of specialization, the distance a patient is willing to travel roughly corresponding both to the fame of the *xiangtou* and to the seriousness of his or her own condition. A child with a minor stomachache will probably not be taken any farther than the neighboring village for treatment. Thus, most villages will have a *xiangtou* like Xu, who specializes in minor ailments, charges little or no money, and sees patients from a very small area. On the other hand, persons with a more serious condition may travel a significant distance to engage the services of better-known healers. Qi, a woman in her early forties with a chronic and debilitating pain in her legs, has traveled to the hospital in Cang County and to numerous *xiangtou* in the area seeking treatment.

Like many other incarnations of local belief, the *xiangtou* in rural Cang County operate with the implicit acceptance, if not approval, of village officials. This is primarily because authorities in these communities, particularly the village head *(cunzhang)* and village Party secretary *(cun dang zhi shuji)*, are first and foremost villagers and are thus realistic about the continued existence of *xiangtou*. Most recognize the village *xiangtou* as a friend and neighbor, rather than an abstract social phenomenon. Moreover, many routinely employ the services of *xiangtou* for themselves and for members of their families. Wang, of Rear Camp, for example, has the respect of not only fellow villagers, but also authorities in his own and neighboring villages. Even those who consider the practices of *xiangtou* to be pure superstition recognize the importance of these individuals to other villagers and the difficulty and ultimate futility of mounting a campaign against them.

As a result, most village and local authorities turn a blind eye to the continued existence of *xiangtou* and leave the policing of small abuses to social pressure. This can be very effective pressure against the *xiangtou,* who live on their professional reputations. For example, although Chen, the *xiangtou* in Yang Camp, is known to be an effective healer, he is also considered greedy and only marginally trustworthy. Beyond harming his reputation as a healer, within the very small world of village society such a reputation is a very heavy burden to bear.

In cases of larger abuses, the village and higher authorities must become involved. The case mentioned above of the Lai Village peasant who was killed during his own exorcism was settled as follows.

During the exorcism, the wife of the peasant had been visiting her home village. When she returned a week later, she was met with the news that her husband had died of an unspecified illness and had already been buried. She pressed her father-in-law for information but, as it was he who had contracted the *xiangtou* in the first place, he was unwilling to tell her anything. Finally, she took the case to the police in Dulin, the township seat. The authorities exhumed the body and determined that he had in fact died of starvation and exposure. Both the father and the *xiangtou* were fined.

Taken together, all of these individuals and tendencies make up the phenomenon known as *xiangtou*, and any one practitioner is also seen within the context of his or her peers. A *xiangtou* can practice in a single village or among local villages, or travel extensively. His or her practice can tend toward folk medicine or rely more heavily on sacrifices and exorcisms. Whatever the characteristics of any particular individual, such healers continue to exist in this and other areas because the beliefs upon which their arts are based are commonly held and because they address a universal need. *Xiangtou* remain an integral part of folk culture and village society.

Conclusion: Local Culture and Contextualized Knowledge

At first glance, the practices of *xiangtou* and the beliefs upon which they are founded might seem rather unremarkable. Indeed, the idea that spiritual forces influence the physical well-being of humans will be quite familiar to students of Chinese folklore, religion, literature, or cultural history. Yet, upon closer examination, these *xiangtou* and their patients reveal much about the nature of religious belief in the context of local society and the geography of local knowledge.

The contrast is that between the practical sphere of the village and the cultural sphere of local society. The previous chapter discussed the role of the village as a node in the network of religious knowledge, by dual virtue of its importance as an affective community of welfare and as a center of religious administration. Despite changes in the composition of the village community itself, this remained the public setting in which religious resources, iconographic representation, and performance were elaborated. In contrast, the case of *xiangtou* represents rather a different sort of geography. On the one hand, it presents a much smaller ritual world than that of village religion. The *xiangtou* themselves act as individuals. They have no formal affiliation with a teacher, are not members of networks, and are not identified with the village community in the way that temples or sectarians often are. Although their ritual activities are largely common knowledge, these activities are more often performed within the confines of the household than in public space. Moreover, the services of the *xiangtou* are not employed for the welfare of the community, but rather for a single afflicted individual.

On the other hand, the context of religious knowledge from which *xiangtou* arts derive is clearly a function of local society. The set of folk beliefs concerning sickness held in Cang County are in many ways comparable to, if not directly derived from, those that have been held throughout

North China for thousands of years. Indeed, many of the beliefs circulated in the villages of Cang County sound as though they could have been taken directly from the classic collections of strange tales. These accounts and stories are extremely personal, however, and almost all of them are taken from within the sphere of local culture and from recent memory. This is not simply a matter of changing names and places in order to make a story more entertaining. Folklorists working in the United States have demonstrated that popular tales are not simply stories, but news, and in many ways reflect present-day fears and concerns. These stories are retold in such a way as to maintain personal significance to the listener, most significantly by grounding them in a commonly understood set of cultural referents or geography. In the case of *xiangtou* and tales of healing, the localization of knowledge reflects both the immediacy and mutability of the sacred, and the central importance that issues of sickness and health have in the minds of villagers.

Finally, I would contend that this local contextualization of knowledge has important ramifications for flow of culture and the exercise of power. Imperial attempts to assert control over local religion, particularly the co-optation and transformation of local cults, have been amply documented. At the same time, the degree of personal and social agency in the reception of centrally propagated forms of worship means that such control is far from total. Certainly, the process of local contextualization represents one aspect of this reception, not of cults, but of themes, such as the nature of divine punishment, the prophylactic power of religious texts, and the caprice of the spirits. Returning again to geography, the referential scope of tales does represent a bounded sphere, even a map of the "imagined" world of peasants; however, even if the scope of this world in some ways resembles that of other local structures, such as the flow of goods in the marketing system, it represents a very different dynamic. Certainly, both the central places at the core of the Skinnerian marketing systems scheme and the networks that comprise Duara's "cultural nexus" formulation each have theoretical significance to our understanding of the structure of rural communication, and the attenuation of each during periods of internal chaos is certainly borne out by the restricted flow of information through rural society during these periods. Nevertheless, the localization of religious knowledge demonstrates yet another dynamic, representing a case in which local belief is informed by an understanding of space that cannot be readily subsumed into any such geographic or institutional hierarchy.

◨ 4 . Monastic Buddhism
The Limits of Institutional Religion

The study of religious history most commonly and instinctively begins with that of ecclesiastical institutions. In the study of Western Christianity, the religious proclivities of scholars themselves have tended to cast ecclesiastical history in the rather pejorative role of parochial apology, prompting scholars of religious institutions to portray their own work in the more sanitized terms of social history.[1] This has generally not been the case in the study of Chinese religion, in which scholars of the ecclesiastical traditions have continued to inspire work of—and largely for—scholars of their own narrowly and institutionally defined fields. This is particularly true in the study of Chinese Buddhism, often referred to as "Buddhology," which as a discipline tends to focus more on the internal evolution of Buddhist theology and doctrinal organization than on the role of these teachings in the larger world of Chinese religion. This tendency has been the subject of criticism among Buddhologists, who note the danger of portraying "true" Buddhism as a lost, classical tradition that is essentially distinct from and in opposition to modern Chinese religious thought, despite the fact that in many ways the two came to form a "complex and comprehensive whole" as early as the Tang dynasty.[2]

Yet, even today, Chinese Buddhism undeniably remains a distinct entity (even if more "imagined" than institutional), with its own clergy, scripture, liturgy, and self-referential history and traditions.[3] As such, it presents a useful test case from which to understand the role of ecclesiastical institutions in local religious life. Thus, this chapter will begin our examination of religious institutions by discussing the state of organized Buddhism in late Qing and Republican Cang County. Just as scholars of medieval Buddhism examine the transformation of South Asian Buddhism under Chinese influence, we must ask the degree to which the Buddhist institution in Cang County shaped or adapted to local conditions.[4] To what degree was the Buddhist church in Cang County part of a larger world, grounded in the historical and scriptural traditions of the teaching and integrated with Buddhist affairs outside the immediate area, and to what degree was it an expression of local religiosity?

Concerning the physical state of the institution, it is clear that in the villages of late Qing and Republican Cang County, as in much of rural North China, the infrastructure of monastic Buddhism was in a state of severe decay. Although local histories proudly detail the significant number of Buddhist monasteries and temples that had been built in Cang County, many of them had fallen into disrepair or ruin by the late Qing, while others had been converted to popular temples or taken over for secular use. In addition, the majority of the Buddhist institution was concentrated primarily in the city of Cangzhou itself and thus was not an important factor in the daily religious lives of peasants in the outlying areas. By the Republican period, few Cang County peasants had regular access to an active Buddhist monastery.

But what then of individual monks, those who traveled in the countryside or took up residence in village temples or mountain hermitages, especially after the large monasteries began to fall into decline? Traveling monks *(you seng)* figure quite prominently in oral literature and certain ethnographic accounts, giving the impression that Buddhist monks were present in significant numbers. Evidence from the period, however, is contradictory. Most statistics on the size of the community of monks and nuns *(sangha)* confirm a picture of very few Buddhist monks in Cang County, in particular, and North China, in general. This contradiction became apparent even within my own fieldwork. Some interviewees described the Cang County countryside as having contained large numbers of Buddhist monks, who acted as the primary ritual specialists for the religious needs of most villagers. Others, in fact, the majority, insisted that Buddhist monks were extremely rare or completely absent and were certainly not present in sufficient numbers to exert a lasting influence on rural religious life.

Nevertheless, the apparent contradiction encountered in source materials and especially in the testimony of the peasants themselves is significant in that it points to a fundamental discrepancy as to who is defined as a "Buddhist monk" and thus to the larger problem of where to draw the boundaries of Buddhism as an institution. Early Qing attempts to control the proliferation of clergy by limiting the number of ordination certificates *(dudie)* were beyond the administrative capacity of the dynasty and soon fell into disuse. By the end of the eighteenth century, areas such as Jiangnan were full of persons identifying themselves as Buddhist monks, but not in possession of *dudie*.[5] Although the weakening of official scrutiny of ordination had allowed Buddhism to thrive in Jiangnan, it had the opposite effect in North China, where the long-term decline of the monastic institution also weakened the force of Buddhism as a self-consciously distinct, doctrinally self-referential, and scripturally pure entity. By the Republican period, the line dividing "pure" Buddhism from popular religiosity had grown very thin. Village monks were only loosely versed in the scriptural tradition of Buddhism and performed many of the ritual functions of popular religion, demonstrating the degree to which they themselves were immersed in local religious tradition. Conversely, popular specialists, including organized sectarian teachings, freely borrowed the terminology, ritual forms, and even costumes of the Buddhist clergy. This blurring of distinctions among officially and unofficially ordained clergy, lay practitioners, and other religious specialists, such as village sectarians, is seen in the imprecise and often confused accounts of local Buddhism given by Cang County peasants.

The State of Monastic Buddhism in Late Imperial North China and Cang County

The first task in understanding the impact of monastic Buddhism on the religious life of rural Cang County is to assess the state of the institution itself—that is, how many monasteries, monks, and nuns existed in the area and whether they were concentrated in cities and holy sites or spread evenly through the countryside. Second, returning to the question of the religion as an intellectual institution, what was the state of Buddhist doctrine and ritual within the monasteries? Were monasteries havens of Buddhist learning within a shifting sea of popular religiosity, or were they also subject to the syncretic tendencies of popular belief? Did monks in Cang County interact with the larger Buddhist world, traveling to the great centers of Buddhist learning to advance their own learning, entertaining well-trained clergy passing through the area on the way to north to Beijing or south to Puto Mountain, or was life in the monasteries more simply a product of local society and religiosity?

On a national scale, the greatest contrast in Republican-era Buddhism lay between North and South China. Throughout the Late Imperial period, monastic Buddhism had been strongest in the Yangzi Delta and the southeast coast. A Qing census conducted between 1737 and 1739 reveals thousands of monks in the southern provinces: 15,364 in Zhejiang and

19,215 in Anhui.[6] During the late Qing and Republican periods, the monasteries of these southern provinces of flourished as never before, many having been reconstructed with massive lay donations after the devastation of the Taiping rebellion (1851–1864). During the 1930s, the large monastic centers of the South, such as Shanghai and Nanjing, were the centers of a Buddhist intellectual and spiritual renaissance. A 1933 census by the newly formed Chinese Buddhist Association estimates that Zhejiang and Jiangsu provinces alone supported more than 150,000 monks.[7]

In contrast, Buddhism in Qing North China was not particularly strong, and certainly never underwent a spiritual or infrastructural revival similar to that in Jiangnan. The 1737–1739 census lists 7,217 monks in Zhili province during the early eighteenth century. This is a significant figure, although still only half that reported for Zhejiang. By the time of the 1933 census, however, this number had dropped to 1,780.[8] Foreign missionaries and scholars who traveled from Jiangnan to North China expressed amazement at the difference between the state of Buddhism in the two regions. More than merely the number of monks, it was the debilitated state of Buddhist learning and activity in North China that shocked these visitors. In his research on Buddhist architecture, Johannes Prip-Møller contrasted the "fervent worship so common in the lower Yangtse valley" with the empty and "quietly decaying" monasteries of outlying areas of North and West China. According to the great scholar of Chinese Buddhism, Holmes Welch, many of the negative stereotypes that characterized Chinese Buddhism during the late Qing and Republican periods—that of indolent and immoral monks who neither understood nor cared for Buddhist doctrine—reflect the fact that most of the Sinological community was concentrated in North China, where such generalizations were quite often true.[9]

Within North China, the majority of monasteries were concentrated within a few cities, particularly Beijing. This is evident in texts such as the *Jifu tong zhi,* a 1910 gazetteer of what is now Hebei province, five sections *(juan)* of which are devoted to Buddhist monasteries. Although the data in this source appear to have been culled largely from earlier county gazetteers and are thus subject to their limitations, they still show the great disparity between the size of the Buddhist institution in Beijing (as Daxing County), which had no less than 256 Buddhist monasteries, and that of the surrounding countryside, which had far fewer. Other than Beijing itself, the greatest concentration of monasteries was in counties immediately adjacent to the capital. Neighboring Ji County, home of scenic Pan Mountain as well as thirty-seven Buddhist monasteries (such as the well-known Singular Happiness Monastery, *Dule si*), was a popular destination for urban pilgrims and pleasure seekers alike, making it something of a religious suburb of the capital. In contrast, counties beyond the periphery of the regional religious life of the capital thus supported a far smaller monastic institution. This is particularly true in southeastern Hebei, where, according to the *Jifu tong zhi,* most counties (including Cang) had fewer than five monasteries listed.[10]

Local surveys from the Qing dynasty afford a rare glimpse of the state of Buddhist monasteries in Tianjin and Qing counties during the nineteenth century.[11] *Baojia* records from 1842 describe the 391 villages of Tianjin County in detail, including the number of temples and their occupants. In the entire county, ninety from a total of 487 temples were designated either "monastery" *(si)*, "hall" *(tang)*, or "nunnery" *(an)*, all of which nominally signify Buddhist institutions.[12] Of them, sixty-two (nearly 70 percent) were located in the city of Tianjin itself. The remaining thirty-one were scattered among 391 villages, an average of one for every twelve villages. A similar record from the 1870s lists a total fifty-two temples in the sixty-eight villages of Dulin Township of Cang County (although Dulin was part of Qing County at the time). Of them, two had likely been founded as Buddhist institutions (one Guanyin Hall and one "big monastery," *da si*).[13] The average number of villages per specifically Buddhist structure, however, is nearly three times that of rural Tianjin, thirty-four compared to twelve. Overall, the trend is unmistakable: the physical resources of Buddhism were more heavily concentrated in and around urban areas. By every measure, the Buddhist institution was far weaker in rural areas, such as Dulin.

The weak state of the Buddhist institution in late Qing and Republican North China, particularly in the rural areas, is superficially borne out by a lack of historical documents. Unlike their southern counterparts, few northern monasteries compiled temple histories *(miao zhi)*. Those that do exist are generally only for the large pilgrimage centers, such as Wutai Mountain, and say little about the smaller, rural monasteries.[14] County gazetteers are often silent or misleading on the details of the local Buddhist institution. As Timothy Brook has recently discussed, the same Confucian literati who compiled county gazetteers were often among the most vocal critics of Buddhism, a trend that generally grew more intense from the Qing through the Republic. Buddhism was regarded as "a breeding ground for sedition and a stimulus to popular superstition," and the traditionally conservative literati of North China often expressed their antipathy to the religion quite openly within the gazetteers themselves. "We Con-

Table 4.1 Relative Size of the Buddhist Institution in Nineteenth-Century Tianjin and Qing Counties

	Urban ———————————————————————————► Rural			
	Tianjin Urban Area, 1842	Tianjin County, Including Urban Area, 1842	Tianjin County, Excluding Urban Area, 1842	Dulin Township, Circa 1875
Number of Buddhist monasteries	62	90	28	2
Total number of temples	161	487	326	52
Temples : Buddhist monastery	2.6 : 1	5.4 : 1	11.6 : 1	26 : 1
Number of villages	...	...	391	67
Villages : Buddhist monastery	...	...	14.0 : 1	33.5 : 1
Number of households	32,857	83,991	51,134	5,399
Households : Buddhist monastery	530 : 1	933.2 : 1	1,826.2 : 1	2,699.5 : 1
Adult population	105,097	265,043	159,946	19,749
Adults : Buddhist monastery	1,695.1 : 1	2,944.2 : 1	5,712.4 : 1	9,874.5 : 1

Source: *Jinmen baojia tushuo, Qingxian cuntu, juan* 12.

fucians," the compiler of the Jinzhou gazetteer of 1690 declared, "do not talk about the Two Teachings [Buddhism and Daoism] and are strict about heterodox ways," and the compiler of the 1756 gazetteer of Qizhou gazetteer proudly announced, "We Confucians most certainly treat [Buddhism] with contempt."[15]

Many of these gentry scholars expressed their distaste for Buddhism by underreporting the number of monasteries in their counties. Although few went as far as the early Qing magistrate of a county in Zhili, who "dared not" list Buddhist or Daoist monasteries in the local history, others did omit smaller structures, those farther from the capital, or those suspected of having been built in defiance of the various imperial prohibitions against monastic construction.[16] Even those local histories that do include a relatively complete list of Buddhist institutions generally do not volunteer much detail about them, offering only a roster of names and rough locations such as "east of the county seat." Almost none includes such information as the number of monks present or any clue as to the life within the monastery itself.

As luck would have it, the Republican-era gazetteers of both Cang and Qing counties do provide significant information on religious construction. These gazetteers, as well as the earlier (1899) prefectural gazetteer of Tianjin, which administered both counties, aimed at completeness and list dates of construction and major repair for a large number of popular temples and Buddhist monasteries. The 1933 gazetteer of Cang County, in particular, appears to have taken the work of recording temples very seriously. This gazetteer lists no fewer than 284 temples, most of which were located in the countryside. In addition, although the Cang County gazetteer, like others, freely refers to earlier editions, it also makes a point of noting recent changes. In contrast, the 1931 gazetteer of neighboring Qing County is more complete concerning temples in the city itself, but less so for those located in the countryside. Taken together, however, these accounts provide a reasonably reliable foundation for understanding at least the physical basis of monastic Buddhism up until the 1930s.[17]

Number of Buddhist Monasteries

The best starting point by which to assess the size and strength of the Buddhist institution is the record of monastic construction and repair. These activities are significant because they reveal not simply the physical presence of a building, but also that of a devoted and organized laity who took charge of and financed a construction project. Specifically Buddhist construction would seem to suggest the presence and leadership of monks, an assumption that will be discussed in detail later in the chapter. Suffice to say now that the history of monastic construction and repair is that of religious life and organization in action.

As mentioned in chapter 1, temple construction in Cang and Qing Counties is relatively well documented in gazetteer sources. Even if many village temples were not documented, the general trends are clear. New temples were built at a steady pace throughout most of the Ming and Qing, with some interruption in the transition between the two. Similarly, existing temples were frequently repaired, with a dramatic increase in temple repair during the late nineteenth and early twentieth centuries. Even if these data do not speak absolutely for the numbers of temples built or repaired, they do demonstrate that votive construction remained an important activity and that, despite reformist campaigns to the contrary, smaller repair projects actually increased in number.

Certain logistical and historical differences must, however, be taken into account when comparing the construction of ordinary temples versus that of Buddhist monasteries. The first is the timing and source of funding. Timothy Brook has shown that during the Ming dynasty, when many of the Cang County temples were built, Buddhist monasteries were very much centers of literate society. Gentry patrons composed odes to the scenery surrounding the monasteries, attended Buddhist lectures, and financially supported construction and renovation projects. During this heyday, when the "seam between the gentry world and Buddhist culture had almost disappeared," support for monasteries came primarily from the gentry, and this patronage was as much participation in the public sphere as an expression of religious piety. This sort of patronage was as short lived, however, and beginning in the late 1600s the gentry began to focus their attention and their philanthropy on other issues.[18]

A second difference is that of scale. If a Buddhist monastery was intended to be occupied, it obviously had to be large enough to house a number of resident monks. In addition, provisions had to be made for their livelihood, usually a small endowment of land to be farmed by the monks themselves. It is true that monastic disciples might take up residence in village temples or that, as monasteries fell on hard times, monks might become itinerant travelers, begging (as opposed to the ordinary period of monastic wandering, *yun you*) or farming a minimal amount of land to care for their own subsistence needs, but the latter state of affairs characterized a monastery in decay. During the time of growth and construction, even a small Buddhist monastery was by necessity a project built on a grand scale.

A final difference between Buddhist monastic construction and that of popular temples involved the various official restrictions placed on the construction of new monasteries. A sign of the perennial imperial mistrust of Buddhism, decrees aimed at restricting the growth of the Buddhist establishment were proclaimed throughout the Ming and Qing dynasties. Ming emperors severely restricted the number of Buddhist ordination certificates to be conferred, increased the interval between ordinations, and proclaimed a ban on founding new monasteries; in each of these measures, their Qing counterparts followed suit. As punishment for illicit construction or enlargement of a monastery, the Qing code demanded one hundred blows with the heavy cane, followed by banishment to a border region.[19] Naturally, numerous monasteries were built as exceptions to or in defiance of this difficult-to-enforce moratorium. According to Holmes Welch, by the final years of the Qing, many monks did not know that many of the laws governing their behavior even existed, and "there were many monasteries built without permission." Even so, the pressure exerted on Buddhist monastic construction was a force not levied upon that of ordinary temples (particularly considering that, as a larger project, a monastery would be more subject to outside scrutiny than a small village temple) and must be taken into account.[20]

On the basis of gazetteer data, monastic construction in Cang and Qing counties was strongest in the Ming, but fell off during the early Qing (Appendix A-2, Temple Construction and Repair Led by Buddhist Monks). The majority of the forty-two monasteries in Cang and Qing counties for which construction dates are recorded were founded during or before the Ming. Eleven Cang County monasteries date to before the Yuan dynasty, although we can assume that many of them had been destroyed during the wars of the Yuan–Ming transition, if not long before. The majority, however, were founded during the Ming dynasty, the highpoint being between the mid-fifteenth and mid-sixteenth centuries. In both counties, the pace of monastic construction fell off sharply during the Qing dynasty; taken together, only three new monasteries were built during the Qing, two of them during the first few years of the dynasty.[21]

The decline in new monastic construction is especially striking when compared to the brisk temple construction throughout the Qing dynasty; however, the divergence of temple and monastic construction from the mid-Qing suggests that the need for new Buddhist constriction may have simply topped out, indicating neither growth nor decline. Once built, however, a temple or monastery required constant repair, particularly to the walls and roofs. A period of extended neglect could see a flourishing monastery literally reduced to ruins. To remain attractive, the buildings of a monastery needed to be renovated at least once each generation. Longer periods of neglect might lead to irreparable structural damage; Timothy Brook quotes one late Ming writer who observed that large buildings should be renovated every fifty years to avoid collapse and another who claimed that after two centuries without repair, nothing of the building would be left standing. Moreover, repair could be extremely costly, usually beyond the means of the monastery itself, and often even beyond the collected resources of the local gentry.[22] Regular renovation of monastery buildings was both important and costly and demonstrates a real interest in maintaining, if not necessarily expanding, Buddhism.

In both Cang and Qing counties, the period of monastic construction during the Ming was followed by a number of repair projects during the

Qing, actually becoming more frequent during the eighteenth and nineteenth centuries. This limited degree of support, however, mostly likely masks a larger picture of neglect, for as many Buddhist monasteries were maintained, many more appear to have been allowed to fall quietly into decay. By the early 1930s, only fourteen of the seventy-four Buddhist monasteries in Cang and Qing counties had been repaired within the previous century, and, of them, only four within the past fifty years. Many of those monasteries for which repair had been specifically recorded list the last instance as having been two or even three centuries earlier. If this record is even close to accurate, we can assume that many of the buildings listed in gazetteers had been reduced to ruins by the time these guides were written. For example, three Dulin temples—the Temple of the Eastern Peak *(Dongyue miao)*, the Hall of Wisdom Nunnery *(Hui tang an)*, and the Shrine of the tutelary deity—were listed as having been repaired during the late eighteenth and early nineteenth centuries; however, none of them appears in the extremely detailed *Diagram of Villages in Qing County* written during the 1870s, leading to the conclusion that these structures must have since been destroyed, abandoned, or converted to other use. The same holds true for Buddhist monasteries. Certainly by the Republican period, it is likely that many of the Buddhist monasteries listed in the gazetteers of Cang and Qing counties existed on paper only.[23]

Buddhist Clergy and Temple Construction

What of the monks themselves? As Vincent Goossaert has recently discussed, very few hard data exist on the size of the Buddhist clergy, particularly at the local level.[24] The number of Buddhist monasteries itself cannot provide much guidance, not merely because the data on the monasteries are themselves less than complete, but also because some monasteries were unoccupied while many Buddhist monks lived in ordinary village temples. In spite of these deficiencies, the record of temple and monastic construction can still give important clues, specifically because Buddhist clergy often took charge of votive construction projects. This is, in fact, one of the few places where monks and nuns do appear prominently in Cang County and Qing County source materials. Although most local histories, including those from Cang and Qing counties, do mention particularly well-known monks or nuns under the heading of "notable personages" *(ren wu)*, few ordinary monks were so recorded. In contrast, clerical leadership of votive projects such as temple construction usually warranted a passing mention in the description of the event, even if the monk himself was not particularly well known. Thus, although the record of clerical influence in temple construction does not demonstrate the actual size of the Buddhist clergy, it can give a rough idea of the relative public influence of this group over the long term.

The gazetteers of Cang and Qing counties together mention twenty-two cases in which a Buddhist monk took charge of organizing the construction or repair of a local temple or monastery (Appendix A-2, Temple Construction and Repair Led by Buddhist Monks). The great majority of these cases—eighteen of twenty-two—concern the repair of an existing structure. In two cases a new temple or monastery was founded, and in two others a ruined one was rebuilt *(chong jian)*. Not surprisingly, most of these construction efforts were spent on specifically Buddhist structures. Only four nonmonastic temples were the subject of a reconstruction effort by a monk: a temple of the White Robe *(baiyi miao)*, a temple of the Medicine King *(yaowang miao)*, a temple of the Eastern Peak *(dongyue miao)*, a Tianqi temple *(tianqi miao)*, and a Queen Mother Pavilion *(wangmu ge)*.

Clerical influence in temple and monastic construction was strongest during the Ming, which is also the period when most new monastic construction took place. Fifteen of the twenty-two instances of clerical involvement took place during the Ming dynasty, particularly the fifteenth and sixteenth centuries. The number of instances declines during the Qing dynasty, with a small resurgence at the beginning of the nineteenth century. The last burst of activity during the early nineteenth century is especially interesting. As the preceding discussion of monastic construction suggests, by the early nineteenth century, many Buddhist monasteries were in need of repair; however, in three of four cases from the nineteenth century and the one from the twentieth, an individual identified as a Buddhist monk is seen leading the repair of a popular temple, rather than a Buddhist monastery. Of these, only the temples of the White Robe and Medicine King are of recognizably Buddhist orientation. The others—the Tianqi, Dongyue, and Pangu temples—could be classified as Daoist or popular temples, but certainly are not Buddhist. In other words, these latter-day efforts show Buddhist monks taking charge of votive projects that were not only external to the monastic institution, but outside of Buddhism altogether. This is an initial indication of the degree to which specifically Buddhist networks (especially those based around a particular monastery) had decreased in importance and to which Buddhism as an institution had blended into a more general religious world.

Size and Importance of the Buddhist Clergy in Cang County

Although it did not always have the power to do so, the Qing was keenly interested in maintaining control over the Buddhist institution. Both they and, later, the Republican government made sporadic efforts to enumerate the number of monks, nuns, and temples and the amount and value of Buddhist property. The Qing effort was based on the *dudie* system of monastic registration, punctuated by occasional nationwide censuses, such as that of 1736–1739.[25] Over the long term, the best local data from the Qing come from the system of *baojia* registration, in which religious personnel were to be listed separately, but these data become less reliable toward the end of the dynasty.[26] During the early Republic, attempts to control the administration of temple property were limited to unpopular and loosely enforced laws, such as the "Temple Registration Statute" *(simiao dengji lu)* of 1919.[27] With the increased military and administrative presence of the Guomindang following the Northern Expedition (1926–1928), however, these efforts were joined by a spate of religious head counts. The first of these came in 1928, at which point a general census of religious personnel was ordered, followed by an even more ambitious census of villages in 1933. As recent research by Rebecca Nedostup has shown, these censuses were ambitious in the extreme and demanded detailed statistics concerning temple property and residents. Perhaps for that very reason, they were rarely carried out according to the designs of government planners, particularly in provinces such as Hebei, in which the Nationalist government still retained only tenuous control.[28]

This official accounting was further joined by similar efforts by the newly formed Chinese Buddhist Association, the organizational and ideological force behind the Buddhist revival in Jiangnan. In 1930, the great religious leader Taixu called for a general census of all of the monks and nuns in China. The results were published in the magazine *Haichaoyin* (Sound of the Tide) and were considered reliable enough for inclusion in the *China Handbook,* compiled by the Ministry of Information in 1947,[29] but even the prestigious Chinese Buddhist Association did not have a particularly long reach into the Buddhist institution of areas such as Hebei, and the data collected there are not likely to be as reliable as those collected in the southern provinces.

Despite these numerous attempts to measure and enumerate the size and composition of the *sangha,* it remains difficult to draw a reliable picture of the Buddhist institution in North China, particularly at the local level. Here, the greatest problem is not a dearth of statistics, but rather that various published statistics are often wildly contradictory. *Baojia* records from Tianjin County listed 321 Buddhist monks and Daoist priests in 1842. Only ninety-seven of them were located within Tianjin city itself (in contrast, the majority of recognizably Buddhist temples, nearly 70 percent, were located in urban Tianjin). This indicates a relatively large number of religious specialists in the countryside, a rough average of one per 1.75 villages or 228 rural households.[30] Statistics published in 1933 by the Shanghai-based *Haichaoyin* listed a total of 1,780 monks and 320 nuns in all of Hebei province, including Tianjin.[31] The Cang County gazetteer from the same year claimed roughly 200 monks and nuns in that county alone. This figure is just under 10 percent of what *Haichaoyin* had estimated for all of Hebei, a rather high concentration considering that many of the monks in the province would have been located in and around the large centers of Beijing and Tianjin.[32] One year earlier, in 1932, neighboring Nanpi County claimed to have had no Buddhist monks but 41 "Buddhist temple residents."[33] The 1994 Cang County gazetteer estimates that the county had 25 monks in 1945.[34] When placed side by side, the rather striking degree of discrepancy in these statistics becomes clear.

When examined more closely, however, a relatively clear and consistent picture of a very small Buddhist clergy begins to emerge. Two of the largest estimates—those of the Ministry of the Interior in 1931 and the Cang County gazetteer in 1933—are poorly explained and not likely to be reliable. Holmes Welch suggests that the former was probably just a "casual guess" on the part of ministry officials. I would suspect that the suspiciously round figure of 200 monks in Cang County is similar in origin. The figure for Tianjin prefecture, as mentioned earlier, represents an urban area and many suburban villages and, though likely reliable, is not typical of a rural area such as Cang. The remaining estimates, though not in exact agreement, still demonstrate a paucity of Buddhist clergy, especially in the rural areas.

Most ethnographic evidence from elsewhere in Republican-era Hebei further confirms the small size of the Buddhist clergy in the rural areas. In his extensive travels through the northern Hebei counties of Xuanhua and Wanquan during the late 1940s, Willem Grootaers found very few Buddhist monasteries, most of which dated from the Ming dynasty and were in a state of advanced decay. Neither they nor village temples housed significant numbers of Buddhist monks. In rural Wanquan, Grootaers found only two monks; in Xuanhua, only one former monastery was populated at all.[35] In his 1933 surveys of Ding County, Li Jinghan compiled the occupation of all adult males from 515 families and discovered not a single Bud-

Table 4.2   Estimates of the Size of the Buddhist Clergy in Hebei Province
and Cang County

Source	Date	Area	Number of Monks	Number of Counties	Average per County
Yellow Registers (huang ce)[a]	1739	Zhili (Hebei) Province	7,217 (plus 1,460 nuns)	94[b]	92
Baojia records[c]	1842	Tianjin Province	321	1	321
Baojia records[d]	Circa 1875	Qing County, Dulin Township	9	1 of 12 districts	108
Ministry of Interior[e]	1931	Hebei Province	21,000	159	132
Nanpi gazetteer[f]	1932	Nanpi County (Cangzhou)	41[g]	1	41
Haichaoyin magazine	1933	Hebei Province	1,780 (plus 320 nuns)	159	13
Cang County 1933 gazetteer[h]	1933	Cang County	200	1	200
Hebei religious survey[i]	1945	Cang County	4	1	4
Cang County 1994 gazetteer[j]	1945	Cang County	25	1	25
Hebei Province Committee[k]	1951	Shijiazhuang, Tangshan, Tianjin, Baoding	217 (plus 246 nuns)	5	98
Hebei Province Committee[k]	1955	Hebei, excluding Baoding	707 (plus 563 nuns)	138	9

[a] Goossaert (2000, 60).
[b] Of a total of 199 counties.
[c] Jinmen baojia tushuo. This includes Buddhist monks and Daoists together.
[d] Qingxian cuntu.
[e] Welch (1967, 411, 415).
[f] Nanpi xianzhi, 1932, 124–125, 503.
[g] Buddhist "temple residents."
[h] Cangxian, 1933, 1623.
[i] Hebei sheng zongjiao yanjiu hui, "Bohai dao zongjiao tuanti diaocha biao" (np, nd).
   In Hebei difang zongjiao tuanti diaocha biao.
[j] Cangxian, 1994, 598.
[k] Hebei shengzhi, v. 68, Zongjiao, 54.

dhist monk or other professional religious specialist. In the entire county, Li found no more than twenty-four monks.[36]

Other ethnographic accounts and episodic evidence, however, seem to reveal precisely the opposite: large numbers of Buddhist monks, who played an important role in village religious life. According to surveys of Xiao and Shajing villages, both located near Beijing, many villages housed a monk in their local temple as late as the early Republic.[37] Although this can be readily explained by the proximity of these two villages to a large urban center, episodic evidence from the Boxer Uprising suggests that a significant number of monks lived in the countryside, as well. Joseph Esherick notes that many of the local Boxer leaders in Zhili were "Buddhist monks or Daoist priests—itinerant types, with no families to bind them to a given locality," a claim further confirmed by peasants in Xiao Village.[38] In the Boxer siege of Cang County, Arthur Peill noted that often the most violent leaders were the Buddhist monks, many of whom seemed to be from outside the area.[39]

This discrepancy is seen even within my own fieldwork in Cang County. Most of those with whom I spoke emphasized the weak state of Buddhism as an institution and, in particular, the paucity of Buddhist monks. Peasants in the Cang County village of Yang Camp knew of only two monks during the Republican era, Benxuan and Benxin, both of whom had lived in the Stone Buddha Monastery *(Shifo si)* in the village of the same name. Benxuan, the older of the two, was killed in 1935, while defending the monastery against bandits, and Benxin, his disciple, left soon thereafter. Nearby Dulin town, the site of significant monastic construction during the mid-Qing, had long since lost its significance as a Buddhist center. According to these sources, by the Republican era the town had neither monks nor operational Buddhist monasteries.[40]

Other peasants, however, gave very different testimony, claiming that certain villages housed large concentrations of Buddhist monks and that *most* villages had at least one monk in residence. Often, completely contradictory testimony came from peasants within the same village. The village of Zhifangtou is a good example. When asked about Buddhist monks during the late Republic, peasants in the neighboring village of Rear Camp insisted that at least ten had lived in Zhifangtou. To our dismay, peasants in Zhifangtou vehemently denied that they had *ever* had Buddhist monks living in the village, and certainly not the large contingent that their neighbors had claimed. Many said that they had never even seen a Buddhist monk, except those portrayed in local opera.[41]

The difficulties encountered in the seemingly simple problem of counting Buddhist monks mirrors the inconsistency of published statistics and stems from a fundamental discrepancy as to who is to be defined as a Buddhist monk. This problem was not specific to the villages of Cang County, nor was it merely a matter of popular misunderstanding. The blurring of boundaries around the Buddhist monastic institution was a long-standing concern for the Qing, who tried to remedy it by instituting strict but impractical laws certifying ordination. Despite the dynasty's increasing wariness of the danger of unlicensed monks in local society, it could do little to rectify the situation. By the waning years of the Qianlong reign, government documents were using the term "monk" to refer to "virtually anyone with a robe and a shaved head, whatever his state of religious commitment or education."[42] By the late Qing, imperial recognition of monastic credentials was no longer necessary, and anyone with a modicum of religious training could simply call him or herself a Buddhist monk or nun. During the Republic, even nominal government control over monastic ordination ceased. The issue soon became so confused that, as a practical solution, a 1929 law recognized as a Buddhist monk "anyone living in a temple."[43]

This was particularly true in the syncretic tradition of popular religion, in which distinct teachings are considered aspects of a greater truth and relatively little attention is paid to the doctrinal affiliation of religious specialists. In ethnographic accounts, as well as elsewhere in my own fieldwork, peasants freely conflated all religious specialists as "Daoists" *(daoshi, lao dao)*, "Buddhists," or even "monks" *(heshang)*. Sectarian groups are often referred to as "Buddhist sects" or "Daoist sects" *(fomen, daomen)*, with little concern as to the difference between the two. The 1933 gazetteer of Cang County, which had claimed the unusually high figure of 200 monks living in the county, illustrates this tendency. Of the 100 temples that reportedly housed monks, all but seven contained lay monks *(youpo)* who "neither shave their heads nor live outside the home, and are popularly referred to as 'People of the Way'" *(dao ren)*.[44] According to this source, such monks performed funerals and popular rituals, but "not two or three in ten have any understanding of Buddhist scriptures." In other words, this source makes no distinction between Buddhist monks, temple residents, and lay religious specialists.

In fact, it is quite possible that many of those identified by outsiders as Buddhist monks were actually sectarians. This was the case with the supposed "Buddhist monks" in Zhifangtou who were, in fact, members of the Teaching of the Most Supreme. Older peasants in Hai Dock village—which once supported a contingent of the Teaching of the Most Supreme and still regularly employs specialists from outside the village to perform funerals and exorcisms—at first described this sectarian group as a "Buddhist sect" *(fo men)*. Pressed further, these same peasants then decided that the group was possibly a "Daoist sect" *(dao men)*. Finally, the group came to the conclusion that the Teaching of the Most Supreme was "either a Buddhist-style Daoist sect, or possibly a Daoist-style Buddhist sect, or maybe both."[45] This degree of casual imprecision demonstrates the low importance in which villagers commonly held the institutional affiliation of religious specialists, as well as the attendant pitfalls of taking such ethnographic testimony too literally.

Finally, at least by the Republican period, the Buddhist monks who were active in Cang County were remarkably similar to local religious specialists in training and ritual function. Peasants living near Stone Buddha Monastery in Cang County remembered seeking out the two resident monks, Benxuan and Benxin, to perform many of the rituals of popular religiosity, such as general blessings, the protective "Jumping over the Wall" ceremony, and funerals.[46] According to informants, none of these rituals was distinctively or exclusively Buddhist, and any could be performed equally well by other ritual specialists, particularly those of the Teaching of the Most Supreme and Heaven and Earth Sect. For quite some time, at least within living memory, nobody had attended the monastery to hear Buddhist scriptures or lectures on Buddhist thought, as Timothy Brook shows that they might have done during the Buddhist heyday of the Ming dynasty. Indeed, nobody had heard of monks in the Stone Buddha or any other monastery having ever held such lectures. Even for local elites, Buddhism held no particular attraction. Large landlord families such as the Wangs of Wang Family Village patronized local temples or sectarian life rather than monastic Buddhism.

By the Republican period, Buddhism was no longer a distinct force in the religious life of rural Cang County. Its teachings had long since been absorbed into popular religiosity, and any original emphasis on scriptural and doctrinal purity was conveniently forgotten. The network of Buddhist teachers and disciples, tempered by strict imperial observance of ordination during the Ming and early Qing, had grown increasingly lax and informal. Local religious specialists, who might call themselves or be locally referred to as "Daoists" or "Buddhist monks," were as deeply imbued in popular and sectarian religious tradition as in Buddhist scripture.

Changes under the People's Republic and Prospects for the Future

In many ways, the story of institutional Buddhism in Cang County would seem to have ended before the founding of the People's Republic. By 1949, most rural monasteries had long been deserted, and even urban temples, such as Water Moon Monastery *(Shuiyue si)*, located on the edge of Cangzhou City, had only a few elderly residents.[47] During the 1950s, the few monks who remained were forced into retirement, and, by the early 1960s, all of them had died of old age. Soon after the outbreak of the Cultural Revolution, the monastery property was confiscated, the buildings torn down, and a coal factory built upon the site.

During the early 1980s, just as villages were rebuilding their local religious infrastructure, faithful in and around Cangzhou City began to take an interest in reviving the monastery. With the coal plant still in operation, it was impossible to rebuild on the original grounds, but when the plant fell upon hard times during the early 1990s, a new plan was conceived. First one, and later a second, idle production hall was rented out to faithful as the new Water Moon Monastery. As of the summer of 2002, the combined rent for these two halls was 8,000 *yuan* per month, a sum donations consistently exceeded.

This monastery is of interest as an example of the expansion of Buddhist networks and suggests the new role that an invigorated ecclesiastical Buddhism could come to play in rural Cang County. During the 1940s, both the monks and faithful of this monastery came from a relatively small area, although one that was only slightly larger than the sphere of local culture of the villager. All of the monks were local, hailing from Cang and Qing Counties, and the more well-to-do faithful might arrive from neighboring villages in horse carts. The monastery had no formal relationship with other temples or monasteries in the area.

Since the 1980s, the newly conceived Water Moon Monastery has expanded its influence. Although the thirty-nine-year-old abbot hails from neighboring Qing County, he frequently travels to neighboring counties, as well as Tianjin and Beijing, to solicit donations and sell calligraphy. He has also written a number of moral tracts, which are published locally and enthusiastically presented to visitors. The ten disciples of the young abbot come from all over North China, one from as far away as Harbin.

The expansion of Buddhist networks in Cang County is both controlled and facilitated by the integration of the local Buddhist institution into the national Chinese People's Buddhist Association *(Zhongguo renmin fojiao xiehui)*. As one of the five official religions of the People's Republic, the doctrine and organization of even local Buddhism are now subject to significant central influence. To retain their official acceptance, monasteries and specialists must present a very standard brand of Buddhism and be ever watchful for the rise of unorthodox ideas or activities among their ranks. At the same time, however, integration into the state-sponsored organization has also exposed local Buddhism to a larger world. Monks from Cang County now receive centrally printed Buddhist publications, attend regional and even national meetings of the Chinese People's Buddhist Association, and decorate their newly refurbished monasteries with iconography mass-produced hundreds of miles away. Although government sponsorship has without question subjected local Buddhism to a great degree of central control, its integration into a wider sphere has arguably made it more "Buddhist"—that is, a stronger and more self-conscious institution—than it had been at any point during the Qing.[48]

The Water Moon Monastery may thus mark the beginning of a new role for Buddhism in Cang County. Increased literacy, particularly in Cangzhou City, makes the writings produced and distributed by the monastery accessible to and attractive for personal devotion. The vastly improved transportation network within the city and to nearby market towns makes the monastery physically accessible to more people than ever. Perhaps more fundamentally, the monastery preaches a brand of Buddhism that will appeal to a wide audience. The dilution of local religious identity in many villages and interruption of public ceremonial has weakened earlier notions of and loyalties to specific religious groups, while the forms and images in the new monastery conform to the expectations of religion as portrayed in the mass media. Finally, although the monastery itself is not government sponsored, it does represent an acceptable form of religious affiliation and expression. The Water Moon Monastery is thus the recipient of generous donations from urban and rural faithful, including those who might be reticent to sponsor more politically questionable religious activities.[49]

Conclusion

Throughout the late Qing and Republican periods, the institutional boundaries of Buddhism were weak and, in many cases, came to disappear altogether. To be sure, most peasants would have identified themselves as Buddhists or, more specifically, as believers in the Buddha (xin fo). This, however, did not demonstrate the universality of ecclesiastical Buddhism as much as the fact that, for peasants and those identified as Buddhist monks alike, the teaching was fundamentally inseparable from the larger world of local religious belief and organization. When such boundaries were drawn around Buddhism, it was generally done by outsiders, either the newly revived Buddhist organizations of the 1930s or, more frequently, the state. State control of Buddhism, through its attempts to police monastic ordination as under the Qing or to sponsor official Buddhist organizations, as continued under the Republic and People's Republic, had as its goal the definition and enforcement of a Buddhist orthodoxy and, by extension, exertion of control over local religion. Ironically, it is under the officially atheistic People's Republic that such state-sanctioned Buddhism has begun to make its most significant headway in the penetration of rural Cang County.

𝄢 5. Pseudomonastic Sectarians
The Li Sect in Town and Country

The Li Sect *(zailijiao)* first developed during the late Ming dynasty and remained one of the largest and most influential religious teachings in China until the early 1960s, when it officially disbanded as an organization in the People's Republic of China.[1] Although the teaching had a wide following throughout late Qing and Republican North China, it was strongest in the city of Tianjin and its rural catchment areas, such as Cang County. The example of monastic Buddhism in Cang County shows that the nominal presence of a religious institution does not necessarily speak for its influence on local religious life. In contrast to formal Buddhism, however, lay sectarian teachings were both a newer and a more dynamic force, and many such teachings developed directly out of rural society. If sectarian teachings were, as J. J. M. de Groot suggested more than a century ago, a popular response to the inadequacies of the Buddhist institution, one might expect to find a higher degree of institutional coherence in precisely those areas in which Buddhism was weakest.[2]

This chapter will discuss the Li Sect from the perspective of its institutional integrity, examining manifestations of this teaching in its national center of Tianjin and the nearby town of Duliu, before finally presenting data from rural Cang County. Such a perspective is necessary because the Li Sect, as it appeared in the villages of Cang County, was both a local phenomenon and an extension of a long institutional evolution, established traditions, and far-reaching networks. In contrast to de Groot's expectations, the Li Sect was organized in much the same way as North Chinese monastic Buddhism, with human resources, both pseudomonastic (formally ordained, celibate, and partially cloistered) specialists and lay devotees, concentrated in the urban areas. As a result, the theological and practical tradition of the Li Sect was the most elaborate and self-consciously distinct in the city of Tianjin. Particularly during the early twentieth century, the Tianjin-based national organization of the Li Sect sought to portray itself as a canonical "great teaching," on a plane with Buddhism or Christianity. The teaching was also active in Republican Duliu, which had four sectarian temples within the town precincts; however, despite the importance of the teaching to town life, Duliu could not support as many religious specialists or as elaborate a ritual calendar as Tianjin. The teaching there was not as specialized, nor was the local organization infused with the same sense of proselytizing mission. Finally, the case of rural Cang County represents the Li Sect in its weakest form. In contrast to Tianjin and Duliu, specialists of the teaching in Cang County were lay devotees and were scattered so thinly that the sect never maintained a significant presence in the ritual or spiritual life of the village. Even had they been able to, the teaching of the Li Sect in rural Cang County was so heavily adulterated with local beliefs that it represented a minimal substantive contribution to local religion.

Nevertheless, it would not do to discount the rural life of the Li Sect entirely. Even in areas in which the teaching was weakest, certain aspects remained intact, most significantly its nominal signifiers and the characteristic prohibition against the use of opium, tobacco, and alcohol. In Tianjin and Cang County alike, many knew the Li Sect simply as the "Temperance Sect" (*jie yan jiu jiao,* literally the "give up alcohol and tobacco teaching"). In Tianjin, where the teaching was theologically and organizationally the most developed, and rural Cang County alike, a great number of ordinary members joined the Li Sect simply to give up one or more of these substances.

Founding and Organization of the Li Sect

The Li Sect was founded during the waning years of the Ming dynasty by Yang Zai (1621–1754, also known as Yang Chengqing and Yang Rulai), a holder of the *jinshi* degree from Jimo County in peninsular Shandong.[3] The scriptural and oral history of the sect paints Yang as a benevolent and filial Confucian scholar who was dismayed by the wars and chaos of the time and sought to ease the sufferings of the people. Although anxious to take up an official position, Yang remained in Jimo to care for and protect his aged mother and, after her death, kept a three-year vigil at her grave. During this time, he formulated the teaching of what would become the Li Sect. Some sources claim that Yang created the teaching himself, whereas others hold that Guanyin revealed it to him in a vision or forest encounter. After the period of mourning had past, Yang gathered a small number of disciples and traveled north, through Hebei, to the mountains of Ji County, about 100 kilometers north of Tianjin. There, he sat in thought and meditation for ten years in Lanshui Cave. During this time, he elaborated his teaching and spiritually and physically purified himself *(xiu lian)*. Later scriptures claim that he was visited by Guanyin, who taught him how to distill mountain plants into medicine.[4] At the age of eighty, he took ten primary disciples, who were sent in separate directions to spread the teaching. Thanks to his advanced techniques of meditation and refinement, Yang reputedly lived for another fifty years, dying at the age of 133.[5]

The early teaching of the Li Sect was characterized by its Eight Proscriptions *(ba jie)*. Originally inspired by the Five Proscriptions of Buddhism, such codified rules of conduct were also relatively common in sectarian teachings.[6] Proscribed conduct within the sectarian tradition generally emphasized Confucian morality and Daoist ideas of purity, the most common proscriptions being against immoral or unfilial conduct and, occasionally, against eating meat or drinking alcohol. The Eight Proscriptions of the Li Sect, however, were concerned primarily with religious practice rather than personal morality. Five of the eight prohibit the ritual activities of popular devotion, such as burning incense and paper to spirits, and reveal a strong Confucian, and even antireligious, element in the original teaching of Yang Zai.[7]

The origins of what would become the most characteristic element of the Li Sect—its strict prohibition of tobacco, alcohol, and opium—and the relative importance of this element in the early life of the teaching, though, remain open to speculation. Li Shiyu, who also conducted an investigation of the Li Sect in his native Tianjin, holds that these characteristic prohibitions, like the Li Sect itself, are direct products of the sectarian tradition. Long before the formation of the Li Sect, teachings such as the White Lotus *(bailian jiao)* and Non-Action *(wuwei jiao)* were also characterized by a strong temperance tradition. The scriptures of the Luo Teaching (particularly its highly influential *Five Part Scripture, Wu bu jing)* directly prohibit the drinking of alcohol (along with eating of meat), as do other scriptures, such as the *Five Part Red Yang Scripture (Hongyang wubu jing)* of the Red Yang Teaching *(hongyang jiao)*. The early Li Sect was certainly well grounded in this larger sectarian tradition. The texts of the Li Sect refer repeatedly to the Luo Teaching, and at least one of the earliest disciples of the Li Sect was also a member of the Red Yang Teaching.[8] Li Shiyu thus concludes that the prohibition against intoxicants, or at least the intellectual seeds from which it would grow, must have existed in the Li Sect from the outset.[9]

Other explanations downplay any direct intellectual links between the early Li Sect and existing sectarian teachings, claiming that the Li Sect began as an anti-Qing secret society and that the prohibitions against alcohol and tobacco represented a later addition. Oral tradition within the sect holds that the teaching was founded primarily as an underground movement in support of the recently deposed Ming dynasty.[10] This is reflected in the secret "Five Character Mantra" *(wuzi zhenyan)*, which originally included such formulations as "Destroy the Qing-Support the Great Ming" *(mie qing fu da ming)*, "Protect the Great Ming with All of Your Heart" *(yi xin bao da ming)*, and "Kill All Manchus on Sight" *(jian manren jiu sha)*.[11] According to these explanations then, the proscription of alcohol and tobacco thus grew out of a general call to moral rebirth, as well as the perception that smoking tobacco was a Manchu custom.[12] As the country began to prosper under the Qing, sentiment against the dynasty began to fade and the Li Sect recast itself as loyal guardians of public morality. The temperance tradition thus took root during the late eighteenth century in the wake of increasingly widespread opium addiction.

These explanations need not be treated exclusively of each other. It is certainly no great leap of logic for a proscription originally made in the context of Daoist refinement to be repeated in the cause of social and moral reform. More significantly, such a shift in emphasis also signals the process by which a relatively esoteric practical tradition was transformed so as to be accessible to the laity and society at large. With the accelerating rise in opium addiction, the temperance tradition would come to take on two layers of significance: for the very devoted, it was one part of a demanding practical and ritual regimen, while for the growing lay following, it was a simple expression of personal morality.

Similarly, as the sect built its popular following, earlier anti-Qing rhetoric was replaced with that of Buddhist salvation, in particular of devotion to Guanyin. It is most likely that the worship of Guanyin was central to the Li Sect from the outset. Later scriptures portray Yang Zai as having been especially devoted to Guanyin, who visited him in visions. At least by the mid-Qing, however, Guanyin had become the primary focus of devotion within the sect. It was most likely during this time that the original Five Character Mantra was replaced by the words "Bodhisattva Guanyin" *(guan shi yin pusa)*.[13]

By the mid-eighteenth century, networks of the Li Sect had proliferated throughout North China, but the mass following was founded on the work of Yin Ruo (1729–1806, also known as Yin Laifeng and Yin Zhongshan), the second great patriarch in the history of the sect.[14] A peasant from the Cang

County village of Keniu, Yin came to Tianjin in 1740 to work at the flour shop of Zhang Wushan, an active member of the Li Sect. Yin joined the Li Sect and continued to energetically spread the teaching throughout the Tianjin suburbs until Zhang's death in 1766. In that year, Yin founded the first "common house" *(gong suo)*, which would become the most basic and characteristic organizational feature of the Li Sect.[15]

Common houses varied in size with the communities they served and had the functions of both temple and meeting house. Among the early common houses founded by Yin Ruo were extra rooms in village temples, but others were simple storefronts or even rooms in private homes.[16] In Republican Tianjin, neighborhood common houses were most frequently buildings of three or four rooms, but the largest ones could grow into elaborate complexes of buildings and courtyards. The common house was the center of ritual activity and organization and also served as a physical center of the teaching within a small area, such as a village or urban neighborhood. Common houses were usually kept unlocked, and believers congregated there informally. Li Shiyu reports that common houses in Republican Tianjin always had a constant sprinkling of faithful, especially the elderly, who would go there to meet friends, drink tea, feed birds, and practice calligraphy.[17]

Reflecting its dual functions, each common house had two strata of local leadership, ritual and administrative.[18] The ritual leader was called the *dangjia*, a term encountered in chapter 2 and used to refer to a variety of sectarian specialists.[19] In Tianjin, each common house housed a single *dangjia*, one room being typically reserved as his living quarters. Although the *dangjia* sat at the center of a local community of believers, he was not so much parish priest as a resident holy man. His ritual role in the daily lives of the local faithful was limited to presiding over the few yearly rituals of the sect; he generally did not preach or attempt to spread the teaching to a mass audience. Rather, he was a highly visible moral and spiritual exemplar, concentrating on personal cultivation through breathing exercises, meditation, and scripture recitation. Like a Buddhist monk, the *dangjia* of the Li Sect was a celibate "outside the home" *(chujia)* professional, rather than a lay faithful. For food, he relied upon the families affiliated with his common house, often eating at their homes on a rotating schedule. According to Bi Wenzhen, a former *dangjia* of the large Old West Common House *(Xilao gongsuo)* in Tianjin, the most convenient situation was to share this responsibility among thirty families, each of which would cook for the *dangjia* one day each month.[20]

Although critics could characterize resident *dangjia* simply as old vagrants who lived off of the charity of neighbors, most appear to have been regarded as exceptional individuals who made a strong impression on their local communities.[21] Later accounts portray the *dangjia* as spending his day in solitary meditation and Daoist exercise, often without a break for food, water, or rest. Personal accounts all stress that the *dangjia* clearly stood out from the crowd. Many remembered such attributes as remarkable personal cleanliness, unusual health and longevity, and a general air of transcendence. Older residents in the center of Tianjin recalled that the *dangjia* who had lived nearby during the 1940s always wore white clothes and shoes, which were always spotlessly clean, in contrast to the mud and filth around him. Another account from Duliu recalls the *dangjia* wearing red Daoist robes, "walking quickly and silently," and never requiring a hat, even in the coldest weather. Regardless of whether such accounts are strictly true, it is clear that *dangjia* was regarded as an exceptional individual, often with a slightly otherworldly quality. Many believed that when a particularly accomplished *dangjia* died, his body would not decay.[22]

The administrative counterpart to the *dangjia* was the "manager" *(chengbanren)*, who cared for the daily affairs of the common house. Unlike the *dangjia*, who lived inside the common house and generally had no family of his own, the manager was a lay faithful who had both a family and outside employment, often one of significant status. The manager collected money for the construction or purchase of the common house, as well as for its maintenance. He organized the festivals of the sect, especially the large vegetarian dinners *(zhaikou)* that followed the ritual activities. He was usually personally wealthy and thus was able to put up the funds for the various expenses of the common house, which he would recoup later through donations from the faithful. The position of manager conveyed great personal prestige and was often a prize fought over by members of the local elite.[23]

Naturally, the spread of the Li Sect in and around Tianjin did not go unnoticed. The earliest known encounter between the Li Sect and Qing officialdom came in 1808, when Yi Chang'a, the viceroy *(zongdu)* of Zhili, ordered Ding Fanlong, magistrate *(xianling)* of Tianjin, to investigate the sect in light of recent White Lotus uprisings. Because members of the sect often worshipped wearing white sashes, Ding took no chances and arrived at the Yangliuqing common house armed with cannon that had been smeared with dogs' blood, to ward off White Lotus magic. Such precautions, however, proved unnecessary. Members of the Li Sect were quick to distance themselves from the White Lotus and other sectarian teachings and emphasized that they were purely orthodox in practice. Investigators agreed, concluding that, "the Li Sect prohibits opium and alcohol, exhorts the way of loyalty and piety, and has no illicit or unorthodox teachings or activities."[24]

A second incident occurred in 1849, when Wang Languang, the new district magistrate of Tianjin, held a similar investigation. After interrogating the leaders of five common houses in Tianjin, Wang concluded that the sect had no heretical practices or beliefs. Like Ding Panlong before him, he presented this opinion to the throne, and his memorial gives us a rare glimpse of the simple but profoundly meaningful morning ritual practiced by members of the sect: "Every morning at sunrise, they burn incense, thank Heaven, earth and the three lumina *(san guang)*. They pray that the earth will give them good crops, that they will live long lives, that the country will have good officials to pacify the people, that their families will produce no troublemakers who argue with their elders, that the four seas will be secure and the Buddha's light will shine on the eight corners of the earth."[25]

The most famous incident occurred in 1884, when Li Hongzhang, then viceroy of Zhili, happened upon a *zhaikou* being held at the Bright and Good *(ming shan)* Common House in Beijing. Suspicious, he launched a large-scale investigation of the sect in Tianjin, in which he estimated that no less than six or seven of ten city residents were members, but finally came to the conclusion that the Li Sect was fully orthodox. He advised the throne not only to recognize the sect as an orthodox teaching *(zheng jiao)*, but even to encourage it in order to shore up public morality and counter the growing influence of Christianity.[26]

The sect expanded rapidly throughout the remaining decades of the Qing and early years of the Republic. By the late nineteenth century, the teaching had already established a strong presence in Manchuria, and, by the early twentieth, it was beginning to assert a national character.[27] In 1913, the Central Common House *(zonghui)* in Beijing began publication of a magazine, *The Li Bell (Li duo)*, followed by the publication of *The Essential Knowledge of the Li Sect (Limen xu zhi)* in Tianjin. By the 1920s, the teaching was established in most major cities in China and beginning to assert itself in the political arena, as well.[28] When the government of Jiangsu province outlawed the Li Sect in 1929, influential leaders in Beijing, Tianjin, and Shanghai mounted a successful appeal to the national government to have the ban lifted.[29] In August 1929, the Ministry of the Interior *(nei zheng bu)* gave backhanded but explicit approval to the Li Sect, stating that it was not a religion, but rather a popular welfare organization that should be allowed to exercise its freedom of assembly.[30] During the height of its influence, important political figures such as the warlord Duan Qirui and even Chiang Kai-shek himself presented the leaders of the sect with gifts of their calligraphy.[31]

By the Republican period, the Li Sect had transformed from a highly specialized tradition of practice to a mass movement, with a role for both pseudomonastic clergy and a devoted laity, as well as an organizational framework in which the two could interact. The specialized techniques passed down from Yang Zai remained the purview of sectarian leaders, who practiced meditation and carried on a strict ascetic tradition, including a series of teachers who took up secluded residence in the Lanshui Cave of Ji County.[32] This, however, did not affect the mass following. In contrast to the demanding esoteric practice of the *dangjia*, ordinary members had few ritual or votive requirements. Activities such as chanting scriptures, visiting the common house, or spreading the teaching to friends were entirely optional.[33]

The Li Sect in the Tianjin-Cangzhou Area, Three Examples

Urban Center: Tianjin

The development of the Li Sect in Tianjin was strongly influenced by the universal recognition of Tianjin as the organizational and spiritual heart of the teaching.[34] When Qing officials first became suspicious of the Li Sect, their investigations began and ended in Tianjin. Peasants interviewed in various parts of Hebei all knew that Tianjin had the greatest concentration of Li Sect members, and pilgrims traveled to the city to visit sites of significance to the teaching, such as the grave of Yin Ruo.[35] The Old West Common House, founded by Yin Ruo in the immediate suburbs of Tianjin, remained one of the most important centers of Li Sect organization, and *dangjia* from the city maintained a clear moral authority over the teaching. Although new members could be inducted at any common house, a large enough number specifically sought to enter the teaching at the Old West Common House that inductions were held there once every two weeks.[36] Even after the formation of the Central Common House in Beijing, Tianjin remained the home of the national organization of the teaching, the United Li Sect Society of China (*Zhonghua lianhe zailijiao hui*). As such, the sect in Tianjin was characterized by a high degree of theological and ritual specialization, although the rank and file membership of the teaching often evinced little understanding of or interest in these innovations.

Production of scripture. The rapid expansion of the Li Sect in Republican Tianjin occurred in an atmosphere of theological exploration and missionary zeal demonstrated by the composition of scripture. Although critics often charged the Li Sect with having no independent system of thought and of plagiarizing common Buddhist scriptures, the teaching did establish a well-developed scriptural tradition of its own, much of which was composed in Republican-era Tianjin.[37] Cai Yucun, the *dangjia* of the large Old West Common House and first head of United Li Sect Society, is known to have penned at least three scriptures, the *Record of the Red Epoch (Hongyangji)*, *The Eight New Debts of Gratitude (Xinba bao'en)*, and *A Complete Explanation of the True Meaning of the Teaching (Kaishi daohua shiyi)*. Secondary and ethnographic scholarship alludes to other texts, such as the *Record of the Truth about the Li Teaching (Lijiao jiuzhenlu)*, the *Way to Enlightenment (Wudao lu)*, and the *Five Sages Deliver Our Teacher (Wufo du zu)*, all of which originated in Tianjin.[38]

Among the longest and most detailed of these scriptures, the *Precious Scripture of the Five Sages (Wusheng baojuan)* demonstrates the degree to which the theological thought of the Li Sect had developed in Tianjin. This scripture, which was considered "indispensable reading to the faithful of the teaching" *(daoqin bu ke bu du)*, was written in Cangmenkou, Tianjin, in 1917 and reprinted there throughout the Republican period, is composed of three parts. [39] The first is a metaphysics of the Five Sages, which relates the pentad cosmology of the Five Phases *(wu xing)* to the worship of Guanyin and four lesser Buddhas, each of whom occupies a "place" *(wei)* that correlates to other earthly and celestial objects and phenomena, such as cardinal directions, seasons, internal organs, senses, holy mountains, stars, colors, and tastes.[40] The second part (see excerpt in Appendix B) contains prayers and liturgies devoted to each of the five places, including incense offerings *(xiangzan)* and sacrificial prayers *(qingshen)*. At the end of these five sections is a sixth, reserved solely for the *dangjia* (others being warned not to look under threat of being struck by five bolts of lightning), which includes diagrams of charms and protective incantations. The third and longest section of the scripture is written in prose and introduces the spread of the Li Sect, including the founding of each common house in the Tianjin area, and an idealized dialogue between Yin Ruo and an unnamed narrator.

The *Precious Scripture of the Five Sages* not only was written in Tianjin, but it and scriptures like it were clearly integral to the theological life of the Li Sect at its organizational and spiritual center. Each of these scriptures was printed with the approval of the United Li Sect Society of China and represented both the vanguard of the intellectual development of the sect, as well as a codification of its standard, accepted doctrine. The scripture also demonstrates the atmosphere of theological exploration and study among the concentrated religious elite of the Li Sect. In Republican Tianjin, where the teaching was well organized and densely populated, such texts circulated in large numbers, both in the hands of private believers and as the corporate property of individual common houses.

Membership and common house activities. The number of religious specialists in Tianjin corresponded roughly to the number of common houses, which grew rapidly during the late Qing and early years of the Republic. Between 1912 and 1934, the number of common houses in the city more than doubled, growing from fifty-six to 128. Although the scale of these common houses varied greatly, even the largest would generally have only one *dangjia*. In many cases, however, the *dangjia* was joined by four lay devotees, corresponding to a pentad cosmology that is elaborated in the scriptures of the sect. Like the *dangjia,* these four devotees had few public ritual functions, concentrating instead on personal regimens of meditation and cultivation.

The ordinary membership of the sect in Tianjin is difficult to estimate, but it certainly did not approach the 60–70 percent claimed by Li Hongzhang. One reason that it could not have been so high is that membership in the Li Sect was personal, rather than familial. Eso-

Figure 5.1   Protective charm from the *Precious Scripture of the Five Sages.* The diagram is accompanied by detailed text explaining the proper steps to be taken when drawing such a charm.

teric knowledge of the Li Sect, such as the content of the Five Character Mantra, was not to be shared even with family members.[41] Division between members and nonmembers was unequivocal; initiates required an introduction from a guarantor *(yinbaoren)* and were inducted by means of a formal ceremony, in which the teaching was transmitted by the *dangjia* physically touching *(dian)* the forehead of the disciple, while the strict prohibitions against opium, alcohol, and tobacco must have severely restricted the mass appeal of joining the sect.[42] More realistic estimates of membership can be extrapolated from extant data. Li Shiyu asserts that the average common house would have at least 300–400 people in attendance at a *zhaikou*, whereas a large common house would have more than a thousand in attendance. With 112 common houses in the city of Tianjin, we can assume a total membership of at least 40,000, but certainly no more than the 100,000 members estimated by the 1934 *Overview of Tianjin.*[43]

The organization of the Li Sect in Tianjin demonstrates the importance of the common house. Most of the ritual life of the sect took place inside the common house and included only inducted members. The most characteristic activity of the sect was the *zhaikou*, which might be held three to five times per year, but many common houses observed additional ritual occasions, including small observances on the first and fifteenth of every lunar month, in emulation of more general Buddhist and popular practice.[44] The *zhaikou* also provided the opportunity for other religious activities associated with the sect, such as the induction of new members or the investiture of a new *dangjia* (called the "descent of the dharma," *xia fa*).

External activities also relied heavily on the common house as a unit of organization. Individual common houses would often organize groups to participate in the processions at large temple festivals, such as the large Empress of Heaven *(Tianhou)* festival on the eighteenth day of the third lunar month, where each group was easily identifiable by a banner or placard.[45] Within Tianjin, the largest single occasion was the yearly visit to the large cemetery on the western outskirts of the city where most *dangjia* were buried. As with the Empress of Heaven procession, each common house would send a few representatives to participate in the "Pilgrimage to the Western Ground" *(chao xi di)*, the formal procession to and around the graves. Some Li Sect members even went on distant pilgrimages, especially to the Lanshui Cave in Ji County, or Mount Puto, considered the birthplace of Guanyin. These were elaborate and expensive undertakings, and often an entire common house would sponsor a small group of representatives to make the journey on their behalf. A record of a pilgrimage to Mount Puto in 1932 reveals close coordination among the common houses of a number of large cities, including Tianjin, Fengtian, Dalian, and Shanghai.[46]

The Li Sect in Republican-era Tianjin saw itself very much as an equal of the great religions, especially Buddhism, the organization and imagery of which it consciously emulated. Yang Zai, Yin Ruo, and *dangjia* were frequently likened to Buddhist monks, and scriptural accounts describe the teaching using Buddhist rhetoric of salvation *(pudu)*. Yet, as with monastic Buddhism, a great practical divide separated the votive lives of the very dedicated, such as the clergy and ordained laity, from that of the rank-and-file membership. Religious specialists had access to a sophisticated theological and practical tradition, and even unordained lay devotees could become involved with the running of the common house or engage in a regimen of personal devotion to Guanyin. For most ordinary members, though, the Li Sect was not as rigorous and was less a religious teaching than a social organization and temperance society. Contemporary sources, such as the 1929 decision by the Ministry of the Interior that legalized the teaching, reflect this perception, praising the temperance work of the Li Sect but discounting its religious significance. Its devotional life, centered on the worship of Guanyin, was hardly unique, and, further, few votive requirements were made on the ordinary devotee. Even in Tianjin, most knew the Li Sect simply as the "Temperance Teaching."

Market Town: Duliu

The market town *(zhen)* of Duliu lies approximately forty kilometers to the southwest of Tianjin. Although the modern town has been nearly engulfed by the urban sprawl of the greater Tianjin area, during the Republic and earlier, town and city were separated by a more considerable geographic and social distance. In 1989, Duliu had a population of roughly 20,000—a slight increase over the 15,600 it had during the 1930s. In the Republican era, as now, the town was best known for its sweet brown vinegar, which is sold widely throughout North China. In addition to brewing vinegar, the town also relied heavily on manufacturing and commerce and, as a result, was strongly influenced by its mercantile elite.[47]

The development of the Li Sect in Duliu is contemporaneous with that seen in Tianjin. As in Tianjin, common houses in Duliu were built during the late Qing and Republican periods. In contrast to Tianjin, however, which had 128 common houses in 1934, Duliu had only four, two of which had been built during the late nineteenth-century Guangxu reign, another in 1927, and the last in 1937. The construction of two large common houses immediately after the 1884 investigation of the teaching suggests that the sect was already a force before the ban on it was relaxed. As in Tianjin, the teaching most likely began to gain a significant following during the middle of the nineteenth century, specifically in the wake of the Opium Wars (1839–1842). Older peasants interviewed during the late 1980s did not know when the sect first came to Duliu, but recalled that it had been flourishing when they themselves were children and that all of the oldest peasants in the town were members at that time. By the early twentieth century, nearly half of the families in the town had at least one member in the sect.[48]

The spread of the sect was certainly aided by the large volume of commercial traffic between Tianjin and Duliu and, locally, within the immediate vicinity of the town. Merchants in Duliu traveled frequently to Tianjin for business and pleasure, and many had significant commercial interests in the city. For ordinary peasants and townsfolk, the trip to Tianjin was more difficult and certainly less common, but not impossible, and many went to Tianjin seeking long- or short-term work. Locally, Duliu was the site of a large periodic market, which attracted peasants from all of the nearby villages and many neighboring towns.[49]

This traffic also provided the opportunity for the exchange of specialists and scriptures. Many of the most influential *dangjia* in Duliu themselves came from or frequently traveled outside the town. The *dangjia* Li Zhongxiang provides a good example. Li was originally from Anhui Province, and encountered the Li Sect while working in a *dofu* (tofu, or bean curd) shop in Duliu. After joining the sect and studying with the *dangjia* of the North Common House, he himself became a *dangjia* and took up residence in the Sanguan temple of Xiliucheng village, about seven kilometers away from town. During this time, he frequently attended rituals in Duliu and the nearby village of Xiliucheng and, in the late Republican Period, returned to Duliu and took up residence as *dangjia* of the West Common House.[50]

Travel to Tianjin also provided an opportunity to exchange or purchase texts, and scriptures such as the *Five Buddhas Deliver Our Teacher* were used in Duliu and carried great weight among the very faithful, although less so among the ordinary membership. One example of the former was the peasant Xu Gongfu. During the 1930s, both Xu and his merchant father joined the Li Sect solely for the purpose of quitting alcohol and tobacco. This type of member was known as "ignorant *li*" (*sha li*). Over time, Xu began to spend time at the West Common House, near his home, and became friends with An Daben, a *dangjia*, who originally hailed from Yangliuqing, the Tianjin suburb where Patriarch Yin had founded the first common house. An shared with him many of the deeper and more esoteric facets of the teaching, and Xu made the decision to spend three years in Tianjin for further study. When interviewed forty years later, Xu was still able to recite numerous prayers and songs from the *Five Buddhas Deliver Our Teacher* from memory.[51]

In all, however, people like Xu appear to have been in the minority. Other members interviewed all understood the rudiments of the history of the sect, knew the Five Character Mantra and abstained from drinking and tobacco, but few knew even the names of Li Sect scriptures, much less their content. In Duliu, as in Tianjin, the Li Sect demanded no daily rituals or devotions of ordinary members. The only regular ritual activities were the *zhaikou,* which the common houses held on different days, and even these were not mandatory. Duliu did have a variation of the annual "Procession to the Graves" in Tianjin, but instead of a procession, this custom of "pressing down the bones" *(yan gu)* was merely a trip to repair the graves at the small *dangjia* cemetery and involved only the managers of the North Common House.[52] Instead, as had been the case with scriptural knowledge, the practical rigor of the Li Sect attracted only a dedicated minority. Like the devoted laity in Tianjin, Xu Gongfu and others like him studied the ritual techniques of the *dangjia* and voluntarily incorporated a regimen of meditation, mantra, and scripture recitation into their own lives, but such was not typical of the rank-and-file membership.

Rather, as in Tianjin, the primary association and attraction of most new members in Duliu was the proscription against alcohol and tobacco. When asked about the daily life of Li Sect members, peasants immediately responded with this admonition to temperance. Later testimony about joining the Li Sect usually includes an immediate statement about abstention, demonstrating the close association between the two. Comments such as "I entered the Li Sect at the age of fourteen, and *afterward never drank or smoked*" are the usual way of speaking about the sect. When asked whether the four common houses in Duliu competed among themselves, Duliu resident Liu Wenguang replied that "every common house had the same goal of abstinence from alcohol and tobacco."[53]

Moreover, the votive and ritual importance of the Li Sect in Duliu was diluted by the prominence of other religious groups and resources. Although most members of the Li Sect kept pictures or tablets of Guanyin and Yang Zai in the front halls of their homes, many also kept those of other deities, such as Guandi, Caishen, and Yue Fei. In addition to the Li Sect, Republican Duliu also supported many other sectarian groups, including the Way of the Sage Immortal *(shengxian dao)* and the Heaven and

Earth and Most Supreme Teachings. Each of these groups had a ritual specialty, such as funerals or healing, and members of the Li Sect freely attended their functions, while some, such as the father of the especially pious Xu Gongfu, even entered more than one sect.[54]

What the religious content of the teaching in Duliu may have lacked, however, its social significance more than made up. By the early half of the twentieth century, nearly half of the families in Duliu had at least one member affiliated with the Li Sect. Each common house drew hundreds of male members to the *zhaikou*, with separate activities arranged for female believers and even for children, who had a catechism called the "children's li" *(tongzi li)*. The four common houses in Duliu were each large, well-decorated buildings of six or seven rooms, "the kind that only a rich merchant or large landlord could live in."[55] The North Common House, the largest of the four, had an affiliated school and a charitable society, which supplied members and nonmembers alike with winter coats, grain, coffins and even burial plots for the very poor.

The most significantly local aspect of the Li Sect in Duliu, and that which interwove the teaching most deeply into local society, was the alliance between the teaching and the commercial and political elite of the town. A local saying characterized this difference: "the poor do not join the Li Sect, the rich do not join the [Green] Gang" *(qiong bu zai li, fu bu zai bang)*.[56] Chiang Chu-shan has suggested that the entry fee of one *yuan*, about the price of a kilogram of good flour, was enough to keep the poorest members out, but the fact that many Li Sect members were in need of charitable donations of clothes and even grain attests to numerous exceptions.[57] Rather, the Li Sect in Duliu was not so much characterized by the exclusion of the poor as by the universal participation of the highest levels of commercial and political society. In particular, most of the managers of the four common houses were from this elite. Similarly, the chamber of commerce openly and actively supported the teaching, particularly the activities of the North Common House. Each of the three chamber of commerce heads during the 1930s and 1940s was a member of the Li Sect, and two of them also served as managers of the North Common House. At least one of the town's four fire-fighting brigades *(shui hui)*, the Spreading Peace Hall *(pu'an tang)*, was affiliated with and supported by the South Common House.[58]

In many ways, the Li Sect in Duliu was the public face of the town. The teaching was certainly an integral part of the local reputation of Duliu; relatively few nearby villages had such a large presence of the Li Sect. Within Duliu, membership in the Li Sect was a must for elite families, who used activities related to the sect to build personal reputations of honesty, piety, and benevolence. This could have tangible benefits. When two Duliu families agreed on a marriage and one member was in the Li Sect, the other side would not require the gifts commonly given to guarantee the agreement. For brewers, merchants, and tradesmen—the core of Duliu society—membership in the sect provided a boost to professional and social standing.[59] The teaching involved such a large percentage of Duliu households and, in particular, the entire commercial and political elite that in and out of the town Duliu and the Li Sect were almost synonymous.[60]

Thus, despite the small distance between the two, Tianjin and Duliu each presented incarnations of the Li Sect that were comparable but in some ways quite different. In each, the teaching had influential supporters and a large public following. In each, the sect provided the devoted few with a forum of worship and public service, whereas the ordinary membership incorporated the sect into a looser regimen of religiosity, the specific contribution of the Li Sect being the passive but singular restriction against alcohol and tobacco. The difference lay not at the bottom levels, but at the top. In Tianjin, the core of the Li Sect was its pseudomonastic religious leadership, supplemented by those local notables who cared for its civil functions. In Duliu, by contrast, the religious life of the teaching played a less prominent role, the more visible and characteristic function of the teaching having been as a charitable organization run by the city's mercantile elite.

Village: Rural Cang County

Within the city of Cangzhou, the Li Sect was quite strong, rather resembling that of Duliu. In Cangzhou City, the sect had devoted *dangjia* (during the late nineteenth century, two *dangjia* from Cangzhou City took up residence in Lanshui Cave), significant membership, prominent common houses, important social and charitable functions, and the blessing of the city's elite. As in Tianjin and Duliu, the professional clergy was joined by a looser lay following, who were attracted to the teaching less by its esoteric practical tradition than as a forum for public piety. For the top levels, this included conspicuous donations to votive and charitable projects and the composition of laudatory essays praising the positive moral influence of the teaching. For those with neither money nor literary talent to contribute, membership was still a public expression of a vow of temperance, along with the respectability and responsibility such a vow implied.[61]

In the villages, however, both the density and nature of the teaching changed dramatically. There, the sect maintained a numerically large but loosely organized rural following. Despite the strength of the sect in the city, neither were records kept of the rural organization nor were rural common houses structured into any sort of hierarchy, except at a very local and informal level. Thus, although the 1933 Cang County gazetteer is able to supply detailed information about the state of the teaching in the city, it is exceedingly vague concerning the state of the teaching in the villages, stating simply that "believers are everywhere . . . those who worship *without established halls* number in the thousands."[62]

In rural Cang County, as had been the case in the outskirts of Duliu, certain villages supported larger or smaller continents of devotees, but, in general, believers were scattered thinly and evenly throughout the countryside. [63] According to peasants in Yang Camp and Quan-Wang Village, most villages in the area had a sprinkling of Li Sect members, usually around ten, but none was known for having an unusually high concentration. One of the largest local concentrations was in Yang Camp itself, which had nearly twenty members and, according to informants, was the only common house in the area.

The life of the sect in Yang Camp would appear to have been modeled upon that in its larger centers, but closer inspection reveals many of the similarities between the two to have been largely nominal. As did those in the larger centers, the faithful in Yang Camp based their local organization around a village common house. Rather than a devoted building, as in Tianjin or Duliu, it was not a permanent structure. It was instead the designation given to the room in which members of the sect were meeting at the time. Even in Yang Camp, the sect lacked a strong public presence and had few regular religious or social activities. In the ritual calendar, as well, the similarities to urban centers of the teaching were primarily a matter of shared terminology. Members in Yang Camp met for an occasion, which they called *zhaikou,* but it consisted simply of a meal in the home of a fellow member. On days of particular significance, members from Yang Camp and nearby communities would gather in the neighboring village of Little Terrace to burn incense before tablets of Guanyin and Patriarch Yang. It might be remembered that such activities are common features of popular devotion but were prohibited by the original teaching of Yang Zai. Although even in more orthodox centers such as Tianjin many ordinary faithful carried on such votive activities in private, the leadership of urban common houses still took pains to emphasize that the sect "neither burns incense nor lights candles" *(bu shao xiang, bu dian la).*[64]

This seemingly minor point reflects a critical difference between urban and rural manifestations of the Li Sect: the lack of a devoted, professional clergy in the latter. In Tianjin and Duliu alike, few among the rank-and-file membership of the Li Sect were particularly well informed about the teaching. Although membership was clearly delineated by a ritual of formal induction, very few ritual or financial requirements were made of devotees. For many, the significance of the teaching was exhausted by its characteristic proscription against the use of intoxicants. This mass following was, however, joined by a stratum characterized either by intense devotion and practice or by engagement of the public sphere. The former included not only the *dangjia,* but also the members who sought lay ordination or sought a more sophisticated understanding of the Li Sect as an act of personal piety. The latter cared for the administrative needs of the common house, made conspicuous contributions to the life of the teaching, and publicly basked in the moral message of the teaching.

In contrast, the Li Sect in Republican Yang Camp had neither a professional clergy nor religious texts. During the 1940s, the *dangjia* of Yang Camp was a married villager who had not undergone any formal period of training or study. Clearly missing from the life of the sect in Yang Camp was specialized knowledge, such as the elaborate meditative techniques or liturgical tradition practiced by the sect in Tianjin and Duliu. Thus, even for the devout, the practical regimen of the Li Sect thus remained very spare, and those who wished to infuse a personal votive regimen into the teaching simply grafted what knowledge they had of the sect onto existing popular and sectarian practices. Some of the more devout in Yang Camp vowed to recite the name of Guanyin (the Five Character Mantra of *"Guanshiyin pusa"*) or sections of the *Lotus Sutra* a certain number of times each day. Nevertheless, both this very common votive act and the worship of Guanyin are very widespread features of popular devotion and can hardly be construed as a product of a specialized sectarian teaching.

Moreover, with little access to the liturgical tradition or ritual specialists of the Li Sect, members in Yang Camp frequently took their ritual needs to other resources, in particular to the more established sectarian groups such as the Heaven and Earth and Most Supreme Teachings discussed in chapter 7. Although the handful of members of the Yang Camp Common House, which also included individuals from neighboring villages, did hold simple *zhaikou* to mark the important days of the liturgical calendar, they also attended the more elaborate rituals held by the Heaven and Earth and Most Supreme. As with the participation of common houses in the temple festival of the Empress of Heaven in Tianjin, members of the Li Sect in Yang Camp participated in village sectarian festivals as an identifiable group, albeit a very small one. In light of the nature of the Li Sect in this village, however, such a gesture was more a show of village solidarity than participation in a ritual capacity. Perhaps most telling, the handful of members of the Li Sect in Yang Camp relied on the Heaven and Earth and Most Supreme Teachings to perform funeral services, even for their own members.

In addition to ritual, the moral and social significance of the Li Sect was also overshadowed by the presence of more established sectarian teachings. Within villages such as Yang Camp, the established teachings not only provided ritual services for free, they also were the most prominent and public expression of devotion and morality, in particular to the degree that they represented the aspirations of the community in village-based rituals. In such a setting, the numerically weak and theologically unsophisticated contingent of the Li Sect was unable to portray itself as the bastion of public morality as it had in Duliu, but rather was content to carve out a small but characteristic niche. Not surprisingly, this was the proscription against alcohol and tobacco. As in Duliu, many of those who joined the teaching in rural Cang County were attracted to precisely this element or, as often, by the hopes that association with the temperance tradition of teaching would improve their social standing within the community. In contrast to Duliu, however, this did not seem to imply a strong status element; in Yang Camp, at least, members included both landowners and day laborers. What many members did share in common, though, was the need to demonstrate responsibility and sobriety. In some cases, this was because of occupational demands, as had been the case in Duliu, but, more frequently, it was to offset a reputation as a drunkard. As peasants in Yang Camp described it, joining the Li Sect was perceived first and foremost as a declaration to gods and men of a lifelong vow of temperance.

Even if its content only reached rural Cang County in a very adulterated form, the terminological markers of the Li Sect were still delineated the teaching as a discrete institution. Key terms such as common house, *dangjia, zhaikou,* and Five Character Mantra were still employed, even if the content only vaguely resembled that in Tianjin. Those outside the teaching, as well, recognized these terms and, especially, the phrase "give up alcohol and tobacco" *(jie yan jiu)* as characteristic of the Li Sect. As Barend ter Haar's work on the White Lotus has demonstrated, albeit in a very different context, such terminological markers have great power to create a sense of unity or tradition, even where none exists.[65]

The reduction of the Li Sect to its characteristic proscriptions and affective markers is seen elsewhere in Republican-era Hebei, where it is clear that the Li Sect was present in name but had not permeated deeply into local religious life. A number of the villages studied by Japanese Mantetsu scholars appear to have supported manifestations of the Li Sect. Henan Village, north of Beijing, built a "Hall of Enlightened Goodness 'antialcohol, antitobacco' common house" *(Wushan tang jie yan jiu gongsuo),* and the ritual life of neighboring Shajing was centered on five occasions called *zhaikou.* Despite these terminological markers, it is not clear that the actual teaching and ritual life of the Li Sect had much other impact on the religious life of these or other villages. This is evident in Shanggulin in southwest Hebei, a village that had a Li Sect *dangjia* who hailed originally from Cangzhou. The *dangjia,* Liu, took up residence in a local temple, which he then renamed the Songbo Common House, and proceeded to attempt to shape local practice to the teaching of the Li Sect. Apparently, however, the message was not sinking in. When questioned about the common house, one peasant identified the deity of the temple as "the Sage Patriarch" *(Sheng zong),* a pseudonym for Guanyin, but did not know exactly who this patriarch was. Like many in the village, he had joined the sect, but did so primarily to stop drinking. The local organization sponsored a number of festivals that he identified with the temple *(miao hui)* rather than with the sect and during which "the *dangjia* would chant scriptures that nobody could understand."[66]

Other reports from North China reveal cases in which the Li Sect nominally occupied an important place in village religion, but the content is so highly adulterated with local practices that cannot be recognized as the teaching seen in Tianjin. In his 1933 investigation of Ding County, Li Jinghan, relates that the local Li Sect was divided into many branches, many of which "sacrifice to bugs and weasels," a reference to the common practice of worshipping animal spirits (such as those presented in chapter 3), and that the adherents "go to altars and make wishes."[67] A 1937 investigation of religion in Jilin revealed the local incarnation of the Li Sect to have been devoted primarily to the worship of fox and animal spirits.[68]

Conclusion: Local Variation in the Teaching and Practice of the Li Sect

As had been the case with monastic Buddhism, the life of the Li Sect was strongest in the cities and changed dramatically in its transition to the villages. In Tianjin, the Li Sect consciously emulated and in many ways resembled Buddhist monasticism. In addition to the cosmetic adoption of

Buddhist imagery and costume by the *dangjia* of Tianjin, the organizational structure of the sect was based on a professional, celibate clergy, while the devoted laity could seek a lesser form of ordination or leadership roles within its civic life. For the great majority, however, membership was more a matter of loose affiliation. Even in Tianjin, many devotees kept no calendar of ritual obligations and had only a loose understanding of the evolving scriptural tradition. For most ordinary members, its social significance, nominal markers, and characteristic admonition against intoxicants defined the sect.

This loose organizational structure allowed the Li Sect to spread quickly and adapt to local society, but also prevented it from making a lasting impact. Being so malleable, the Li Sect was able to establish itself in local society without necessarily confronting established religious traditions, but, at the same time, it contributed little to them. In the villages of Cang County, the teaching attracted a thin layer of support in numerous villages but never took center stage or grew beyond the role of supplementing an extant religious life and religious public sphere. As had been the case with monastic Buddhism, the dearth of trained clergy in the countryside did not restrict the spread of the Li Sect, though it did both reduce the teaching to its simplest form and leave it open to significant adulteration. The Li Sect in Cang County represents less a case of a religious teaching transforming the countryside than a case of local religiosity appropriating the nominal and practical markers of the teaching.

6. Apocalyptic Sectarians
The Way of Penetrating Unity
and the End of Days

The Way of Penetrating Unity *(yiguandao)* began as one of the greatest sectarian success stories of the Republican era.[1] From obscure beginnings in rural Shandong, this sect rose rapidly during the first half of the twentieth century and within a single generation had spread throughout China and attracted an immense following. Even considering the popularity of the Way of Penetrating Unity in Taiwan and Southeast Asia today, the 1930s and 1940s were clearly the height of its influence.

The greatest attraction of the Way of Penetrating Unity during this time was its millenarian vision and the promise that those who entered the sect would be spared the coming destruction *(rujiao bijie)*. This sort of apocalyptic vision is a familiar element of Daoist, Buddhist, and sectarian theology alike and struck a very responsive chord during the turbulent 1930s, allowing the Way of Penetrating Unity to gain a firm foothold in urban and rural North China. The greatest expansion, however, occurred during the Japanese occupation (1937–1945) in villages brutalized by the Japanese occupation and civil war that followed. This was the case in Cangzhou, where the teaching developed a following of nearly 30,000, buoyed by predictions that a nuclear attack, natural disaster, or Communist military victory would be the event to usher in the apocalypse.

The phenomenal growth of the Way of Penetrating Unity during this period proved to be its undoing after 1949. Soon after the founding of the People's Republic, the new government accused the sect of having collaborated, first with Japanese and later with the Guomindang, by using popular belief in the apocalypse to sap the strength of the Revolution. Within months, the sect was targeted for complete eradication as the first objective of the "Suppress the Counterrevolutionaries" *(zhenya fan geming)* campaign of early 1951. During this movement, leaders were captured and imprisoned or executed, and believers were subjected to a barrage of anti-sectarian propaganda. Nevertheless, although its recruitment networks reached every province of China, and its nationwide membership may have numbered in the millions, this campaign provoked no significant resistance. Rather, the vast majority proved very willing to abandon the teaching and its millenarian vision. By the end of the three-month campaign, the Way of Penetrating Unity had effectively disappeared.

The rise and fall of the Way of Penetrating Unity in Cangzhou reflects the distinct role and organizational dynamic of millenarian teachings in local religious life. It is not difficult to imagine why promises of an imminent paradise would have a special appeal during times of crisis. This appeal, however, is not merely escapism for the masses or opportunism among the leadership, nor is it exhausted by the event of the apocalypse itself. The Way of Penetrating Unity preached the millennium, but it did so in vague terms. Neither the national nor the local organization in Cangzhou ever set a date for the event, nor did they separate themselves from society in preparation for it. As much as it promised salvation from the horrors of the day, the apocalyptic message of the Way of Penetrating Unity also provided comfort in a metanarrative context, as a theodical explanation for human suffering. When the end came for the teaching, it was not done in by the disconfirmation of its predictions or by the show of force by a new government committed to their dissolution, but rather by the cessation of decades of war and the optimism of the early 1950s. With the threat of war and famine seemingly behind them, most members of the teaching lost their interest in the millenarian message of the teaching.

Early History and Teaching of the Way of Penetrating Unity

Origins and Spread before 1937

Although Chinese scholars have discussed the intellectual origins of the Way of Penetrating Unity in terms of an earlier sectarian legacy, the Way of Penetrating Unity as an independent movement dates to the late Qing dynasty.[2] The first leader of the teaching is traditionally said to have been Wang Jueyi, an impoverished orphan from Qingzhou in peninsular Shandong, who founded the teaching in 1878 while studying with Yao Hetian, a sectarian teacher in Shanxi.[3] Recent work by Lu Yao has called this idea into question by crediting the founding of the Way of Penetrating Unity to Liu Qingxu, a Confucian scholar and student of Wang Jueyi. In either case, Liu Qingxu is the first person who can be clearly identified with the teaching. During the late 1880s, Liu returned with the teaching to his native Qingzhou and began to spread it among his fellow scholars.[4]

Upon the death of Liu Qingxu in 1918, the teaching passed to a second patriarch, named Lu Zhongyi, who left Qingzhou and brought the teaching to his native Jining, in southwestern Shandong. It was here that the Way of Penetrating Unity first took root, largely because Lu Zhongyi, unlike Liu Qingxu before him, sought his converts in large numbers and among the peasants. Within a few years, Lu had attracted a few hundred devotees, based around a small core of twenty-five disciples, some of whom were sent to the neighboring provinces of Henan, Hebei, and Shanxi to spread the teaching. Among these disciples was Zhang Guangbi—also known as Zhang Tianran—a thirty-year-old former soldier who would soon emerge as the greatest leader of the Way of Penetrating Unity.[5]

During the mid-1930s, Zhang Guangbi gained control of the Way of Penetrating Unity, and it was under his leadership that the teaching began to take on national prominence. With the death of Lu Zhongyi in 1925, the leadership of the sect was passed to his younger sister, Lu Zhongjie. The next few years most likely saw a power struggle between Lu Zhongjie and Zhang Guangbi, possibly, as Lu Yao suggests, over the increasingly lucrative "merit donations" (gongde fei) being collected by the teaching. Whatever the cause of the split, Zhang left Jining in 1932 and traveled to Ji'nan, the provincial capital, to continue spreading the teaching there. In 1934, he founded the first *tan* (shrine, the basic organizational unit of the Way of Penetrating Unity) and began to gather disciples.[6] From Ji'nan, the Way of Penetrating Unity began to spread throughout North China. Within a year of the founding of the first *tan* in Ji'nan, four more had been established in that city. In late 1935, members were sent to Tianjin, where they rented a building to serve as the first *tan*. Soon thereafter, missionaries established a base of faithful in Beijing and as early as 1936 were reaching into Anhui, Jiangsu, and Manchuria.[7]

The experience of early missionaries in Tianjin gives a good indication of the problems the sect faced in establishing itself in a new city. The first was simply that, with so many sects, teachers, and temples in the city, few people took notice of the Way of Penetrating Unity. To call attention to the teaching, missionaries were sent each day to chant scriptures in public parks and set up eye-catching displays of statues and religious parapher- nalia. These techniques attracted a few dozen members, and the founding of the first *tan* in that city raised this number to a few hundreds. As the teaching established a series of *tan,* the membership took on more mean- ingful numbers. According to Sung Kuang-yü, more than 100 *tan* of the

Way of Penetrating Unity were established in Tianjin during the 1930s. Even if the majority of these were simply altars in the homes of the faithful, local membership would have numbered in the thousands.[8] In Tianjin and many other cities of North China, the Way of Penetrating Unity had established a firm base for further expansion.

This auspicious beginning can be traced to the eschatological vision of the Way of Penetrating Unity, which was characterized by a sense of divine mission and destiny. Like most teachings in the sectarian tradition, the Way of Penetrating Unity subscribed to the eschatology of the Eternal Venerable Mother *(wusheng laomu)*, a supreme and all-loving deity. Dismayed by the immorality of her bemused children on earth, the Eternal Venerable Mother devised a plan for their salvation, over the ages sending a series of prophets and teachers to guide them to truth.[9] Humankind knows these as the great religious figures of history, such as Confucius, Laozi, and the Buddha, a fact that provides inspiration for the syncretist belief that "all religions are one" *(wanjiao gui yi)*. This sequence of events was designed to prepare the world for the revelation of a greater truth, and culminated in the revelation of the true teaching, the Way of Penetrating Unity.

Although it was only now being revealed to the world, the Way of Penetrating Unity was said to have existed since the beginning of time and been transmitted secretly through a chain of teachers. The first of these was none other than Pangu, the mythical being who divided the heavens from the earth. Thus, within the Way of Penetrating Unity, Wang Jueyi is not considered the founder of the sect, but rather its sixty-fifth patriarch, while Zhang Guangbi is considered the sixty-eighth.[10] The "Penetrating Unity" of the teaching was this unbroken genealogy and was visibly represented in the "Diagram of the Veins of the Way of Penetrating Unity" *(Yiguan daomai tujie)* hung in every hall of worship.[11] The deification of sectarian patriarchs also included those of the present day, who were revealed to be reincarnations *(huashen)* of buddhas and immortals. Lu Zhongjie, the sister of Lu Zhongyi, was the Venerable Mother of the Great Ultimate *(taiji laomu)* and revered as the earthly form of Guanyin, the "Ancient Buddha of the Southern Sea" *(nanhai gu fo)*. Lu Zhongyi was known both as the Living Buddha Jigong *(Jigong huofo)* and, more significantly, as the Buddha Maitreya *(mile fo)*.

The claim of Lu Zhongyi to be Maitreya deserves notice, because it marks the bridge between simple eschatological exploration and an actual millenarian movement. Taking its cue from comparable traditions of thought in Daoism and Buddhism, the eschatology of the Eternal Venerable Mother envisions a tripartite division of cosmic time into epochs *(jie)*, each of which is presided over by a single Buddha.[12] The current epoch is the second of three and is the charge of the Sakyamuni Buddha. The arrival of Maitreya on earth augurs the transition to the third epoch, during which the current world will be swept clean in a period of apocalyptic chaos and destruction. On its ruins, the Eternal Venerable Mother and the Maitreya Buddha will build a new world, the "Homeland of True Emptiness" *(zhenkong jiaxiang)*, a paradise on earth, free of war, hunger, and tyranny. This tradition of apocalyptic thought permeated the sectarian tradition, and its logic and participants were stock figures in uprisings throughout the Ming and Qing dynasties. In proclaiming himself to be Maitreya, Lu Zhongyi did more than simply clothe himself in the divine. In effect, he had announced the imminent end of the world.

The coming apocalypse imbued the work of missionaries with a sense of urgency and, under the leadership of Zhang Guangbi, became the focal point of the teaching's energetic recruitment drive. Within the sect, members referred to missionary work as "opening up new ground" *(kai huang)*, and, within a few years, techniques for attracting converts were well refined. Teachers painted vivid pictures of the destruction urged people to "join the sect to escape the disaster" *(rujiao bijie)*. Li Shiyu noted that a practiced missionary could easily speak for more than three hours on end and employed a well-polished routine that could both captivate an audience and respond to even the most hostile skeptics. Although not all speakers were as proficient or convincing, actively spreading the sect to friends and family was considered among the most basic responsibilities of the Way of Penetrating Unity members. As a saying within the teaching put it, "Because they are your family, you must save them, because they are your friends, you must save them" *(yin qin du qin, yin you du you)*.[13]

The rapid expansion of the teaching across North China was facilitated by its ability to replicate its elaborate hierarchy of command at the local level. Soon after the death of Lu Zhongyi, Lu Zhongjie formally renounced her position within the teaching, making Zhang the undisputed and increasingly deified head *(shizun)* of the sect, a place he would hold until his death.[14] Below Zhang came a strict hierarchy of leaders, including *daozhang* (Leader of the Way), *dianchuanshi* (Transmitter of Rites), *tanzhu* (Altar Master), and *jiangshi* (Lecturer). Except for the *daozhang*, the very highest circle of leaders, all other leaders were present at the local level. This concentration of leaders at the lower levels allowed local incarnations of the sect to operate independently, with the result that particular individuals or *tan* could exert considerable influence over the local life of the teaching. This was especially true in rural areas, where the teaching was spread through seed *tan,* located centrally in the county seat, from which the teaching would radiate into the surrounding villages.[15] Within local communities, ordinary membership was strictly policed. New members were admitted in a ritual in which the *dianchuanshi* would physically touch *(dian)* the forehead of the initiate and could enter only with the recommendation of a guarantor, who would then be held partially responsible for the conduct of his pledge.[16]

In addition to its promise of salvation from the apocalypse, the Way of Penetrating Unity enabled direct contact with the gods through spirit-writing rituals *(fuluan).* Spirit writing was characteristic of many sectarian movements during the late Qing and Republican periods and consists of a human medium transcribing the words of a deity during a state of possession.[17] In Republican North China, spirit-writing séances of the Way of Penetrating Unity were conducted rather like they are in Taiwan today, with three highly trained specialists *(luanshou,* also called the "three talents," *san cai)* working together to channel the voice of the gods. Although these three underwent a period of intense training and refinement, earning them a special place in the religious hierarchy of the teaching, the use of spirit writing séances represents an important part of the process by which the teaching reached out to a mass base.[18] According to Lu Yao, the first use of spirit writing by the Way of Penetrating Unity was in 1923, the period when Lu Zhongyi was shifting the focus of proselytizing efforts from intellectuals to peasants, when a Jining temple scheduled spirit writing séances twice per month.[19] Spirit writing left ordinary believers in awe of the teaching; Sung Kuang-yü quotes a former soldier from southern Shandong who recalled that peasants would travel for miles to visit a séance and wait in line for hours to pose their personal questions to the spirits.[20]

The ability of any *tan* to hold its own spirit-writing séances reveals the weakness of central control and enhanced the autonomy of local leadership structures at its expense. Despite the large number of texts produced, the Way of Penetrating Unity produced no single systematic doctrine. Instead, spirit writing served as a source of doctrinal authority at the local level.[21] This fact combined with the rapidity with which the teaching spread across China resulted in a great deal of local variation. Sung Kuang-yü notes that major centers of the teaching each trained their own spirit-writing specialists, and the large number of such specialists present in Cangzhou demonstrates that minor ones did so as well.[22]

Within local incarnations of the teaching, however, spirit writing made an especially strong impact. The writings transmitted through the "three talents" usually appeared in stylized prose or poetry, such as five- or seven-character poems or Song dynasty–style *ci,* the complexity of which demonstrated that they were not merely spontaneous compositions. Their content was often vague moral precepts, but could also include messages from the gods, charms *(fu)* for various sorts of protection, or even direct healing by the painting of a dot *(dian)* on the forehead of the afflicted person during the ritual.[23] By some particularly negative accounts, local leaders used the forum of spirit-writing séances to brainwash members. These report that some *tan* would irregularly hold "Buddha and Immortal Research Sessions" *(xian fo yanjiu ban),* or "Confessions" *(chanhui ban),* in which members would be asked questions by the gods and beaten if they answered incorrectly. In addition, spirit writing also had an important economic element. Members were often told to make cash donations or to buy items, such as charms, incense, or statues from the sect.[24]

What was missing, however, was the apocalypse itself. The Way of Penetrating Unity had not assigned a specific date to this event and continued to speak about it in immediate but still vague terms. Nor was a countdown to apocalypse necessarily needed. The Way of Penetrating Unity attracted an audience for its message as the culmination of cosmic time, attracting disciples with its mysticism and spirit-writing séances and using this epistemological framework to serve as "the seed crystal of a new social organization."[25] It was not, however, steeling its ranks into a core of firm believers, nor had it required significant financial or personal contribution from the rank and file. Despite its aggrandizing claims and awe-inspiring mysticism, the claim that the Way of Penetrating Unity used the specter of the apocalypse to gain "strict thought control" over its members is rather an exaggeration.[26]

Nevertheless, by 1937, the Way of Penetrating Unity was off to a very auspicious start. The teaching was already found in a number of major cities of North China, and its spread showed no signs of abating. In the space of just over ten years, the Way of Penetrating Unity had grown from a small teaching in southwest Shandong to one of the most wealthy and influential sects in the Chinese Republic, covering most of North China.

Growth and Evolution, 1937–1949

The period between the Japanese invasion of North China in July 1937 and founding of the People's Republic of China in 1949 was one of constant warfare, and it was in this atmosphere of panic and dismay that the

Way of Penetrating Unity experienced its most rapid growth. By the early 1940s, the teaching had reached as far as the southern province of Jiangxi, and by the Japanese surrender in 1945 it was present in almost areas of the country. The greatest gains, however, came in the areas most affected by the occupation, the cities and villages behind Japanese lines. Later statistics give an indication of the sect's rapid growth. In 1951, members numbered more than 178,000 in Beijing and at least 140,000 in Tianjin. Data from the countryside is even more striking. A *tan* established in 1942 in Wutai County, Shanxi, grew to reach 150 villages and gain more than 9,000 converts. In Hu County, in neighboring Shaanxi, the Way of Penetrating Unity was present in no fewer than 337 villages, with membership at nearly 17,000. In the Jiangnan city of Wuxi, a single *tan* founded in 1942 served as a seed for fifty-four others and is said to have attracted an incredible 160,000 members in Wuxi County alone. Even taking into account the fact that the Way of Penetrating Unity was strongest in North China, the total number of members appears to have grown phenomenally during this period and, by 1949, must have easily numbered in the millions.[27]

During this period, the Way of Penetrating Unity further intensified its mystic and apocalyptic teaching, and the cult around Zhang Guangbi himself continued to grow. Within the sect, Zhang was known as the "Gong-Chang teacher" (*gong-chang shichuan*, the two characters *"gong"* and *"chang"* placed together forming the character of Zhang's surname). This was not merely a convention; Li Shiyu reports that many ordinary believers were afraid to say the name of Zhang Guangbi aloud; nor was it permitted to print the characters together. The deification of Zhang Guangbi was given substance by numerous hagiographical texts, of which the following account is typical:

> When our great teacher was born, his eyes and eyebrows were perfectly shaped, and there was depth and wisdom in his eyes. . . . On his forehead, he had a third eye. His nose was straight like that of a dragon, and his head was like that of a god. His mouth was perfect and he already had a long beard. His earlobes touched his shoulders and his arms were very long (all signs of great wisdom and ability). He walked beautifully and perfectly, with long strides, and was obviously not of the mortal world. On his left hand, he had a red birthmark shaped like the sun and on his right one like the moon; they were so red that they would leave a mark when he touched his hand to paper. On his left foot, he had the seven stars of the Big Dipper, and on his right foot, the six stars of the Southern Dipper.

Because of this, although he had been born into the mortal world, everyone knew that he was one with the universe—the Living Buddha Jigong, who was sent by Heaven to save humanity.[28]

The increasing deification of Zhang Guangbi as a messiah figure is significant in its relation to the apocalyptic vision of the teaching, which took on increasing significance after the Japanese invasion. During this period, Zhang was revealed to be both the True Heavenly Buddha (tianzhen fo) and the deified sectarian leader Piaogao, both of whom are associated with the coming of the epoch.[29] The Way of Penetrating Unity continued to prosper during the Civil War that followed the Japanese surrender, but as a Communist military victory became more likely, the sect braced itself for the inevitable showdown. Beginning in 1949, with the founding of the People's Republic just on the horizon, a number of local and provincial governments made initial movements against the teaching, but the greatest move against the sect came in early 1951, when it was targeted for complete eradication in the first "Suppress the Counterrevolutionaries" campaign. This movement linked the arrest and execution of higher-level leaders with an intense propaganda campaign intended at winning over ordinary members and turning the populace firmly against the sect. Activities were coordinated on a national scale, demonstrating the importance and intensity of the campaign, which was one of the first mass political campaigns of the newly formed People's Republic. The Tianjin-based New Life Evening News (Xinsheng wanbao) devoted most of its front page to propaganda against the Way of Penetrating Unity for three consecutive weeks in April 1951—including even a serial cartoon showing the decline of a young man tricked into joining the sect. Similar articles were published throughout the country at roughly the same time. This propaganda condemned the teaching on charges similar to those leveled by mainland scholars today: collaboration with the Japanese and, more prominently, with the Guomindang and its "imperialist" allies, and the maintenance of a network of spies and traitors. Other alleged crimes—such as stealing money, raping women, and breaking apart families—were also strongly emphasized and became stock phrases associated with the sect.[30]

Although scholars cite the close relationship between the high levels of sectarian leadership and members of the Wang Jingwei government, as well as the propaganda (often originating in spirit writing) that promoted "Chinese-Japanese friendship" and discouraged peasants from supporting the Communists, neither the Japanese nor the Guomindang ever gave open, institutional support to the teaching at any stage, and both ap-

Figure 6.1   Two consecutive frames from a serial warning readers
against the evils of the Way of Penetrating Unity. In the first, a *dianchuanshi* receives a case of handguns from one of "Chiang Kai-shek's
bandit generals" (i.e., a Guomindang officer). In the second, a female
believer who had been kidnapped and raped by a younger *dianchuanshi* is killed while attempting to escape. The scowling woman on the
far right is Sun Suzhen, wife of Zhang Guangbi.

pear to have had misgivings about allowing the Way of Penetrating Unity to expand unchecked.[31] Both the Japanese and the Guomindang restricted the movement of top leaders, including Zhang Guangbi, and even suspected the teaching of having a role in resistance, prompting them to destroy a number of *tan* in and around Tianjin.[32] Soon after their flight to Taiwan, the Guomindang declared the teaching "harmful" and "heterodox" *(xie)* and outlawed the teaching in 1953. Whatever the activities or sentiments of top levels of leadership may have been, the Way of Penetrating Unity was not simply an expression of sympathy for the Japanese occupation or the religious arm of the Guomindang.

The difficulty in assessing the wartime activities of the Way of Penetrating Unity lies in the large degree of organizational and doctrinal autonomy enjoyed by local leaders. Despite the prominence of top-level leaders such as Zhang Guangbi, they exerted little control over the day-to-day affairs of the quickly expanding sect, particularly at the local level, where doctrine was produced largely in spirit-writing séances. In 1939, high leaders of the Way of Penetrating Unity met in Beijing to attempt to standardize ritual practice of the sect, but even at this early stage, the teaching was already fractured into a number of recognizable schools *(pai)*. This splintering continued during the Japanese occupation and grew particularly intense following Zhang's death in 1948.[33]

Finally, although the Way of Penetrating Unity remained focused on the coming apocalypse, the appeal of the teaching was not exhausted by this singular event. Throughout the late 1940s, predictions of the millennium, such as this one from rural Henan, became increasingly vivid:

> The Communists and the Guomindang can't stop their running around, but the sins of the people are too great, they cannot ascend to heaven and the great apocalypse will come. There will be forty-nine days of darkness, during which the sun and the moon will lose their brightness, lamps will not light the way and fires will not burn. All sorts of demons will come looking for their enemies from the former world. Debts once incurred and lives once taken shall then be repaid. Nobody shall escape this destruction, only those who enter the Way of Penetrating Unity will be protected.[34]

It is clear that this sort of vision was the center of the life of the teaching as a social organization and repositioned the individual and the events of the day in light of a larger chronology of universal significance. This vision was not, however, a call to action, but rather one for patience. Believers were not told to hasten the apocalypse by supporting one of the many factions, but to remain aloof from them by avoiding military service alto-gether.[35] The world was destined for a purgation of its sins, and regardless of whether the apocalypse was to come at the hands of the Japanese, Com-munists, civil war, nuclear holocaust, or natural disaster, it was both in-evitable and the will of Heaven.

The promise of the apocalypse was thus more fundamentally one of salvation and one that believers found easy to adapt to include deliverance from earthly woes, as well. Thus, it is not surprising to see the teaching come to incorporate more general sectarian and popular practice, such as healing. Testimonies from former sectarians in Tianjin included the promise of healing as a major attraction to joining the Way of Penetrating Unity. More telling are the methods used. In addition to the healing per-formed during spirit-writing séances, Leaders of the Way sold decoctions of blessed incense ashes as medicine, a method taken directly from popu-lar spiritualism.[36] Another element was the promise of invulnerability to bombs and bullets. As demonstrated by Joseph Esherick in his landmark work on the Boxer Uprising, invulnerability through charms or rituals is an important part of the popular religious tradition of North China.[37] In Tianjin, many reported that they had joined the sect to protect themselves or their sons from being killed in the fighting. Many local leaders, includ-ing high-ranking *dianchuanshi* in Tianjin, made this promise explicitly.[38]

The Way of Penetrating Unity in Cangzhou

Arrival and Spread

The Way of Penetrating Unity was probably brought to the Cangzhou area during the mid-1930s and was certainly well established there by the end of the decade. Under the leadership of Zhang Guangbi, the Way of Penetrating Unity had spread from Ji'nan to Tianjin, and, by 1936, the Tianjin base was already organizing missionary drives as far away as Man-churia and South China. Because Cangzhou is located on the railway line linking Ji'nan and Tianjin, it is almost certain that the teaching reached Cangzhou during this initial phase, either directly from Ji'nan or indirectly from Tianjin.

As with its national expansion, the teaching in Cangzhou grew most rapidly in response to the military insecurity of the late 1930s and 1940s. Cangzhou was held by the Japanese from 1937 through 1945 and was heav-ily contested during the civil war that followed. It was during these periods that the Way of Penetrating Unity experienced its greatest growth. The first mention of the teaching in Cangzhou was in 1938, when faithful from Cang County began missionary work in neighboring Hejian County. This reaped a vast harvest of faithful. In 1941, a *tan* was established in Hejian that could reach 106 villages and served to attract more than 6,000 members.[39] By the end of the 1940s, the Way of Penetrating Unity had a sizable membership, as evinced by data from the 1951 movement against the teaching. A January 1951 report estimated the total number of the members in the twelve-county Cangzhou Special Region at 28,590 and the number of villages in which the teaching was active to be roughly 500. This proved to be short by about half. After the conclusion of the campaign, the number of members was changed to 41,500 and number of villages to 1,200. In Botou Township alone, 14 percent of the population was estimated to be members of the Way of Penetrating Unity, while in Jiaohe County 35 percent of all villages had members in the teaching.[40]

Within most of these villages, the Way of Penetrating Unity represented a small but distinct minority of believers. As had the Li Sect, the Way of Penetrating Unity spread thinly and relatively evenly through the countryside. Among the roughly 1,200 villages in which the teaching was active, an average of just more than 12 percent of village households were affiliated with the teaching. Within each such household, only a few members were actual inductees. Even among the villages in which the teaching was active, such individuals represented only 5.5 percent of the total population. Although their numbers were small, these individuals were clearly distinguished from their neighbors. In contrast to local manifestations of the Li Sect, which represented the addition of nominal markers and a temperance tradition to a well-established world of popular religiosity, the apocalyptic element of the Way of Penetrating Unity presented the teaching as radically new and fundamentally different. This was not simply in the minds of believers, but also reflected in their behavior. Far more than had the Li Sect, members of the Way of Penetrating Unity in rural Cang County demonstrated a sense of purpose and distinction with a clear regimen of ritual obligations, secret initiation ceremonies, and dietary restrictions.

Also in contrast to the Li Sect, the Way of Penetrating Unity in rural Cangzhou maintained an elaborate structure of local leadership, which served as a self-referential center of spiritual authority. As table 6.2 demonstrates, the highest local leaders, the *dianchuanshi*, were present in every county, often in rather significant numbers. For each *dianchuanshi*, there were roughly two to five *tanzhu,* who formed the bulk of the leadership

Table 6.1   Concentration of Believers in the Way of Penetrating Unity (W.P.U.) within 1,206 Villages

County	Villages with the W.P.U.	Households in the W.P.U.	Individuals in the W.P.U.
Suning	72	554 (11.5)	1,050 (6)
Hejian	106	744 (10.7)	1,362 (4)
Renqiu	93	405 (14.6)	1,134 (5.7)
Xian	59	200 (12.7)	437 (6.3)
Jiaohe	194	500 (20)	843 (8.8)
Qing	95	548 (13)	1,256 (5.3)
Jianguo	131	575 (12.4)	1,107 (15)
Huanghua	152	1,375 (20)	3,919 (3.3)
Cang Township	22	106 (14)	197 (4.8)
Cang County	259	1,179 (7.1)	2,417 (3.1)
Botou Township	13	458 (24)	789 (10)
Total	1,206	6,687 (12.5)	14,516 (6.5)

Note: Numbers in parentheses are percentages.
Source: CA, appended table 2.

within the villages. Lower-level leaders and specialists, including the "three talents" of spirit writing, *jiangshi,* secretaries, and the like, were numerically not as important as the *tanzhu.*

The number of leaders is especially striking when compared to the total number of faithful. In each of the counties, there was one leader or specialist of the Way of Penetrating Unity for every ten to twenty members and for every one to three villages. The presence of specialists in such numbers further suggests that the Way of Penetrating Unity represented an independent and discrete force within the village. With a devoted leader and a core of believers, a single village or a cluster of neighboring villages could operate as an independent religious community, performing its own religious rituals and meeting for group prayer.

The Way of Penetrating Unity in Cangzhou made frequent use of spirit writing, as demonstrated by the number of texts uncovered by investigators. Peasants in Yang Camp recalled having heard of spirit-writing séances, although none had seen one in person. Moreover, there is a great disparity in the number and sort of texts collected, suggesting that they were produced locally. Investigators in Cang County found seventy-five of these texts, but turned up none in Botou Township. Botou did, however, produce a text called the *Scripture to Exhort the World (Quanshi jing)* in large

Table 6.2   Leadership of the Way of Penetrating Unity in 1,206 Cangzhou Villages

County	Dianchuanshi	Tanzhu	Leaders below Tanzhu	Total Number of Specialists	Ratio of Believers to Specialists
Suning	21	47	4	72	14.6
Hejian	17	85	30	132	10.3
Renqiu	5	25	15	45	25.2
Xian	7	30	4	41	10.7
Jiaohe	9	19	22	50	16.9
Qing	13	30	16	59	21.3
Jianguo	11	36	15	62	17.9
Huanghua	24	103	46	173	22.7
Cang Township	9	6	6	21	9.4
Cang County	13	63	14	90	26.9
Botou Township	1	36	3	40	19.7
Total	130	480	175	785	18.5

numbers.[41] More than a thousand copies of the *Scripture to Exhort the World* were found in Botou Township alone, which suggests that this text was short and easily reproduced. It was also quite localized. Despite the large numbers produced in Botou Township, nearby Qing and Xian Counties produced few or no copies of the text, and older peasants in Cang County had not heard of it (see Appendix C-1, Materials Confiscated in the Course of the Campaign against the Way of Penetrating Unity, March 1951).

Showdown with the People's Government

As the civil war between the Guomindang and the Communists drew to a close, the latter began to take a more aggressive stance toward local sectarians, especially the Way of Penetrating Unity. Within Cangzhou, the local governments of Cang and Jianguo Counties and Botuo Township outlawed the Way of Penetrating Unity in 1949. At that time, none of these local governments seemed to have made any attempt to enforce this policy by arresting sectarian leaders, concentrating instead on interrupting the dissemination of propaganda, particularly in the villages, where the teaching was the strongest. This early experience is instructive. Botou Township and Jianguo County both reported that many ordinary members were willing to abandon the Way of Penetrating Unity upon hearing that it had been outlawed. Those that remained were characterized as "exceptionally superstitious." Of greater concern was the reaction of leaders, who remained with the sect as it was forced underground. The report from Jianguo County gives the most candid assessment. "Since it was outlawed," it said, "the Way of Penetrating Unity has become more secretive in its movements, and a greater threat overall."[42]

In Cangzhou, and throughout China, the real push for the eradication of the Way of Penetrating Unity came soon after the founding of the People's Republic. In June 1950, the government of Hebei province officially outlawed all sectarian organizations. On October 10, 1950, the central publication, "Concerning Directives for Suppressing Counterrevolutionary Activities" *(Guanyu zhenya fan'geming huodong de zhishi)*, initiated a systematic purge of the enemies of the new state. This movement, which was to deal with different kinds of "counter-revolutionaries" such as landlords, occupation-era officials, and Guomindang officials in turn, first set its sights on the eradication of sectarians, particularly the Way of Penetrating Unity. An article in the *People's Daily* run on February 22, 1951, anticipated the campaign against the Way of Penetrating Unity by outlining the punishments for those who "use feudal sectarians to hinder the revolution," the most severe of which was death.[43]

In early January 1951, the organizational groundwork for the campaign against the Way of Penetrating Unity was laid.[44] On January 6, the Hebei provincial government sent a directive to the Cangzhou Prefectural Committee, declaring that the first two months of 1951 were to be devoted entirely to the eradication of "reactionary sects," of which the Way of Penetrating Unity was the most important. Within days, a more detailed directive was sent from Cangzhou to each of the twelve local governments (ten counties and two townships) where the movement was to be centered. Instructions were then passed down from county governments to township and finally local and village cadres.

These directives were produced independently, but all outlined essentially the same demands. Cadres at all levels were given orders to destroy the organizational and leadership structure of the Way of Penetrating Unity, especially its "spy organization"; round up and publicly try high-level leaders (such as *dianchuanshi*); launch a campaign of education and political training in order to turn receptive low-level leaders (such as *tanzhu* and *daoshou*), ordinary members, and the general populace firmly against the Way of Penetrating Unity; and safeguard the party and People's Liberation Army against infiltration by the sect—cadres and soldiers who were members of the Way of Penetrating Unity were to receive stringent education and either give up the sect or be expelled.[45]

Before any of these directives could be achieved, however, cadres were instructed to make a thorough investigation of the Way of Penetrating Unity, including the number of members, important villages, and the movements of the leaders. Many of these reports took advantage of earlier surveillance and movements against the teaching and are impressive in their detail. For example, a January 14 preparatory report from Cang County names two *dianchuanshi* who were to be arrested and made to give information about the rest of the organization. The report mentioned not only the home villages of these two individuals, but also included personality profiles. The former, surnamed Jia, was characterized as a coward, who was likely to talk under pressure, whereas the latter, a Mrs. Feng, was a hardened criminal who would require more creative persuasion.[46]

Higher-level leaders were to be captured immediately and then dealt with on an individual basis. The "criminal, landlord, and traitorous elements" (estimated to comprise about 90 percent of the higher leadership) were to be executed publicly, no doubt as a lesson to those who might doubt the resolve of the new government. Execution was the fate of all five of the highest leaders (one *daozhang* and four *qianren*), thirty-three of forty-seven *dianchuanshi*, as well as fifty-two others. Otherwise, those with some merit to balance their crimes were to receive lesser punishment or no punishment at all. More than half of the new *dianchuanshi* had their punishment thus lessened to imprisonment, and ten new *dianchuanshi* were released into "the custody of the masses."[47]

Of equal importance was to divide the middle-level leaders, such as *tanzhu* and especially *daoshou*, by their willingness to cooperate. Those with a history of collaboration or anti-Communist activity were to be executed or imprisoned; this was the fate of only twenty of the nearly 350 *tanzhu* captured. Others, particularly village-level leaders, were to undergo a period of intense political education, usually lasting twenty to thirty days, in which they would be shown the evils of the Way of Penetrating Unity in the hopes that they would give up the sect willingly.[48] Thus reformed, these mid-level leaders would then become part of the apparatus put to work against the teaching, lecturing peasants against the Way of Penetrating Unity and volunteering intelligence about its organization. Of course, the reality was not always so ideal. A report from Jianguo County complains that one *tanzhu* was taken in for "training" eight times, only to return to his old ways immediately upon release. Upon his final capture, he was executed.[49]

Extra effort was made to purge the Way of Penetrating Unity from the ranks of the Communist Party and its military. Results from the movement show that this effort was well warranted. In neighboring Hejian County, of the 1,168 the Way of Penetrating Unity members who came forward to renounce the teaching, no less than 156 were cadres or party members. Moreover, of them, twenty-one were *tanzhu* and five were high-ranking *dianchuanshi*.[50] Returning to the question of collaboration, the involvement of significant numbers of party members and affiliates in the Way of Penetrating Unity provides ample evidence that such activities were not prominent in the life of the teaching in Cangzhou.

The greater part of the educational campaign was aimed at ordinary believers and the peasants in general. Cadres were encouraged to employ a variety of methods to spread propaganda denouncing the Way of Penetrating Unity, especially taking advantage of the idle time of the peasants around Spring Festival. The most basic method was to mobilize supporters and cadres to lecture the peasants directly. Jianguo County organized three teams of students to travel to the countryside and conduct lectures. According to its own report, the Huanghua County government prepared 1,100 people for propaganda work against the Way of Penetrating Unity. The

Table 6.3   Communist Party Member and Affiliate Participation in the Way of Penetrating Unity

	Village Cadres[a]	Party Members	Total	Dian-chuanshi	Tanzhu	Leaders below Tanzhu	Ordinary Members
Cang County	99	58	179	1	2	…	176
Renqiu	95	25	159	5	21	…	133
Xian	31	55	70	…	…	1	69
Huanghua	3	8	17	…	…	…	17
Qing	53	11	78	…	1	2	75
Suning	25	11	47	…	2	…	45
Cang Township	118	17	177	…	…	…	177
Jiaohe	45	17	80	…	1	2	77
Jianguo	6	4	10	…	…	1	9
Botou Township	86	13	235	…	2	…	233
Hejian	17	24	116	…	1	1	114
Total	578	243	1,168	6	30	7	1,125

Source: CA, appended table.
[a] Including National Assembly members and Youth League members.

most characteristic, and quite possibly the most effective, method was to use creative techniques that would reach large numbers of illiterate peasants, such as short, easy-to-remember poems, *kuaiban* (rhymed speech to rhythm beaten on a small wooden board), mobile exhibitions, and popular songs. A short antisectarian poem spread by party cadres in Cang County alluded to the attraction of the healing practices of the teaching:

> The Way of Penetrating Unity,
> what bunch of nonsense!
> They cheat real money
> and sell fake medicine!
> (*Yiguandao, xia hu'nao. Pian zhenqian, mai jiayao*)[51]

This and other propaganda initiatives appear to have met their mark, and the greatest success of the movement appears to have been at the level of ordinary believers. As had been the case in the initial movements against the teaching, most reports agree that the great majority of peasant adherents were willing to formally renounce the Way of Penetrating Unity soon upon hearing that it had been outlawed.[52] Nor was this success simply inflated by cadres. Testimony of Cang County villagers affirmed that the popular following of the Way of Penetrating Unity all but disappeared in the two months of the campaign.

Attraction of the Way of Penetrating Unity

The Hebei provincial government was especially concerned with the leadership of the Way of Penetrating Unity, which it estimated to be 90 percent "reactionary elements." Most other reports, including the original directive sent by the Hebei provincial government, make numerous references to the leadership of the Way of Penetrating Unity being composed primarily of traitors, local toughs, spies, ruffians, and landlords.[53] But what would make millions of city dwellers and peasants alike rush to join an organization that was obviously working for the Japanese? Certainly by 1940, the horrors of the Japanese occupation were common knowledge in all but the most remote areas, and the Way of Penetrating Unity propaganda urging "Chinese-Japanese friendship" must have sounded patently hollow, if not ridiculous. Yet in the Cangzhou area alone, the Way of Penetrating Unity was present in more than 1,600 villages, with ordinary believers numbering in the tens of thousands. Are we to believe that these were all "traitorous and reactionary elements"?

Certainly the organizers of the campaign did not. A common theme that runs throughout the directives sent down to county governments and reports sent back up to the prefectural and provincial levels is that the majority of ordinary members were ignorant, superstitious peasants who were "tricked" into joining, and thus a major task of the movement was to use education to reveal the true nature of the Way of Penetrating Unity and turn peasants against the sect. The Cangzhou directive gives voice to one of the greatest fears of the Communists: that the movement against the Way of Penetrating Unity might appear to be a general religious purge. It strongly cautioned cadres that for "very superstitious old men and women who are not political, and not important to the sect, the greatest concern is to stop them from holding activities of the Way of Penetrating Unity."[54] In this same vein, one of the strongest concerns was to prevent public suicides of Leaders of the Way or members. The above document mentions this fear specifically, and other reports made after the conclusion of the movement specifically emphasize that there were no religiously induced suicides.[55]

The "superstition" of the masses aside, peasants joined the Way of Penetrating Unity for a variety of reasons. The broad range of concerns among members in Cangzhou is best suggested by a 1947 investigation of the Way of Penetrating Unity conducted during land reform in Dai County, Shanxi. In this single village, where nearly three-quarters of all peasants were in the Way of Penetrating Unity, Communist cadres asked 502 "poor peasants" why they had joined the sect.[56] Not surprisingly, the largest number (46 percent) stated that they had joined the Way of Penetrating Unity to "escape disaster" *(duozai taonan)*. After witnessing years of brutal war and famine, it was certainly no leap of faith for most peasants to believe in the existence of such a disaster and natural for them to seek spiritual assistance to pass through it unharmed. This phrase, however, is equivocal in its meaning: it can refer to *the* disaster *(da nan)*—that is, the apocalyptic change of epoch—as well as to difficulty in general. Because the apocalypse itself was never given a specific date, and no call was made for military or other drastic action, one could join with little harm, attain a sense of security concerning the possibility of millennial change, and rely on the spiritual protection of the sect for other problems, as well.

In addition to this general concern, peasants in Dai County joined the Way of Pervading Unity for very specific reasons, and reports from Cangzhou also confirm the particularistic attraction of the teaching. In Dai County, the second-most-common goal for joining the teaching was "to get rich" (14 percent) followed by prayers for children or the safety of family members; twenty-one members (3 percent) joined specifically to give up smoking. In Cangzhou, the most common reference is to healing. The provincial directive urged local cadres to demonstrate to peasants that "not only is the Way of Penetrating Unity unable to cure sickness, but they are also harmful and illegal."[57] The report from Jianguo County also confirms that many people joined the Way of Penetrating Unity to be healed or because of the popular belief that doing so would bless their children with long life.[58] Certainly the apocalypse might come, but the rush to join the Way of Penetrating Unity and later to abandon it was not simply a function of that single event.

Politics and the Aftermath of the 1951 Movement

Although both the directives sent down before the campaign and the reports sent back up two months later emphasize the counterrevolutionary nature of the Way of Penetrating Unity, few substantiate this claim with any kind of detailed account. The Cangzhou Special Region report is the most cautious, calling the organized mass following of the Way of Penetrating Unity a "potential base for antirevolutionary activities."[59] Local directives allude to the "evil deeds" of the Way of Penetrating Unity, often in the stock phrases about the infiltration of the sect with Japanese, Guomindang, and American spies. (With the outbreak of the Korean War, the latter were of particular importance.) The Cang Township directive against the Way of Penetrating Unity informed local cadres that the sect "spreads rumors in order to start a panic."[60] A more specific report comes from neighboring Huanghua County, where spirit-writing séances had produced detailed predictions of the end of the epoch. Leaders were said to be telling villagers that a third world war was coming. Reflecting the fears of the day, they reported that "Beijing and Tianjin would be destroyed by lightning, and Manchuria by a nuclear bomb." More alarming to the Communists were rumors that "the end of the Eighth Route Army would come in May" and that "Mao Zedong is a demon king [mowang], and soon the demons will all get their just punishment!"[61] In nearby Jianguo County as well, Leaders of the Way spread predictions about a third world war and the White Yang epoch.[62]

As such, the campaign against the Way of Penetrating Unity was steeped in political overtones, and its success may to some degree reflect both popular loyalty to the Communists and the increasing politicization of rural life. Especially during the war years, many peasants had entered the sect with a low degree of commitment as a hedge against the possibility of the coming apocalypse and because there was little personal or financial cost associated with joining. The 1951 campaign against the sect, however, raised these costs considerably. Although older peasants in Cang County strongly refuted the claim that local members of the sect had in any way been involved with the Japanese occupation, the charges levied against the teaching as a whole did find a receptive audience. To avoid the taint of collaboration, former members were pressured to distance themselves from the teaching, and most did so willingly. As this and subsequent propaganda campaigns saturated village society during the early 1950s, the Way of Penetrating Unity became a stock member of the reactionary rogues gallery. A report from Jianguo County adds with obvious pride that children fighting in the schoolyard would reserve the names of Harry Truman, Chiang Kai-shek, and the Way of Penetrating Unity as their greatest insults.[63] By this time, however, most members had long since abandoned the teaching.

After the conclusion of the 1951 movement, the teaching continued to resurface, but it was a shadow of its former self. Subsequent sources claim that in Cangzhou, a few leaders had escaped the dragnet and attempted to revive the teaching. According to the 1995 Cang County gazetteer, Leaders of the Way returned to the area after the movement against them had died down and again began to preach that the apocalypse was at hand and would be triggered by a war to overthrow the Communists. This same source cites an investigation in 1955 that revealed a close network of the Way of Penetrating Unity stretching across four counties, the leaders of which were not discovered until 1957, at which time they were immediately executed.[64]

Sources on such individuals are few and highly suspect, not least of all because the Way of Penetrating Unity was subjected to numerous campaigns throughout the 1950s and 1960s. Former leaders were again brought out and subjected to public "struggle" and the sect was made synonymous with reactionary forces.[65] It is not inconceivable, however, that a number of Leaders of the Way did escape and continued to practice deep underground, as they had in parts of Shandong.[66] Nevertheless, the very real danger of being associated with the sect after 1951 makes this smaller core membership a very different phenomenon than the large casual following it had gained in the two decades previous.

The political demonization of the Way of Penetrating Unity has shaped its place in local historical memory. The evidence of limited sectarian resurgence through the 1950s not withstanding, for most peasants the teaching itself was already a distant memory by the end of the decade. The teaching, however, was to remain a focus of various political campaigns through the early 1980s and reemerged in its former role as universal villain in the context of the movement against Falungong in 1999. For those under fifty, who knew the teaching only through decades of propaganda, this was an effective tactic. Even those who had seen the sect in its heyday, and felt that the charges of collaboration, theft, and rape charged against the sect were exaggerated, still spoke of the teaching in terms that reflected the decades of political scapegoating. Many had become accustomed to referring to the sect using a pejorative name that was employed in the propaganda against it, loosely translated as "the Way of Penetrating Harm" *(yiguan hairen dao)*. When asked to give his overall assessment of the Way of Penetrating Unity, one older peasant explained that the charges levied against it spoke only for the higher-level leadership of the teaching. After contemplating briefly and reformulating his thoughts, he suddenly but significantly shifted his vocabulary to reflect the influence of decades of political education. "On the whole," he said, "the Way of Penetrating Unity seems to have been a reactionary cult *(fandong huidaomen)*, after all."[67]

Conclusion: Millenarianism with No Millennium?

Perhaps the greatest question to emerge from the campaign against the Way of Penetrating Unity in Cangzhou is why the sect offered no organized resistance. Many of the large and small sectarian uprisings of the Qing dynasty had also been prefaced on religious vision, and certainly from the point of view of the late Imperial state, this was the danger of allowing sectarian religion to go unchecked and even more so of challenging it, once established. Yet, not only did the nearly 30,000 members of the Way of Penetrating Unity in Cangzhou fail to raise military resistance, they did not take the sect underground.[68] When the time came, the great majority appeared very willing to renounce the teaching.

The answer to this may lie in the nature of the Way of Penetrating Unity as an apocalyptic movement. In his introduction to *Apocalyptic Time*, Albert Baumgarten outlines a four-part trajectory along which such movements develop.[69] The first two parts, the arousal of public opinion to the millenarian message and the search for scriptural confirmation, are characteristic of the early years of the Way of Penetrating Unity. The intense missionary work of the teaching in urban and rural China was predicated on constant revelation of its divine mission. New confirmation appeared in the form of spirit-writing séances and, as had Protestant exiles in early modern Europe, reexamination and reinterpretation of the extant scriptural tradition to reveal a deeper, hidden thread that connected the past and portended the arrival of the true teaching as a matter of preordained, cosmic significance.[70]

The second half of this trajectory, however, never came to pass. Baumgarten refers the third part of this scheme as "upping the ante," that is, the tests or trials by which the dedicated core commit to the movement. Fundamentally, this is a matter of faith, characterized by the "sacrifice of individual identity" and renunciation of the world by giving up personal property, abandoning one's family, or remaining with the sect in defiance of custom or law. In other words, it is a decisive act by which the committed core chooses to follow the vision of a future world, by breaking ties with the present one. This is followed by the fourth phase, the inevitable disconfirmation of the millennium and the aftermath, in which the teaching either retreats from its apocalyptic scheme or dies out.[71] The event that prompts the transition from part two to three, and transforms the intensification of vague millenarian longings into a discrete movement, is the revelation of a specific date for the apocalypse, which is usually not far in the future. Although some local leaders may have been more specific than others in their allusions to the apocalypse, the Way of Penetrating Unity never made such a concrete prediction, certainly not one with the authority of nationally recognized figures such as Zhang Guangbi, and thus never steeled its large membership into a committed core. Nor did civil authority force its hand. Although the Japanese occupation, Guomindang, and Communists had each demonstrated a degree of mistrust for the Way of Penetrating Unity, there was no concerted movement against the teaching until the 1951 campaign, by which point Zhang had already died and his wife fled to Taiwan.

This trajectory, however, does not necessarily need to proceed to its conclusion. As Stephen O'Leary has discussed, scholarly understanding of apocalyptic movements is often hampered by the paradigm of scientific rationality, viewing millenarian vision as a hypothesis that can be disproved by experiential evidence, in particular the failure of Armageddon to materialize. By contrast, the appeal of the Way of Penetrating Unity transcended this one event. The Way of Penetrating Unity offered spiritual protection against disasters great and small and provided tangible benefits in form of healing. The attraction of the apocalyptic message, though, was not simply spiritual opportunism, peasants hedging their bets against a possible apocalypse by joining a sect that offered protection. Even as a millennial movement, the Way of Penetrating Unity did not require an immediate apocalypse. Rather, the apocalyptic message was ongoing; it gave comfort by framing earthly suffering in a metanarrative of preordained cosmic significance and gave refuge in the message of the eventual triumph over it in the millennial kingdom.[72]

In this context, the greatest enemy of Way of Penetrating Unity was peace and prosperity. Regardless of whether they expected the Communists to make good on their promises of social reform, most peasants in Cang County greeted the founding of the People's Republic in 1949 as the end of a decade-long nightmare of war and famine. This newly optimistic view of the future eroded the appeal of the millenarian vision of the Way of Penetrating Unity and contributed to the willingness of all but the most committed members to abandon the teaching.

7. Village Sectarians

The Most Supreme and
Heaven and Earth Teachings

Each of the teachings discussed thus far—monastic Buddhism, the Li Sect, and the Way of Penetrating Unity—exerted a distinct force on the development of local religious life in the villages of Cang County, but none could be said to have maintained an active, enduring presence as an institution. Organizationally, both monastic Buddhism and the Li Sect were characterized by highly specialized theological and liturgical traditions that remained the purview of a small, primarily urban, stratum of experts and were not brought to bear upon the local life of the sect. The apocalyptic vision of the Way of Penetrating Unity afforded comfort during a time of war and crisis, even if this vision never provided a plan of action to bring about the coming millennium and proved unable to thrive under less threatening conditions. Theologically and organizationally, each of these teachings satisfied a particular niche, but they were not oriented toward the needs of everyday religious life.

In rural Cang County, that role was played by two sects, the Teaching of the Most Supreme *(taishang men)* and Heaven and Earth Teaching *(tiandi men)*, which I will characterize as village sectarians.[1] Each of these sects has exhibited great longevity in rural Cang County: local organization of the Teaching of the Most Supreme can be traced back to at least the mid-nineteenth century and that of the Heaven and Earth to the early eighteenth. Although they were subjected to intense pressure during the 1950s and 1960s, both began a revival during the late 1970s and have remained active through the end of the twentieth century. Throughout this entire period, affiliation with each of these teachings has remained relatively constant, neither expanding in response to social crisis nor collapsing under political pressure. The reason for this tenacity lies in their importance to village society and personal piety. Both the Most Supreme and the Heaven and Earth teachings perform the vital ceremonials of public and private religious life: the calendar of annual festivals, occasional ceremonies, such as prayers for rain, as well as blessings, exorcisms, and funerals.[2] Outside of their ritual capacity, specialists of these two sects also serve as an important source of knowledge about the sacred and are often portrayed as moral exemplars.

The village sectarians of Cang County represent yet another example of the interaction between institutional networks and local society. Each of the two teachings was originally transmitted to Cang County by extensive missionary networks that crossed North China, but soon lost contact with these networks and developed as local phenomena. Within the local sphere, as well, the two teachings demonstrated different degrees of institutional integrity. Historically, the Teaching of the Most Supreme was the larger, but less unified, of the two. The Heaven and Earth Teaching, in contrast, was present in a smaller number of villages but maintained a stronger cooperative network among them. This difference came to shape the local development of the two teachings, particularly in the period of sectarian revival since the 1970s. With its loose local network, the Teaching of the Most Supreme was less able to adapt to the strains of reorganization, and, as of the late 1990s, was present in only about half of the villages that had supported it a half century earlier. In contrast, the tightly knit Heaven and Earth Teaching was able to reconstitute its earlier networks and doctrine almost completely intact.

Origins of the Teaching of the Most Supreme

The precise origins of the Teaching of the Most Supreme must remain to some degree a matter of speculation. The teaching as it appears in the villages of modern Cang County retains no scriptural tradition that would outline its history, nor have I encountered the teaching mentioned by name in any historical sources. Although ethnographic work in and around the city of Tianjin has turned up groups of the same name and similar description, this provides no more information on the origins or history of the teaching.[3]

The Teaching of the Most Supreme is clearly a product of sectarian currents of mid-Qing North China. In light of the lack of historical or scriptural documentary evidence, it is not possible to posit a conclusive pedigree from which the teaching evolved. As with all sectarian teachings, tracing this genealogy is difficult because, despite their appearance as distinct intellectual and organizational entities, these teachings tended to merge together, their characteristic theological contributions outlined in texts that had limited circulation and significant practical innovation occurring at the local level, under the influence of charismatic teachers.[4] The case could be made, however, that the Teaching of the Most Supreme descended from an eighteenth-century tradition of teachings known collectively as the Primordial Chaos and Return to the Origin Teachings. On the one hand, the Teaching of the Most Supreme reveals a number of nominal ties to this intellectual tradition. More striking, it resembles the Primordial Chaos and Return to the Origin tradition in its loose organization, specifically the high degree of institutional vagueness and local autonomy.

In the late eighteenth century, the Primordial Chaos and Return to the Origin Teachings were active in throughout North China and are best known for their central role in the misnamed "White Lotus" sectarian rebellions of the mid-Qing dynasty, but the ideas after which each is named demonstrates an intellectual pedigree that both predates and transcends the two teachings themselves. The term "Primordial Chaos" is a Daoist referent to a time before the separation of heaven and earth and has been in use since at least the Tang dynasty to refer to the divine and transcendent manifestation of Laozi.[5] It was also the name of a distinct tradition within Daoism. A Yuan dynasty source mentions a branch of Daoism called Primordial Chaos alongside other established schools, such as the Complete Perfection (quanzhen). At this time, Primordial Chaos was not so much a sect of Daoism as a tradition of individual inner alchemical (neidan) practice. This tradition had neither clerical organization nor scriptures, the Ming dynasty tradition of popular scriptures (both "precious scrolls" and apocryphal Buddhist sutras) bearing the Primordial Chaos name actually being the product of the older Vast Yang Teaching.[6]

The name of the second teaching, the "Return to the Origin," also descends from a preexisting term, which can be rendered by at least three distinct sets of homophonous characters, each of which shares the theme of returning mankind to a heavenly home. The term first appears in an exposition on the theme in the *Sutra of the Imperial Ultimate Cause and Effect (Foshuo huangji jieguo baojuan)*, a precious scroll from 1430, and sectarian scriptures of Ming and Qing continue to refer to this return specifically in terms of the eschatology of the Eternal Venerable Mother.[7] One of these, the late Ming *Precious Scripture of the Ancient Buddha, Heavenly Perfected Verifiable Dragon Flower (Gufo tianzhen kaozheng longhua baojing)*, refers specifically to a Return to the Origin Teaching:

The Return to the Origin Teaching, established the dharma sect,
   to save the sons and daughters,
The Return to the Origin Patriarch, guides the good people,
   to meet at the Dragon Flower [Assembly].[8]

The task of isolating the precise genealogy by which the earlier intellectual traditions of Primordial Chaos and Return to the Origin evolved into the sectarian teachings bearing the same names is a matter of some debate and beyond the scope of this study. Most locate the common ancestor of the two as either the Ming Dynasty Vast Yang teaching or the homophonous (and possibly identical) Red Epoch Teaching. It is certain that the Vast Yang Teaching was responsible for the Ming tradition of Primordial Chaos scriptures, and sources from the mid-Qing record the existence of a "Primordial Chaos Red Epoch Teaching" *(Hunyuan hongyang jiao)*.[9] Whatever their antecedents, the formation of these two teachings into distinct lineages can be definitively traced to early eighteenth-century Shanxi, and specifically to Zhang Jindou, a highly influential leader of the Non-Action Teaching. Zhang gathered numerous disciples, and two of these, Feng Jinjing and Tian Jintai, each founded independent branches, which became the Primordial Chaos and Return to the Origin Teachings, respectively.[10] Over the eighteenth and nineteenth centuries, these two networks intertwined and proliferated across China.

What is significant is that, although Primordial Chaos and Return to the Origin teachings each traced themselves to a distinct missionary lineage, both were characterized by the autonomy of local networks. Over the nineteenth century, the Primordial Chaos and Return to the Origin Teachings each branched into numerous smaller teachings, including the Clear Water *(qingshui)*, Heavenly Principle *(tianli)*, and Eight Trigrams *(bagua)* teachings, each which further divided into independent networks.[11] To be sure, each of these teachings developed a characteristic theological core, as expounded in scriptures, but this alone did not stem the processes of diversification and localization. This was particularly true of local leadership of eighteenth-century Primordial Chaos and Return to the Origin sects, which ranged from messianic visionaries such as Zhang Ren to opportunists such as Zhang Jindou. Occasionally, these local networks would clash, but what was it issue was less a conflict of scripture than of leadership styles and goals.

One aspect of this tradition that has received relatively little attention was the ability of these groups to function quietly as stable local institutions. Unless somehow drawn into political intrigue, such groups remained beyond the interest of most government investigators and appear only tangentially in historical records.[12] Yet, evidence demonstrates that the practice of such groups remained very close to the needs of everyday life. One group calling itself a "Return to the Origin Assembly" *(shouyuan hui)* thrived in the suburbs of Beijing during the late eighteenth century under stable leadership of a southern Zhili woman named Hu Er Yinjin. Hu attracted visitors with homilies (known as "divine thoughts," *shen xiang)* and her ability to heal, while ordinary members of the group recited simple mantras and scriptures for talismanic value.[13] Following the early nineteenth-century Linqing rebellion, leaders of the Red Yang Teaching, with close (although ambiguous) ties to both the Primordial Chaos and Return to the Origin traditions, were arrested and deposed. Despite the fact that their testimonies were taken in the context of a criminal investigation, they still demonstrate the importance of activities similar to those conducted by Hu, including votive scripture recitation, vegetarianism, healing, and the performance of simple ceremonials, such as funerals to the local community of believers.[14]

A number of clues link the Teaching of the Most Supreme as it developed in Cang County to this large and shifting tradition. First, it is clear that similar sectarian teachings were well established in Cang County by at least the early nineteenth century. In 1813, Huang Yübian, the magistrate of Cang County and compiler of the *Detailed Argument against Heterodox Religions*, discovered among the people a large number of Primordial Chaos scriptures. Although these scriptures are originally attributable to the Vast Yang Teaching, they were also employed by teachings in the Primordial Chaos tradition.[15] A second clue is in the name of the teaching itself. The monikers "Lord Lao Most Supreme" *(taishang laojun)* and "Lord Lao of the Primordial Chaos" *(hunyuan laojun)* were often used interchangeably for the deified form of Laozi or else combined, as in a 1013 edict that refers to Laozi as the "Emperor of Supreme Virtue, Most Supreme Lord Lao of Primordial Chaos" *(taishang laojun hunyuan shangde huangdi).*[16] Further evidence confirms the existence of a Li Trigram, Lord Lao Teaching *(ligua laojun jiao)* in early nineteenth-century Cangzhou.[17]

A third concerns a deity called the Venerable Ancestor of Primordial Chaos *(hunyuan laozu).* This deity is discussed in detail in the Vast Yang Scriptures that bear his name and is identified occasionally as the Amithaba Buddha or, more frequently, the sect's sixteenth-century founder, Piaogao. According to the latter formulation, the Venerable Ancestor of Primordial Chaos is a favored son of the Eternal Venerable Mother and a vital architect and participant in her design for the salvation of 9.6 billion of her purest human children. It was he who sent the heavenly messengers to be born as the great religious figures of history, and his own human birth as the patriarch Piaogao marked the culmination of this process. Although other teachings do not deny the importance of Piaogao or the Venerable Ancestor of Primordial Chaos, active worship of the deity was characteristic of the Vast Yang Teaching and its descendants. This includes the Teaching of the Most Supreme in modern Cang County, for whom this deity occupies a central role in ritual practice.[18]

It should again be emphasized, however, that, if Teaching of the Most Supreme is indeed a branch or descendant of the Primordial Chaos or Return to the Origin Teachings, it is in practice a very distant relation. Although a scriptural tradition suggestive of the Primordial Chaos tradition was present in early nineteenth-century Cang County, the modern Teaching of the Most Supreme has no memory of these texts, nor indeed of ever having had a scriptural tradition of its own. At least since the 1940s, it has relied primarily on general Daoist and Buddhist texts, such as the "Universal Gateway" *(pu men)* chapter of the *Lotus Sutra*, also known as the *Guanyin Scripture (Guanyin jing)*, the *Jade Emperor Scripture (Yühuang jing)*, and the Daoist classic, the *Daode jing*. When presented with the names of some of scriptures associated with the Vast Yang Teaching, current members responded that they had never heard of these texts, much less used them in a ritual setting.[19] More fundamentally, the tendency of eighteenth-century Primordial Chaos and Return to the Origin networks was to branch out and establish local independence. Just as these two teachings developed into numerous sects during the nineteenth century, so too would the evolution of the teaching over time would proceed in tune with local realities and needs, largely independent of any sort of standardizing or centralizing influence.

The Teaching of the Most Supreme in Cang County to 1949

No conclusive historical record of the Teaching of the Most Supreme in Cang County exists either in written texts or memorized liturgy or even among its current leaders. As such, knowledge of the origins and spread of the sect is sketchy. Oral histories collected in the late 1980s hold that the Teaching of the Most Supreme was founded in northern Shandong and transmitted to Cang County during the Daoguang period (1821–1851) of the Qing dynasty.[20] My own fieldwork could not confirm this belief, primarily because a number of the older leaders had since died and much of their knowledge had not been passed on. Nevertheless, the claim that the Teaching of the Most Supreme originated in mid-Qing Shandong does seem plausible, as this was both a time and place of intense sectarian activity.

According to these histories, the teaching was brought to Cang County by a missionary who, quite significantly, is not remembered by name. This teacher passed through Cang County and transmitted the teaching to two local disciples. Each of these disciples was entrusted with a *gui*, a chest of objects used in the ritual life of the sect, and sent to spread the teaching among surrounding villages. This was the beginning of the characteristic organizational pattern of the Teaching of the Most Supreme in Cang County: the division of villages into two groups, North Chest *(beigui)* and South Chest *(nangui)*. It is significant that the Teaching of the Most Supreme in Tianjin is not organized by chest, nor is this system mentioned in ethnographic work on the sect in Duliu. Most likely, this system is unique to the teaching in this part of Cang County, one of many examples of the institutional localization of sectarian culture.[21]

Indirect evidence suggests that each chest of the sect may have once acted as a single ritual network. The *gui* to which this name refers is more specifically called a *jinggui* (scripture chest) and is a basic feature of sectarian organization. A scripture chest contains the ritual objects of the sect, such as flags, scriptures, spirit tablets, and musical instruments, which give a community the ability to perform ritual functions independently, and the physical possession of such a chest is often a symbol of authority within the ritual community. Today, the Teaching of the Most Supreme uses the term "chest" to refer obliquely to an independent ritual community; the person who leads and organizes ritual functions can be referred to as "leader of the chest" *(guitou)*. Perhaps most telling, the greatest division in the ritual practice of the Teaching of the Most Supreme remains that between villages of the North and South Chests. Although few ordinary villagers can distinguish between the two, specialists insist that the scriptures, music, and costume of each of the two Chests are distinct enough that the villages from two different chests are unable to perform rituals together.[22]

The first clear picture that can be drawn of the sect in this area is during the 1940s, at which time the teaching was a regional network based on ritual groups within individual villages. By that time, it was clear that the sect did not maintain any extralocal ties. Although the Teaching of the Most Supreme was active in and around Tianjin, groups in Cang County had no contact with these or other branches of the sect outside this area. In fact, if they ever had, such relations had been long forgotten before the memory of my oldest informants. None of the oldest members of the sect had even heard of the existence of the Teaching of the Most Supreme out-side the immediate area, and many were convinced that the two chests of the teaching in Cang County constituted the entirety of the teaching.[23]

In contrast, within the Cang County area, the organization of the villages of the Teaching of the Most Supreme was quite intimate. Older members of the sect (as well as many villagers not affiliated with the teaching) could easily recite the names of all or most of the Cang County villages in which the teaching had been active during the 1940s. Most informants concurred that, during this time, the Teaching of the Most Supreme was present in fifty-two villages, characteristically divided between North Chest and South Chest. The North Chest was the larger of the two, consisting of thirty-six villages, while South Chest had only sixteen.

By the 1940s, however, each of the two Chests of the Teaching of the Most Supreme, which had once cooperated as ritual networks, had evolved into a loose confederation of ritually independent villages. Older peasants confirmed that by this time there was no organization of either chest as a whole, and neither met to conduct ritual functions as a single community. Instead, the center of organization was the individual village. By the 1940s, most villages that maintained the teaching possessed scripture chests of their own, and almost all were able to perform ritual functions independently. To do so, the primary consideration was to have a critical number of specialists (*daoye*, literally, Elders of the Teaching) who had mastered the musical and liturgical tradition of the sect. Rituals of the Teaching of the Most Supreme required a core of at least ten such specialists (three *wenchang* to chant and perform ritual activities, accompanied by seven *wuchang* who chant and perform accompanying music) and agreed that, as of 1949, each of the villages mentioned as having supported the Teaching of the Most Supreme had this critical number.

Although villages with the critical number of specialists were ritually independent, groups from individual villages would frequently cooperate as a matter of custom or to perform ritual functions on a grander scale. One such occasion was the large-scale ritual conducted annually by villages of the North Chest at the Balang Temple festival in Zhao-Guan Camp as late as the 1930s.[24] A number of the villages with the North Chest of the Teaching of the Most Supreme, including Zhao-Guan Camp, Tea Tent *(Chapeng)*, and White Horse Village, would chant scriptures at the festival, sometimes together and sometimes as individual village-based groups. Peasants throughout the area, many of whom were affiliated with the South Chest or with other groups such as the Heaven and Earth Sect, were free to visit the festival as worshipers or onlookers, but only specialists from North Chest villages participated in a ritual capacity. A similar gathering occurred during the Guanyin temple fair of Hai Dock Village, at the time a center of the South Chest of the Teaching of the Most Supreme. Peasants in Hai Dock recalled that, during this festival, groups of specialists from neighboring villages would arrive to chant scriptures. Although these groups were all from the South Chest of the same teaching, they would not chant together. Rather, they engaged in a kind of friendly competition to see who could draw off the largest portion of the festivalgoers by making the best music. In both cases, the ritual component was composed of individual groups of the same chest, who came to showcase their own piety and skills, while adding to the scale and grandeur of the festival.

In addition to cooperative participation in sectarian festivals, village contingents of the Teaching of the Most Supreme strengthened their bonds by training new specialists with leaders in neighboring communities. This extension of the formal bond between teacher *(shifu)* and disciple *(tudi)* across village boundaries both cemented the ties of friendship between communities and standardized ritual practice. During the 1940s, the leader of the Teaching of the Most Supreme in Hai Dock, a septuagenarian surnamed Zheng, was particularly well regarded, and young devotees from a number of neighboring communities studied under him, often taking advantage of the agricultural slack season during winter to remain in the village for weeks at a time. This established the reputation of Hai Dock as a local center of the teaching and developed strong ties of friendship and cooperation among villages. Thus, although the ritual core of the Teaching of the Most Supreme in the 1940s was the village-based contingent, in practice small clusters of villages were also bound by close personal and customary ties of cooperation.

As discussed in chapter 2, however, even though sectarian groups such as the Teaching of the Most Supreme were organizationally based on the village, its ritual core represented a distinct group within the community. Like the Li Sect and the Way of Penetrating Unity, they generally did not incorporate unaffiliated villagers into their activities and made relatively few demands of nonmembers. But, unlike the Li Sect and the Way of Penetrating Unity, the Teaching of the Most Supreme performed ritual functions on behalf of the community and its members, particularly the performance of funerary rites, in which fellow villagers were given preferential treatment. Although unaffiliated villagers did not participate in ritual activities and had no mark of membership or religious prohibitions related to the sect, all were felt to benefit from the presence of the ritual group and to be socially obliged to provide financial support for ritual functions.

Origin and Beliefs of the Heaven and Earth Teaching

The Heaven and Earth Teaching was founded in northeast Shandong by Dong Sihai (1619–1650, also known as Dong Jisheng and locally as the "Great Teacher") during the waning years of the Ming dynasty.[25] A theme common to the histories of late Ming sectarian groups, Dong is said to have been dismayed by the social decline of the day created a teaching to bolster decaying public morality.[26] The teaching of the Heaven and Earth Sect, like that of the Teaching of the Most Supreme, is thus a product of Ming dynasty sectarian tradition. In practice, however, it represents a different pattern of organization, one that is more discrete and self-consciously distinct than the Teaching of the Most Supreme. This is evident in rural Cang County, where the Heaven and Earth Sect represents a more immediately unique contribution to local traditions of belief and practice than does the Teaching of the Most Supreme. In terms of belief, the Heaven and Earth Sect is characterized by the deification of Dong Sihai and its keen understanding of its own identity and history and emphasis on Confucian morality. In practice, this is reflected in the strong emphasis placed on scripture and the great demands on ritual specialists to become versed in this tradition.[27]

Within the Heaven and Earth Sect, Dong Sihai himself is a primary object of devotion, and his deification is linked to the eschatology of the Eternal Venerable Mother. As had the Way of Penetrating Unity, a central belief of the Heaven and Earth Sect is that the founder of their teaching was a divine figure, an avatar sent by the Eternal Venerable Mother, as the apex of her divine plan for universal salvation. The following scriptural passage is typical:

> The Eternal Venerable Mother looked down at the [mortal] world
>   of red dust and called forth the wind,
> Then she asked the Powerful and Auspicious One [Dong Sihai],
> What if I were to ask if you could descend into the mortal world?
> The Powerful and Auspicious One was surprised at these words . . .
> [He asked,] "What use are all of these Ten Thousand Buddhas sitting
>   before the Lotus Throne?"
> He thereupon crossed the Eastern Lands and descended into the
>   world. . . .
> He arrived in Taiping Village, in Dong Family Grove [Dongjialin],
> Exactly on the first day of the first month, he left his [Eternal Venerable] Mother and descended into the world.[28]

The importance of this cosmology is visually expressed in a ritual setting, in which the tablets *(paiwei)* of Dong Sihai and the Eternal Mother are placed side by side in the center of the altar.

Inherent to this cosmology is the acceptance of past teachers and existing beliefs as lesser players in this same scheme, rather than dismissing or confronting them. Reflecting this practice, other deities are included in ritual functions, as seen in the diverse collection of spirit tablets erected during sectarian rituals, as well as the text of the ritual itself. A common feature of popular liturgy, rituals of the Heaven and Earth Teaching begin with an "invitation to the spirits" *(qing shen)*.[29] The names of spirits to be invited make up a set scriptural passage called "Hymn of Invitation to the Sages" *(qing sheng zhi)* and includes such deities as Confucius, the Buddha, the Medicine King, and household gods. It does not, however, invite any of the marginal, dangerous spirits of popular religion, who are commonly invited to such rituals to appease them. Despite the expansive nature of their pantheon, the sacred addressed by the Heaven and Earth Sect maintains a self-consciously orthodox orientation to its ritual. (For one such litany, see "Litany of Gods Invited to Heaven and Earth Festivals," Appendix D.)

The moral absolutism implied in the worship of only orthodox cosmic forces is one indication of the strong Confucian element in the teaching. The name itself alludes to the Confucian relationships of obligation to Heaven, Earth, Ruler, Father, and Teacher *(tian, di, jun, qin, shi)*. These values are visibly represented in the Heaven and Earth tablet, which appears in the front hall of all members and many sympathetic villagers, and are actively articulated in the ritual life of the teaching. In addition to an uncompromising stance toward the demonic (for example, the healer Wang —introduced in chapter 3—who heals by confronting, rather than appeasing, demonic forces), the scriptures of teaching, of which the following passage is typical, expound upon these five relationships at great length:

> First, we show gratitude for the kindness of Heaven,
> Second, for the kindness of Earth,
> Third, for the kindness of the Emperors and Kings of Land and Water,
> Fourth, for the kindness of those who raised us from infancy,
> Fifth, for the kindness of our Teacher.
> We bring together the mass of believers to show gratitude for these
>   Five Kindnesses.[30]

The simple, repetitive nature of these scriptures is indicative of their didactic function. Another such passage (translated in *Heaven and Earth*

Scripture, Drawing in the Clear River [Qingjiang yin], Appendix D) is accompanied by a ritual in which a single stick of incense (an alternate name for the sect being the "Single Stick of Incense Teaching," *yizhu xiang jiao)* is lit for each of the Five Kindnesses. Such a graphic yet straightforward ritual, accompanied by the chanting of scripture, is an extremely effective device for disseminating the moral message of the teaching.

The Heaven and Earth Teaching in Cang County to 1949

The emphasis on obligation and duty extends to the worship of past teachers, making the genealogy of missionary networks a very simple matter to trace. Soon after the founding of his teaching, Dong Sihai began to gather disciples, and the sect gained a large following during his lifetime. In a pattern common to sectarian organizations, Dong trained eight primary disciples, one for each of the eight trigrams *(ba gua)*.[31] Just before his death, Dong sent each of these disciples in a different direction to spread the teaching. One of these disciples, Ma Kaishan, took the teaching to the north (the *kan* trigram), passing through Cang County on his way to Tianjin.[32] Just as Dong is revered as the divine founder and patron of the teaching, Ma Kaishan remains an object of devotion within the *kan* trigram.[33]

The earliest official reference of the Heaven and Earth Teaching in Cang County is a memorial dating from 1813, which describes a fusion of the Heaven and Earth (under an alternate name, the As You Wish Sect, *ruyi men)* and Li Trigram (*Li gua)* teachings. This document describes the teaching as making basic moral injunctions to be filial to one's parents, burning incense and praying three times each day, and having techniques for healing and *qi* circulation *(yunqi gonfu)*. Memorials from roughly the same period show the teaching to have been present throughout Hebei and Shandong provinces.[34]

Other sources, however, confirm the teaching to have been active in Cang County for at least a century before that. According to scriptures, Ma Kaishan passed the teaching to Li Longjiang, a peasant from Xiaoli village near the southern gate of the Cangzhou city walls. Li then brought the Heaven and Earth Teaching to the village of Rear Camp, which remains its local center even today. From Li Longjiang, the third generation of the Heaven and Earth teachers, the sect was passed to Liu Lisan, who is buried on the outskirts of Rear Camp, and then to Tu Pinyi. Of the thirteen generations of the Heaven and Earth Sect teachers that followed Tu Pinyi, eleven have the surname Tu, a dominant name in Rear Camp, an earlier name of which is Tu Family Camp. With this evidential confirmation of scriptural tradition, we can reasonably conclude that the Heaven and Earth Sect has been present in at least one Cang County village continuously for roughly fourteen generations, from the early eighteenth century to the late twentieth.[35]

Throughout its history in Cang County, the local organization of the Heaven and Earth Sect has demonstrated remarkable continuity within a small number of villages. Like the Teaching of the Most Supreme, the Heaven and Earth Sect was organized around village-based ritual groups. In contrast to the large and loose organization of villages with the Teaching of the Most Supreme, though, the Heaven and Earth Sect maintained a smaller, tighter network. The first picture of the local organization of the sect comes from an 1863 record of ritual donations to the annual Heaven and Earth festival of Dizang (on the twentieth day of the tenth lunar month, correspondent to the Lower Primordial).[36] This record, a 1.5-meter-long piece of cloth painted to resemble a stone inscription, is still displayed at important Heaven and Earth Sect functions and confirms the participation of a few widely scattered villages.

Table 7.1   Village Contributions to the Lower Primordial Festival of the Heaven and Earth Teaching, Second Year of the Tongzhi Reign (1863) and circa 1915[a]

Village	Number of Contributors
1863	
Tu Family Village (Rear Camp)	72
White Yang Bridge	50
You Family Village (You Village)	14
Zhifangtou	12
Five other villages	15
Circa 1915	
[Little] White Yang Bridge	104
Tu Family Camp (Rear Camp)	63
You Family Village	46
Yang Family Camp (Yang Camp)	29
White Horse Village	16
Quan Camp	12
Other	4

[a]No date is given for this second record, but, based on the names of the contributors, many of whom were ancestors of interview subjects, it can be placed during the first years of the Republic.

A second record of the same festival, dating from the 1910s, shows remarkable continuity with that from 1863, which demonstrates that, during this time, the internal organization of the Heaven and Earth Sect in the area changed relatively little. Indeed, even that change is largely illusory. The participation of Zhifangtou, a minor contributor in 1863, was probably nominally subsumed under that of its larger neighbor, Rear Camp, in the second scroll. The most significant change is the addition of the two adjacent villages of Yang Camp and Quan Camp in the latter scroll. Yang Camp, however, is known to have had five generations of the Heaven and Earth Sect teachers, taking the history of the sect in that village back to the late nineteenth century. Its immediate neighbor of Quan Camp was also probably brought into the sect at this time. Thus, the few villages that supported the Heaven and Earth Sect in the 1940s had already done so for at least fifty years, or, in the case of Rear Camp, nearly two centuries earlier.

The scriptural tradition of the Heaven and Earth Sect not only describes the local propagation of the teaching, but has also shaped it. Within Cang County, the Heaven and Earth Sect has no written scriptures—all are transmitted orally from teacher to disciple. This custom is not universal. Early nineteenth-century sources concerning the sect in Shandong do speak of unwritten scriptures *(wuzi jing)* but also mention the copying and propagation of standard written texts, such as the *Scripture of the Ten Kings*.[37] Devotees in Tianjin do have written copies of Heaven and Earth scriptures, including the *Great Scripture (Da jing)*, *Heart Scripture (Xin jing)*, *Root Scripture (Genben jing)*, *Book of Vows (Liaoyuan jing)*, and *Great and Bright Ten Character Buddhist Scripture (Da ming shizi fo jing)*. In Cang County, these same texts are used, although the teaching has no record or memory of their have existed in written form. This explains how the teaching largely escaped the scrutiny of Qing investigators such as Huang Yübian. Neither memorials presenting intelligence on the sect nor the *Detailed Argument against Heterodox Religions* makes mention of these texts.[38] Certainly, this lack of written texts helped the teaching to maintain a low profile in the face of concerted antisectarian purges.

The reliance on orally recited scriptures restricted the spread of the Heaven and Earth Sect within Cang County to nearby villages, but also gave the teaching particularly deep roots within a limited number of communities. The task of committing the entire scriptural tradition of the teaching to memory, as well as the music and rituals that accompany these scriptures when chanted, can take more than ten years and places demands on novice specialists. Like those of the Teaching of the Most Supreme, rituals of the Heaven and Earth Sect require a core of at least ten such specialists, making it very difficult for the teaching to take root within a new community. Once established, however, the teaching remained tenaciously anchored within these few villages. The time, effort, and devotion required to become a specialist of the Heaven and Earth Sect was well known and reflected in the respect shown them by fellow villagers. In addition, because specialists not only learned the ritual forms of the teaching, but also mastered the content of its scripture, they developed a strong sense of its own history and identity. In striking contrast to those of the larger but less-organized Teaching of the Most Supreme, which had no scriptural tradition of its own, any specialist of the Heaven and Earth Sect could speak in great detail about the founding of the teaching and its spread north by Ma Kaishan as well as about the doctrines of the teaching itself.

Like the Teaching of the Most Supreme, the primary activities of the Heaven and Earth Sect were the performance of a number of public and private rituals. The largest of them were the three yearly ceremonies (the Upper, Middle and Lower Primordials) and occasional pubic rituals that attracted onlookers and devotees from within the village and neighboring communities. Although the 1813 memorial describes the teaching in terms of individual activities, such as healing and the ritual of lighting one stick of incense and kneeling three times per day, it is silent on the more organized activities of the sect. One of these, the Upper Primordial Festival (held on the fifteenth day of the first lunar month) is described in a passage from the 1933 Cang County gazetteer:

> On the last day of the year . . . peasants go to the entrance of the village to "invite the spirits" *(qing shen)*. They place a stick of incense upright in a small pile of dirt, light firecrackers, and sacrifice, but do not *ketou*. They light the incense, carry it back, and put it into a burner. Then they choose an appropriate place in the village . . . make a ring out of stalks of sorghum, place the incense burner in the middle, and burn a yellow paper tablet *(paiwei)*, on which are written the characters "great teacher" *(da shi)*. This is called the Heaven and Earth Tent. They take a few dozen fried snacks *(youtiao* —to be distributed to children later) and hang them in the tent. At sunset, they play cymbals and drums and light lanterns.[39]

Attrition and Entrenchment, 1949–1976

This sketch of the Most Supreme and Heaven and Earth Teachings before 1949 reveals the importance of these two groups to religious life, not only to the devotees themselves or to the villages that supported them, but to neighboring villages as well. Nevertheless, such groups still only organized on a relatively small scale. Although they might travel to neighboring communities or occasionally organize extravillage activities, in general, they did not travel beyond the local marketing town and so kept a comfortably low profile. Thus, although they and all sectarian teachings had been officially outlawed for hundreds of years, in practice neither of these two teachings ever developed into much of a concern to the state and they were allowed to quietly remain active.

This changed dramatically after 1949, when the People's Republic brought its social policies to bear on village society, the first sweeping religious campaign being that against the Way of Penetrating Unity in 1951. As discussed in the previous chapter, this campaign demonstrated both the resolve and ability of the new government to enforce its social program against unauthorized religious organizations, as well as the direction that policy would take. Although many accepted the charges of treason, fraud, theft, and rape levied against the Way of Penetrating Unity at face value, others suspected that these had been exaggerated for political purposes. Despite such skepticism, the Way of Penetrating Unity was still an alien teaching without deep roots. Even in light of the degree of misgiving that some might have felt about the campaign levied against it, the teaching was easy to jettison once the conditions that had fomented its spectacular rise had passed, and, indeed, many were happy to see the teaching eradicated.

This was not the case with the Most Supreme and Heaven and Earth Teachings. Not only did each of these two have a long history within the villages of Cang County, but their leaders were respected and their ritual services considered vital to village welfare. In contrast to the Way of Penetrating Unity, it would be hard to charge either sect as being in any way exploitative. Neither accepted payment for their many ritual services, and there were few who did not at one point been the beneficiary of these services, be they the healing or funeral rites held for a relative or simply the general feeling of well-being and protection that the ritual occasions of the sect offered the community. This alone was certainly not enough to ensure the survival of the Most Supreme or Heaven and Earth Sects; after all, many formerly respected villagers came to suddenly find themselves in hot water during the various mass campaigns of the 1950s and 1960s. Nevertheless, neither villagers nor cadres could equate these two teachings with the Way of Penetrating Unity simply by virtue of their common sectarian heritage.

By all accounts, the eradication of the Most Supreme and the Heaven and Earth Sects was never a priority for rural or higher level cadres, as had been the campaign against the Way of Penetrating Unity. Instead, throughout the first two decades of the People's Republic, local cadres concerned themselves with suppressing the external manifestations of belief, in particular village ritual activities. Rituals performed by the Most Supreme and Heaven and Earth Sects were condemned as backward "superstition" *(mixin)*, but the groups themselves were never labeled as "reactionary" *(fandong,* as had been the Way of Penetrating Unity), a charge that would have necessitated their eradication. Instead, hope remained that an awakened populace would willingly shed these customs on their own (as they had those of the Li Sect), but there was no immediate need to root them out. In any case, the strength of these groups in the villages clearly showed the difficulty of forcing them to do so.

Increasing Pressure, 1949–1966

The intensity and depth of the 1951 campaign, which promised to be the first wave of a more sweeping social revolution, portended a new, uncertain era for local religious groups. To be sure, groups such as the Most Supreme and Heaven and Earth Sects were not necessarily antagonistic to the Communists. Many sectarian leaders in these villages had fought the Japanese as members of the Eighth Route Army, and many sectarian strongholds, such as Yang Camp, had taken on immense risks by storing grain and supplies for guerrilla troops. Local cadres were careful not to undermine this base of support by attacking venerable village institutions such as the Most Supreme or Heaven and Earth Sects. Instead, they were quick to isolate the Way of Penetrating Unity, distancing it from other popular religion, even encouraging other religious groups to take a stand against the teaching.[40]

Nevertheless, many sectarian leaders began to sense that the tide had turned against them. Although they still enjoyed relative freedom to pursue their ritual activities, village contingents of the Most Supreme and Heaven and Earth Teachings had already witnessed the sudden and intense movement against the Way of Penetrating Unity, and some feared that the winds of political favor could just as easily turn against them. Such fears were further compounded with similar examples from the various social campaigns of the next fifteen years. As the countryside passed through the restructuring of Land Reform and the Great Leap Forward (1958–1960), intense pressure was placed on village society to root out old customs and thinking. Even if these sects had no overt political ideology, their thought was considered to be backward at best and reactionary at worst, and most began to fear that they would eventually fall victim to the growing tide of "socialist education" and restructuring. Such fears were compounded during the late 1950s, which brought news of conflict between the government and the Heaven and Earth Teaching in Shandong and especially the arrest and execution of sectarian leaders in its birthplace of Dong Family Grove.[41]

As this pressure became more tangible, both the Most Supreme and Heaven and Earth Sects began a gradual retreat from public life. The first casualties of the period were the large, extravillage festivals, such as the annual Teaching of the Most Supreme festivals held in Hai Dock and Zhao-Guan Camp. Many of these large-scale festivals had already been interrupted by the chaos of the previous two decades and had only just recovered during the latter half of the 1940s, whereas others never recovered at all under the new regime. The Teaching of the Most Supreme festival held in the Balang temple of Zhao-Guan Camp reached a highpoint during the 1920s and early 1930s but ceased throughout the Japanese occupation and Civil War period. After a short-lived attempt to revive the festival immediately following the establishment of the People's Republic, it was abandoned permanently during the early 1950s. Extravillage festivals of the Heaven and Earth Sect, such as the Upper Primordial rituals, were still held, although they began to decrease in scope (both number of participants and scale of ritual activity) over the course of the first decade after the revolution.

The decline in large-scale sectarian activity reflected a kind of self-censorship in the face of increasing political and social scrutiny. Considering the uncertainty of the times, religious leaders sought to retain a low profile, particularly outside their home villages. The rhetoric of the campaign against the Way of Penetrating Unity had stressed the unethical methods that the sect had allegedly employed to gain a mass following, implying that the crime was not one of improper belief, but rather the use of religion to defraud the masses. In the face of these charges, the Heaven and Earth Teaching in Yang Camp attempted to impress its orthodoxy and loyalty to the new People's state by altering its traditional five-character tablet, replacing the "feudal" obligation to the ruler (jun) with one to the people (min).[42] The more common response for both the Most Supreme and Heaven and Earth Sects was to voluntarily curtail their most public and visible activities in the hope that doing so would avert the charge that they were corrupting public morals or using their religious teaching to exploit the masses. Both teachings thus reached an unspoken truce with rural cadres, which would continue until the outset of the Cultural Revolution. Later campaigns against social ills in 1955 and 1957, which usually included a revived movement against former Way of Penetrating Unity members, still never reached the Most Supreme or Heaven and Earth Teachings in Cang County.

Even at this early stage, however, village sectarians did face very real pressure. During the summer of 1953, a small group of cadres visited Quan-Wang Village, just as the village contingent of Most Supreme sectarians was in the middle of the Prayer for Rain ceremony.[43] The cadres declared the activities "not revolutionary" (bu geming) and confiscated the ritual objects of the group, including musical instruments, costumes, and flags.[44] Within a few weeks, these objects were returned through the intercession of an influential friend of the village head, but the impression had been made. Local tradition, related to me by sectarians and unaffiliated villagers alike, holds that this particular village was spared any further intrusion by an instance of divine intervention. After this incident, overzealous cadres were kept at a distance by a miasma that confounded the road to the village, preventing unwelcome visitors from finding it. Such a belief itself anticipates the increasingly strained relations between the village and local government on the question of religious practice.

Overt government pressure aside, the increasingly antireligious sentiment of the time, combined with the new economic realities of collectivization, further weakened the draw of the Most Supreme and Heaven and Earth Sects in village life. By the mid-1960s, a new generation had grown up almost entirely under the People's Republic, and the realities of the social revolution of the new government pervaded every aspect of life. To be sure, no amount of political education could obviate religious specialists. Beyond ideology, as long as "life and death" matters remain unsolvable, religious customs will exist to address them. Moreover, villages still felt a strong sense of pride and well-being while their sectarian group remained active. Villagers continued to respect specialists for their moral fiber and personal devotion, in many cases as much to the goal of socialist reconstruction as to the sacred.

Such conditions are not absolute, however, and over time, in certain villages in which the sectarian culture had been weakened, perhaps through the natural death of a number of senior specialists, the teaching slowly began to die out. In Hai Dock, once a local center of the Teaching of the Most Supreme, the older generation of leaders was not followed by enough novices to continue the teaching. By 1960, too few specialists remained for the village to conduct rituals without help from neighboring communities. The diminished presence of the teaching within the village further accelerated the social decline of the Teaching of the Most Supreme; by the mid-1960s, the teaching was abandoned and the Scripture Chest was put into indefinite storage in the corner of a barn. It is no surprise that this phenomenon was more pronounced in the large number of Teaching of the Most Supreme villages than in the small but tightly knit group of Heaven and Earth Sect villages.

Cultural Revolution, 1966–1976

The years of and following the Cultural Revolution saw the nearly complete cessation of all forms of religious expression throughout China, including Cang County. The Most Supreme and Heaven and Earth Teachings, by this point the only two surviving sects in this area, were forced completely underground and were unable to perform any sort of public ceremonials within their own villages. Even funerals, the most important ritual events in rural religious practice, were reduced to simple, atheistic ceremonies.

The strict social policies of this period were enforced by groups of Red Guards, who maintained a strong and visible presence within peasant villages. Among the Red Guards themselves, an important division separated those who visited the village in from the outside, usually the nearby town of Dulin or the city of Cangzhou, and the peasant Red Guards recruited from and operating within their home communities. Those Red Guards who visited the villages from the town or city tended to be the more ideologically motivated, but less informed about conditions inside the village.[45] In general, the activities of these groups were restricted to the surface accouterments of religion: smashing statues, pulling down any remaining ruins of temples, overturning graves and markers, and occasionally subjecting very high-profile religious specialists, such as former members of the Way of Penetrating Unity, to political struggle sessions. Red Guards from within the village, to be sure, were also highly motivated ideologically. Like their urban or semiurban counterparts, they engaged in political struggle against landlords, chanted slogans, and fervently studied Maoist thought. In this area at least, however, they did not target the teachings of the Most Supreme or Heaven and Earth within their own villages, nor did they go out of their way to reveal the existence of these groups to outsiders. Apparently, even Red Guards were still members of village society and retained personal respect for the knowledge and conduct of sectarian specialists. Convinced that these groups had stopped their activities and changed their superstitious ways, both village and outside Red Guards were content to let them be.[46] Despite the extreme political fervor of the time, there was never an organized purge of either group in rural Cang County.

Nevertheless, during the ten years of the Cultural Revolution, the public activities of these two sects ceased completely. The largest regular activity, the Upper Primordial ritual, was replaced by a staged New Year rally of "art for the masses" (qunzhong yishu) featuring songs praising Mao Zedong, local Hebei opera (Hebei bangzi), which had been rewritten along revolutionary lines, and patriotic speeches. Even then, some Heaven and Earth groups, such as those in Yang Camp and Rear Camp, did manage to perform a smaller version of the ceremony (xiaoban, literally "doing it small"), which consisted of two or three specialists gathering to whisper the scriptures of the teaching before a small paper altar that was then burned in the family stove. These exceptions, however, were rare. All other annual and occasional ceremonies were completely discontinued. Of all of ceremonies, those most sorely missed were funerals, the most profound expression of piety and gratitude toward a deceased relative. Despite the passage of some thirty years, many of my informants wept bitterly as they recalled the shame and horror of having buried a parent with no ceremony, or even a proper burial—because Cang County did not yet have a crematorium, bodies were often interred in "scientific" mass graves outside the village.[47]

The interruption of sectarian ritual during this period not only frustrated the ritual needs of ordinary and sectarian peasants alike, but also diminished the place of these groups in the public life of the village and, further, disrupted the transmission of knowledge from senior specialists to young novices. The place of sectarian groups within the village, their knowledge of the sacred, their piety, and the respect that they receive from other peasants all relied on a public forum for their expression. Without such a forum, the importance of the sectarian teaching to the community was not impressed upon the younger generation, further reducing the number of young recruits who were sufficiently committed to the teaching to train as ritual specialists. Moreover, the ten-year process of training a novice specialist itself takes place in the context of an active ritual life. Thus, although these teachings were never subjected to an active purge, the effects of this decade-long hiatus reached beyond the years of the Cultural Revolution itself and shaped the revival of sectarian groups during the 1980s.

Guarded Renaissance after 1977

The arrest of the Gang of Four marked the end of a decade of political and social chaos and the beginning of a period of painful but optimistic reform. With a perceptible change in central policy, many members of the Most Supreme and the Heaven and Earth Teachings sought to revive and continue their earlier religious practices. In light of the ritual hiatus of the previous ten years, however, each faced great difficulty reviving even in the freer political climate of the late 1970s and 1980s, the main impediment being replacing of the members lost to sickness or age during the previous fifteen years.

At the end of the 1970s, many village groups of the Teaching of the Most Supreme and Heaven and Earth Teaching were eager to begin revival but lacked either a strong leader (*dangjia*, the same term used by the Li Sect), peripheral ritual specialists, or both. When interest in reviving the group was strong, the problems that the sect faced were logistic: how to train a new leader or the requisite number of specialists. A more difficult case arose when the village in general, or even the former specialists themselves, had simply lost interest in reviving the sect. With the Teaching of the Most Supreme, this was the case in a number of villages, such as Hai Dock, which had voluntarily abandoned the teaching just before the beginning of the Cultural Revolution and felt no impetus to revive it. Differences between the tightly knit Heaven and Earth Teaching and loosely organized Teaching of the Most Supreme villages became especially pronounced during this period of sectarian revival. Unlike the Teaching of the Most Supreme, the Heaven and Earth Sect retained strong roots in village society and close ties between villages and thus revived in each of the four communities that had supported the teaching in 1949.

Sectarian Networks

Both before and after their revival, the Most Supreme and Heaven and Earth Teachings remained organizationally based around the village; however, the extravillage relations of each sect have developed along notably different lines since 1977. Before 1949, villages with the Teaching of the Most Supreme occasionally cooperated in the performance of ritual functions to strengthen customary networks. Since 1977, this has often become a matter of necessity, rather than choice. Even with the need to combine resources in order to perform ritual functions, there is no formal relationship among villages of each chest or the teaching as a whole. Individual villages maintain a sense of their own sectarian history, but the self-conscious identity of the Teaching of the Most Supreme as a distinct teaching is very weak. In contrast, each of the four villages with the Heaven and Earth Sect revived their teaching with a remarkable tenacity and clearly evident sense of purpose. Beginning in the late 1970s, these villages shared both physical and human resources to help each community revive the sect. The difference between the two teachings is also evident in their extended ritual networks. Even when they pool resources, specialists of the Teaching of the Most Supreme generally perform activities close to home, rarely straying more than five kilometers. In contrast, Heaven and Earth groups will travel within a much larger radius, further demonstrating the extended personal and devotional networks of the sect.

The Teaching of the Most Supreme: Limited Networks and Commercialization

Before 1949, villages of each chest of the Teaching of the Most Supreme formed cooperative clusters, cemented by ties of friendship, reciprocity, and custom. With the weakening of its organization in the post–Cultural Revolution revival, however, such clustering in the Teaching of the Most Supreme has in many cases changed from a courtesy to a necessity. This is most evident in the need for villages to band together to assemble the number of ritual specialists needed to chant scriptures. Villages such as Guo-Bu Village or Qian-Hai Camp, which had once supported independent contingents of specialists, can now organize rituals only with the help of a village in which the teaching remains active, usually Quan-Wang Village. In the former two cases, the teaching is no longer truly a village sect. Although villagers do continue to enjoy the benefits of affiliation with the Teaching of the Most Supreme (such as preference in the planning of ritual activities), the ritual life of the sect no longer holds a high profile in the ritual life of the community. As a result, the sect is unable to recruit young men in significant numbers to rebuild the ritual independence of the community. Within a matter of years, it is almost certain that in many of these dependent villages, the Teaching of the Most Supreme will die out completely, and villagers will be forced to turn to look elsewhere to have their ritual needs met.

Villages have proved unable to revive the Teaching of the Most Supreme for any of a number of reasons. The village of Shi Family Camp, for example, could not revive its sectarian group because the the *dangjia* had died

Table 7.2   Villages with the Teaching of the Most Supreme, 1949 and 1997

South Chest	North Chest
1949	
Wang Family Village	Ni Camp
Shi Family Camp	Zhao-Guan Camp
Zheng Camp	Ren-Xing Village
Little Terrace	Chenyu
Feng-Guan Village	Qijiawu
Tian Family Village	Guanting
Xinkailu	Chapeng
South Xiao Camp	Front White Horse Village
Hai Dock	Rear White Horse Village
Liu Dock	Wanliang si
Dulin	E Village
Chenxin Village	Zaolin
Dai-Qi Camp	Big Cheng Village
Zhang Family Camp	Little Cheng Village
Bu Village	Big Qutou
Guo-Bu Village	Little Qutou
	Yang Village
	Chongxian
	Banqiaohe
	Front Wuyuan
	Rear Wuyuan
	Taiyuan
	Mumendian
	Wotou
	Big Pangu
	Little Pangu
	Tashizhuang
	Liang-Lai Village
	Zhu-Xing Village
	Tao-Guan Camp
	Zhao-Guan Camp
	Han-Zheng Village
	Little Zhao Village
	Little Feng Village
	Xu Village
1997	
Quan-Wang Village	Ni-Yang Camp
Shi Family Camp	Zhao-Guan Camp

Table 7.2   *continued*

South Chest	North Chest
	1997
Zheng Camp[a]	Ren-Xing Village
Feng-Guan Village	Qijiawu[a]
Xinkailu	Guanting
Dulin[a]	Chapeng
Chenxin Village[a]	Front White Horse Village[a]
Dai-Qi Camp	Zaolin[a]
Zhang Family Camp[a]	Front Wuyuan
Bu Village[a]	Rear Wuyuan
Guo-Bu Village[a]	Wotou
	Big Pangu
	Little Pangu
	Liang-Lai Village
	Tao-Guan Camp
	Zhao-Guan Camp
	Xiao-Zhao Village
	Little Feng Village[a]
	Xu Village

[a]Currently unable to perform rituals independently.

during the late 1950s and no leader of comparable stature came forward following his death. With the two-decade hiatus of ritual activities, such an individual was even less likely to appear during the period of revival. Older specialists within the village still remember some of the rituals, but not enough to perform the ritual activities of the teaching. In Zheng Camp, the situation is reversed; the former *dangjia* is still alive, but the number of peripheral specialists is not sufficient to perform ceremonies. Again, this situation creates a spiral of decline. With few or no public rituals, the sect loses its place in the religious life in the village, which, in turn, is what draws new recruits into the teaching.

Within this area, the South Chest of the Teaching of the Most Supreme is now firmly anchored in only four villages: Quan-Wang Village, Feng-Guan Village, Xinkailu, and Dai-Qi Camp. Hai Dock, where Yang Guorui, the recently deceased *dangjia* of Quan-Wang Village, had studied, had been the unquestioned center of the Teaching of the Most Supreme during the 1920s and 1930s, but it fell into decline after the death of the *dangjia* in the 1950s.

Figure 7.1   A Teaching of the Most Supreme funeral in Yang Camp.

Quan-Wang Village, in contrast, rallied around the teaching under the influence of the charismatic and widely respected Yang Guorui, a situation that continues even after his death.[48] Similarly, strong centers such as Dai-Qi Camp and Zheng Camp retain close ties to Quan-Wang Village because many of their own leaders, particularly those who sought to revive the teaching after the Cultural Revolution, had trained under Yang Guorui.

   Other communities, such as Bu and Guo-Bu Villages, have revived some ritual ceremonies, but only by forming dependent clusters with larger villages, such as Quan-Wang Village. These villages retain a handful of specialists, but, like Shi Family Camp and Zheng Camp, they were unable to revive the sect as an independent ritual entity within their own communities. With no village sectarian group of their own, these specialists might act as auxiliaries for the ritual functions of larger villages or as local representatives of the sect in their own community, arranging religious activities though relying on the aid of outside specialists to perform ritual functions.

Figure 7.2
Prayer during the
Heaven and Earth
New Year festival.

The geographic scope of Teaching of the Most Supreme is visible in the ritual obligations of any single village group. Of these, the most numerically significant are funerals, for which the groups are usually contracted by a third-party referral. An analysis of funerals performed in a two-month period in late 1997 by the Teaching of the Most Supreme branch in Quan-Wang Village demonstrates how these referrals follow extant patterns of cooperation among the Teaching of the Most Supreme villages, resulting in a very busy schedule.

The Teaching of the Most Supreme has endured a gradual commercialization of its activities since the Cultural Revolution. As late as 1949, no groups within this teaching, North or South Chest, accepted money for the performance of ritual services. Over the next decade, however, all villages in the teaching began to evolve on a trajectory, some faster and some slower, that placed increasingly specific monetary demands on its clients.

The case of Xinkailu is typical. Like other villages, sectarian leaders here had originally followed the custom of refusing money even if offered, only taking part in the banquet that followed the ceremony. This first changed during Collectivization, in which the labor of the individual had to be accounted for by the production brigade. Ritual services were thus paid for (informally, naturally) by a donation of work points. In their immediate post–Cultural Revolution revival, the Teaching of the Most Supreme had begun accepting money if offered, and by the early 1980s each group charged a set sum for services. By the early 1990s, the fee was calculated at 30 *yuan* (roughly what a laborer working in Cang County might earn in a day) per specialist. According to Teaching of the Most Supreme members in Quan-Wang Village, the group in Xinkailu has even begun making specific demands for the sort of food and alcohol that they will be served following the ritual.[49] Although other villages may follow this pattern a bit more slowly, the larger picture of rapid commercialization is clear.

In the space of two months, the sectarians of this village performed a total of eleven funerals, more than one a week, if evenly spaced. Paradoxically, it is the commercialization of their activities that has allowed the sect to regain popularity. As before, when performing services for fellow villagers, the sect does not charge money and is usually contacted directly; the family or its representative approaches the *dangjia* and requests a funeral on a certain date. For deaths outside the village, however, sectarian leaders are usually contacted through an intermediary, either a fellow sectarian or a commercial funeral planner *(zongli)*. The latter organizes funerals for a set price, providing a tent, the white mourning clothes *(xiaofu)*, the banquet, and a contingent of sectarians to read scriptures at the funeral. As of the late 1990s, a large funeral, including the services of a contingent of Teaching of the Most Supreme specialists, cost a total of 600 *yuan*.[50] Because their services are commercial in nature, groups of specialists from the Teaching of the Most Supreme are easily approached, even by strangers, but their services rarely take them far from home. The farthest that the group from Quan-Wang Village had traveled recently, the village of Dai-Qi Camp, is only about five kilometers (ten *li*) away.

The Heaven and Earth Sect: Strong Tradition, Extended Networks

Compared with those of the Teaching of the Most Supreme, Heaven and Earth Sect villages have maintained stronger networks over a larger dis-

Figure 7.3   Heaven and Earth festival in Huanghua County.

tance. Villages with the Heaven and Earth Sect are few and relatively far from each other. The distance from Rear Camp to Yang Camp or White Yang Bridge is roughly thirty *li* (fifteen kilometers), a two-hour bicycle ride, just under an hour by tractor, or—to put it into the context of the 1940s—a full morning on foot.

Despite this distance, Heaven and Earth Sect villages maintain quite close relations, and all recognize Rear Camp as the center. Although most specialists in this area were trained by the *dangjia* of their own village, a significant number make the effort to go to a neighboring village to study under another *dangjia*. In the post–Cultural Revolution revival, Zheng of White Yang Bridge traveled to Rear Camp to study with Tu, with the aim of reviving the Heaven and Earth Sect in his home community. Not surprisingly, relations between these two villages remain extremely close. The other villages in the teaching also routinely cooperate to perform rituals at festivals and activities.

The strength of these customary ties is seen in the annual visit made by members of the Heaven and Earth Sect in Duliu, which is roughly 100 kilometers away, in the suburbs of Tianjin. Despite the distance between them, this group maintains very close ties with Rear Camp, the home village of Teacher Xiao, who first brought the Heaven and Earth Sect to Duliu. Representatives from Duliu return to the grave of Teacher Xiao every year on his birthday and on the anniversary of his death. In addition, they participate in the Dizang Bodhisattva activities held in White Yang Bridge (the same festival as that recorded in table 7.1), often staying for the entire three days. After the festival, a contingent from Rear Camp will travel to Duliu to attend its festival, which is held five days later. Finally, and perhaps most significantly, a portion of new specialists from Duliu (roughly one per year) train under the *dangjia* of the Cang County area, especially Tu of Rear Camp.

The wide but tight network of relations among villages of the Heaven and Earth Sect ensures that the specialists of any one village will travel much more than those of the Teaching of the Most Supreme. As is the case with the Teaching of the Most Supreme, the Heaven and Earth Sect performs most of its funerals within a relatively close radius, the majority being within Yang Camp itself and the neighboring village of Little Terrace.

Table 7.3   Funerals Performed by the Most Supreme and Heaven
and Earth Teachings

Location of Funeral	Number Performed	In Conjunction with Villages	Distance from Village/Camp (km)
Teaching of the Most Supreme, Quan-Wang Village, October–November 1997			
Quan-Wang Village	1	None	...
Shi Family Camp	5	Shi Family Camp	1+
Qian-Hai Camp	1	Shi Family Camp	3
Zhang Family Camp	1	Guo-Bu Village,	3
Dai-Qi Camp	2	Dai-Qi Camp	5
Dulin	1	Dulin	2
Heaven and Earth Teaching, Yang Camp, 1990–1998			
Yang Camp	15	Most Supreme, North	...
Little Terrace	>10	Most Supreme, South	1
Chapeng	3	Most Supreme, North	1+
Qian-Hai Camp	3	Most Supreme, South	4
Hai Dock	2	Most Supreme, South	3
Liulaitang	2	Most Supreme, North	6
Xiao-Jin Village (in Cangzhou City)	1		14
Rear Camp	3	Heaven and Earth Sect	8
White Yang Bridge	1	Heaven and Earth Sect	13
Dulin	2	Most Supreme, South	1

Source: Interviews in Quan-Wang Village and Ni-Yang Camp, November–December 1997.

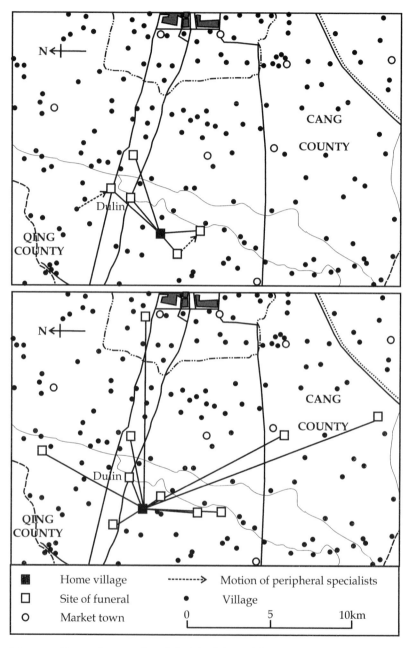

Map 7.1 Funeral networks of the Teaching of the Most Supreme as viewed from Quan-Wang Village *(top)* and of the Heaven and Earth Teaching as viewed from Yang Camp *(bottom)*.

Conversely, the most distant funerals are in those villages with which the sect has the closet relationship. The farthest that the Teaching of the Most Supreme *daoye* from Quan-Wang Village traveled was to Dai-Qi Camp, about five kilometers away, and then because of a special tie between those two villages. A similar situation exists with the Heaven and Earth Sect, with the relationships being geographically more distant and cooperation more close.

The ritual functions of the Heaven and Earth Sect cover an extremely large radius and often involve the cooperation of one or more villages. Unlike the temple festivals of Hai Dock and Zheng Family Camp, former showcases of cooperation within the Teaching of the Most Supreme, the Heaven and Earth Sects continue to organize on the larger scale. Locally, the largest event is the Dizang festival, held in White Yang Bridge on the twentieth day of the tenth lunar month. This festival is attended by each of the Heaven and Earth Sect villages in the area and is vital to maintaining the networks of cooperation as well as the orthodoxy of teaching and ritual among these villages. These ties are particularly clear in the special relationship between Rear Camp village and the town of Duliu, separated by nearly 100 kilometers (which, as of the late 1990s, was traversed in an open-bed truck). Despite the great distance between them, these villages continue to maintain close ritual and affective ties.

Unlike the Teaching of the Most Supreme, the Heaven and Earth Sect has remained completely uncommercialized, giving it a special relationship with the village but also reducing the number of outsiders who request its services. Not only are funeral services uncompensated, but Heaven and Earth specialists are further obliged to perform such rituals for anyone who asks—*you qiu bi ying,* literally "any request must be answered," a phrase also seen in temples to praise the benevolence of particular deities. In contrast, the Teaching of the Most Supreme may refuse a ritual request. This has had the effect of limiting the number of funerals that the Heaven and Earth Sect specialists perform—particularly outside of their own villages. Unlike the specialists from Teaching of the Most Supreme of Quan-Wang Village, who perform an average of one funeral per week, the Heaven and Earth Sect of Yang Camp does so only about once every ten weeks. The reason is that, because the Heaven and Earth Sect are not compensated their ritual services, those from outside the village or who do not have a close relationship with a specialist are reluctant to approach them with such a request. Instead, most will take their request to the Teaching of the Most Supreme, preferring the straightforward exchange of ritual services for cash.

This further shapes the local reputation of the Heaven and Earth Sect and is indicative of the role that organized religious groups can play in the moral landscape of Chinese villages. A peasant in Dulin, with no ties with the teaching, spoke with admiration of a recent instance when the Heaven and Earth Sect group of Rear Camp performed a full-day funeral for an old woman in a neighboring village. To do so, the ten sectarians had to leave their recently harvested crop in the rain for one day—leading to serious economic losses for each of the specialists. Such news circulates widely in local society and acts as a magnet to draw like-minded peasants into the teaching.

Not only was the Heaven and Earth Sect able to recreate its local networks over the course of the 1990s, but it even began to expand beyond its pre-1949 boundaries. This is in part a result of improvements in the transportation infrastructure, which allow members greater physical mobility than ever before. At the beginning of the decade, the *dangjia* of Rear Camp Village made a personal pilgrimage to the Shandong village Dong Family Grove, the birthplace of Dong Sihai located approximately 100 kilometers to the south. Since the mid-1990s, members of the sect from White Yang Bridge and Rear Camp Villages travel together to participate in a sectarian temple festival in neighboring Huanghua County. This trip takes about two hours in open-bed truck and arrives at a scene reminiscent of the festival held by the Teaching of the Most Supreme in pre-1949 Balang Temple, with village-based groups of Heaven and Earth Sectarians each chanting scriptures and performing sacrifices in a fog of incense smoke and a sea of some 40,000 faithful. Because of the distances involved, this sort of travel was simply not feasible for all but the most devoted before the expansion of the transportation infrastructure that began in the 1970s.

Conclusion

Of the sectarian groups that have arisen in Cang County over the nineteenth and twentieth centuries, only the two that are the subject of this chapter remain active. It is clear that the tenacity of these two groups is a result of their importance to the enduring concerns of everyday religion and to their role in village society. Here, the contrast with the experience of the Way of Penetrating Unity could not be greater. Not only did the apocalyptic predictions of the Way of Penetrating Unity thrive in an atmosphere of panic and dismay, but the group itself was perceived as a foreign network that divided village society. Indeed, after the commencement of the 1951 Suppress the Counterrevolutionaries campaign, the existence of the Way of Penetrating Unity in a village represented a tangible threat to the community. In contrast, although both the Teaching of the Most Supreme and the Heaven and Earth Teaching are organized around a discrete group of ritual specialists, the religious needs that they address are more common to everyday life, and the benefits extend to the entire community, in terms of either general spiritual protection afforded the village or the preferential treatment given fellow villagers in the performance of individual ritual functions. In addition to their ritual efficacy, and despite centuries of propaganda portraying sectarians as superstitious and seditious, these groups represent a relative orthodoxy in the village. Other forms of power, including that of local cadres, build upon this orthodoxy in the exercise of their own moral authority.

Village sectarians represent another aspect of the interaction between institutional religion and local society. Unlike local incarnations of the Li Sect or monastic Buddhism, these sects are largely self-referential. The local incarnation of the sect cannot be simply written off as a misunderstanding of a more sophisticated urban tradition. Like the Way of Penetrating Unity, the local life of the Most Supreme and Heaven and Earth Teachings is independent of the national organization. In the case of the Way of Penetrating Unity, however, this autonomy is based on the ability of local leadership structures to claim the authority of the sacred through spirit-writing séances, whereas that of the Most Supreme and Heaven and Earth Teachings is a function of the organizational tradition and, more fundamentally, the spiritual goals of the sect. Like the Primordial Chaos teaching of Hu Er Yinjin, the Most Supreme and Heaven and Earth Teachings in Cang County operate on a very small and realistic scale. Their moral influence and spiritual efficacy are not trained on the world or the nation, but rather on the locality and, specifically, on the village. As such, local concerns and history are freely incorporated into the life of each sect. This process is seen in the characteristic organization of the Teaching of the Most Supreme into chests and in the inclusion of the local genealogy of the Heaven and Earth Teaching, from the *kan* trigram of Ma Kaishan through fourteen generations of *dangjia* in Rear Camp Village, in the canon of sectarian scriptures. Far from a misunderstanding of a larger tradition, village sectarians have the authority to reproduce and alter it.

回 Conclusion

Cang County and Chinese Religion

Rather than attempting to reduce the changes in the local religion of Cang County to a single story, this study has sought to demonstrate their inherent complexity. The root of this complexity is not merely the diverse mosaic of actors and institutions involved, but also the degree of latitude enjoyed by the individual in the perception of and interaction with them. To be sure, certain long-term trends, such as the increasing ability of the state to exert influence over local society and ecclesiastical institutions, played an undeniable role in the shaping of local religion. Nevertheless, both the forces of historical change and the intellectual contribution of religious teachings and traditions were transformed as they passed through various filters, the cultural filters of local and village society and, ultimately, the cognitive filter of individual religious consciousness. With this in mind, let us briefly revisit some of the issues raised at the outset of this study.

Local Religion and the State

Central and local authorities have always been keen to monitor the religious activities of village society, and such scrutiny reached its peak during the first three decades of the People's Republic. Before this period, official desire to police local religion exceeded its ability to do so, and, since the late 1970s, the reverse may be true. To a large degree, the degree of scrutiny depends on the proclivities of local officials, but the overall trend is unmistakably a retreat from the extreme rhetoric and policies of the Cultural Revolution and perhaps the recognition that some amount of religion is inevitable and maybe even desirable for the stability of local society.

It is tempting to compare the religious policies of the post–Deng Xiaoping People's Republic to those of the late Qing dynasty. Both allowed local religion a degree of autonomy and were concerned primarily with the preventative isolation of heterodox religious groups, sectarians in the former instance and groups such as Falungong and underground Christian churches in the latter. In terms of positive ideology, both proclaimed a religious and cultural orthodoxy, complete with its symbols, rituals, and (less frequently) texts, which acted as the social capital of local society. Like any commodity, the social capital of the religious orthodoxy was only as valuable as it was a scarce—hence the desire of certain parties to appeal to and dominate it.

The local economy of orthodoxy is hardly within the grasp of the state, however, and local actors appeal to religious sensibilities in many different ways. This fluidity is perhaps best seen in groups such as the Heaven and Earth Teaching and its relationship other religious actors. In villages such as Rear Camp, the Heaven and Earth Teaching presents itself very much as the voice of orthodoxy, from its strong Confucian (and Communist) rhetoric and uncompromising stance toward demonic spirits to their open dislike for groups such as the Way of Penetrating Unity and, more recently, Falungong. Most villagers respond in kind, regarding the teaching with a great deal of respect, despite the fact that, strictly speaking, the teaching is illegal and has been frequently the target of antisectarian campaigns. Even with the entirely unprecedented reach of the state into village society, orthodoxy remains largely in the eye of the beholder.

The Geography of Local Religion

Like state power and orthodoxy, culture is not simply forced upon local society, but actively recreated by it. This is very much true in the case of religious belief and organization. On the one hand, the strongly functionalist attitude that most devotees have toward the sacred demands confirmation of the immediacy of divine action and efficacy, in particular through the medium of miracle tales. In the case of *xiangtou,* such tales engage a larger tradition of knowledge about sickness and healing by reconstituting it within the context of "real world" of the peasant, that is, from the present day and within the immediate vicinity. Within the sphere of local society, the flow of information connects all points, carried not only by men going to and from the market town, but also by wives returning to their natal homes, goat herders meeting on the road, and children visiting festivals in neighboring communities.

On the other hand, patterns of religious organization have a similar "localizing" effect on religious institutions. This is evident in each of the teachings presented in this study. Its limited resurgence since the 1980s aside, monastic Buddhism was the largest yet ecclesiastically weakest of the teachings. Despite, or perhaps because of, its long history in Cang County, rural monasteries were only vaguely distinguishable from other temples, and the specialized textual and ritual tradition of a self-consciously distinct Buddhism was a distant memory. Even if most peasants had only a vague idea of where the boundaries of the Buddhist institution stopped, however, the teaching and its specialists maintained as important a role in the economy of religious knowledge and services as did the locally distinct incarnations of Islam studied by Clifford Geertz in Indonesia.[1]

Nor is localization the fate of only very old religions. The Li Sect and Way of Penetrating Unity, each of which rode to Cangzhou on a wave of national popularity, were accepted into local society only as much as they were transformed by it. The former never developed a large following, representing as it did a public declaration of temperance, and added little to the world of local religion beyond a handful of nominal markers of its identity. At first glance, the Way of Penetrating Unity would seem to represent imposition of a powerful religious institution onto local society, especially considering the speed with which the teaching spread through North China. The speed of its collapse, however, reveals that the teaching did not conquer North China as much as its apocalyptic vision gave voice to the mass desperation of the war years. Even the two teachings that did take deep root, the Most Supreme and Heaven and Earth Teachings, did so at the expense of their extralocal ties. Of the two, only the Heaven and Earth Teaching has retained any idea of its history outside the area and, until the 1990s, little contact with branches farther than a day's walk from home.

The second arena of significance is the village itself. Despite the free flow of information and culture within local society, each village maintains a degree of distinction in the shape of its religious life owing to both the concentration of religious resources and religious knowledge within the village and the importance of individuation to village identity. Ritual activities within the village thus revolve around local religious resources, while the lore surrounding them shapes perception of the sacred realm and its actors. Thus, in the village of Hai Dock, with its Guanyin temple, individual prayers, public rituals, and miracle tales focus largely upon the large statue of Guanyin. In contrast, those in communities such as Yang Camp center on the morality, traditions, and rituals of village sectarians.

Passive versus Active Religiosity

The public religious life of the village was an important arena in which the floating culture of tales and stories was made into a concrete regimen of rituals and locus of identity, but this did not coerce the participation of the individual in a way similar to the Christianity of early modern Europe. To the extent that the village had a common political or economic fate (which was increasingly true from the late Qing onward, but had always been so in the case of natural and manmade disasters such as drought or bandits), it often addressed the sacred as a community. In terms of village ritual practice, though, most members of the community remained passive beneficiaries. All that was demanded of them was a financial contribution, because the ritual acts themselves were performed by a small core of specialists on behalf of the community. As a political entity, the village could police the lives of its members to some degree by keeping out unwanted influences, such as certain sectarian groups. Because the disparity of engagement with the sacred within the community was a matter of individual piety, however, the religious life of the individual was by no means merely a function of village society.

Rather, the degree and manner in which the individual engages the sacred in a votive or ritual setting is largely a personal decision. Within any community, certain households will be far more devout than others, and, even within the household, individual members often display a great deal of disparity in their attitude toward religious devotion, especially across generations. Now in his sixties, Yao Gui has been the head of the Heaven and Earth Sect in Yang Camp for three decades. In contrast, his adult son expresses public ambivalence and private contempt for the activities of the sect. Perhaps more typical is the reaction of the elder Yao's daughter-in-law, Wang Chun. Since her marriage to the younger Yao ten years prior, she has attended numerous rituals of the Heaven and Earth Sect, as well as those of the Teaching of the Most Supreme in neighboring Quan-Wang Village. Despite her proximity to the teaching, Wang understands very little of its ritual practice and none of the chanted scriptures, although she can distinguish scriptures of the Heaven and Earth Teaching from those of the Most Supreme based on the sound of the accompanying music.

Nor is there a necessary impetus for her to develop a deep personal understanding of the sect or the sacred. In contrast to Pauline Christianity, in which the individual is always in intimate contact with the sacred, the logic of popular theology places only minimal emphasis on belief and understanding. The root of Christian devotion charges the individual with a debt to the sacred that can never be repaid, thus demanding constant penance and worship with no promise of earthly reciprocity, but the greater mission of coming to know God through suffering and obedience. In theological terms, the individual must remain constantly engaged with the sacred, and falling into religious passivity becomes a lapse of faith and reneging on the devotion owed to God. As such, the practicality of popular worship frustrated Christian missionaries, such as the late-nineteenth-century Hampton DuBose, who characterized it as "[lacking] all of the elements of true devotion" with "nothing like deep moral earnestness and solemnity."[2] Perhaps because the comparison to Christianity is unavoidable for most Western readers, scholars such as Wing-tsit Chan, Clarence Day, C. K. Yang, and Poo Mu-chou have placed great emphasis on the intense worldliness of Chinese popular belief. Such ideas return us to the debate between orthodoxy and orthopraxy, and James Watson's assertion that the correct performance of ritual, rather than belief or consciousness, is the main priority of popular religiosity.

In the villages of Cang County, however, even the *ritual* regimen of the individual is policed to only a very minimal degree. What few rituals are socially and theologically required are those associated with death, such as funeral rites and maintenance of the gravesite. These rituals placate the soul of the deceased, not only preventing it from returning and wreaking vengeance on the living, but also upholding a general level of morality and filial piety. Most other aspects of religious and ritual life do not immediately affect spiritual or moral well-being of the community and are thus matters of personal choice. Even in communal rituals, such as prayers for rain, the ritual participation of most individuals is superfluous. Instead, the efficacy of the ritual comes from the actions of a small core of specialists.

In terms of both belief and ritual action, a distinction must thus be made between active and passive religiosity. The former draws the individual into participation in a ritual setting or religious act, whereas the latter involves the individual doing nothing offensive to the sacred but does not draw him or her to become actively engaged with it. Of course, in any religious tradition, most individuals will have a primarily passive relationship with the sacred. Few have the time, luxury, or interest to maintain a votive regimen as a primary activity. In Cang County, even ritual specialists, such as those of the Heaven and Earth Teaching, are still ordinary peasants. They share the same economic, social, and familial concerns as their neighbors, and even the most devout will punctuate an otherwise full day with only a few votive activities. The majority of peasants, however, spend even less of their time in and pay less attention to active engagement with the sacred. Most approach the sacred only in times of need or at intervals to maintain a reciprocal relationship of protection for devotion. Nevertheless, even in these activities, the individual is very often simply the beneficiary of specialized ritual action, of which he or she might have only minimal understanding.

In contrast, active religiosity in Cang County is not a matter of responsibility but of individual choice. To be sure, certain aspects of the textual tradition in which popular religiosity is grounded do emphasize a votive debt toward the sacred, but the logic of popular practice is otherwise, if only because the sacred realm is perceived not as a monolithic, unchanging truth, but rather as a collection of interested, individual actors. Even sacrifices to ancestral spirits and care of family graves are not theological necessities, but social ones. These are not the debt of the individual to the sacred, but rather a filial obligation to secure the postmortem welfare of one's own parents.

This said, there are those individuals who do voluntarily maintain an active votive regimen: not only sectarian leaders, but also solitary religious specialists, such as *xiangtou,* as well as the faithful who flock to engage the sacred at temples and rituals. In contrast to Watson's correct characterization of the many faithful who neither understand nor necessarily believe in the rituals performed on their behalf, there is still a large proportion of villagers who have made a strong personal investment in their religious lives, and these individuals often possess an impressive store of knowledge. Specialists of the Heaven and Earth Teaching spend as many as ten years to master their ritual repertoire and scriptural canon. At the extreme of this tendency are sectarian leaders such as Tu of Rear Camp, who has devoted much of his adult life to religious study and reflection. Tu is literate and has read numerous Buddhist scriptures, as well as the Bible and Qur'an, and has developed a detailed personal theology that combines elements of these scriptural traditions with the basic moral tenets of peasant society. Moreover, feelings of curiosity and genuine devotion toward the sacred extend beyond ritual specialists. Individuals with a very loose understanding of organized religion (in particular, the sectarian traditions, rather than Buddhism), will form a personal theology based on local tales of morality, fate, and a divine justice. Even those who employ ritual specialists solely for the satisfaction of personal needs, such as healing, will do so with some understanding of who populates the sacred realm, how they intact with the human world, and why.

Religious life within the villages of Cang County consists of the interaction between active and passive religiosity. With no theological impetus to coerce the individual into a lifestyle of active religiosity, those who join a religious teaching or engage in a votive regimen do so voluntarily, whereas those who do not do so are not viewed as failing in their duty to the sacred. Moreover, just as any community will demonstrate a range of personal responses to the sacred, certain individuals serve as storehouses of religious knowledge. To the extent that less religious villagers will defer to the ritual and scriptural knowledge of the more actively devout, their interaction with the sacred conforms to Watson's characterization of orthopraxy. Taken as a community, however, villages have unofficial experts on the divine, just as they do on more mundane topics, such as folk medicine or tractor repair. The former individuals often perform ritual actions on behalf of the community and serve as sources of orthodoxy (or at least authority) in questions concerning the nature of the sacred or proper ritual conduct. Thus, although the villages of Cang County are thick with religious influences, organizations, and specialists, the choice of how to engage and understand the sacred remains primarily with the individual.

Religious Institutions and Individual Belief

In 1961, C. K. Yang proposed a dichotomy between "institutional" and "diffused" religion. The former was characterized by an independent theology, ritual practice, and organization and referred most immediately to the textual traditions of Buddhism and Daoism but could certainly apply to sectarian traditions as well. In contrast, diffused religion is defined as the eddying mass of beliefs and practices that pervade society but with no identifiable glue to hold them together into a coherent religious system. Customary funerary practices, belief in Heaven, and the *yin-yang* cosmology are all examples of this sort of religion.[3]

As the experience of Cang County shows, however, "institutional" religion is often quite diffuse, while "diffused" religion is, in a way, institutionalized. As each of the major religious teachings was introduced to rural Cang County, it was transformed and remolded to become a local institution inside the nominal shell of a national one. Nevertheless, the shuffling of institutional and terminological boundaries occurs even within local society. Many of the rituals and symbols of village sectarians are subject to significant misinterpretation (perhaps "reinterpretation" is a better term) by those outside the teaching. The most obvious example concerns the hagiography of leaders such as Patriarch Dong Sihai of the Heaven and Earth Teaching. Those within the teaching can speak about

Patriarch Dong, his background, and the beliefs upon which he founded the teaching in great detail because this knowledge is enshrined in the scriptures that ritual specialists commit to memory. Many occasional devotees, such as Wang Chun, do not understand the text of the chanted scriptures, tend to know very little about Dong, and freely conflate him with other male deities, such as Guandi. Outside the narrative tradition, ritual knowledge can also be obscured. For example, when Heaven and Earth sectarians chant scriptures inside a home, they often sit on the family *kang* without first removing their shoes, in violation of common custom. Members of the teaching explain that this is because a true believer must be modest and cast his eyes downward as he walks, one ancillary benefit of which is clean shoes. By not removing their shoes, these specialists are thus making a statement concerning personal morality; however, very few of those outside of the teaching knew the reason behind this custom. Most attributed it to the more pedestrian causes of laziness or simply cold feet.

In contrast, those beliefs and traditions characterized as "diffused" reveal patterns of customary usage and understanding that approach a clear, though rarely articulated, systemization. The interaction between human and sacred actors, in particular the exchange of favors that is the core of popular devotion, proceeds according to a distinct morality that is understood by all, but designed by none. Belief in the healing power of fox spirits derives from an immediate and constantly evolving oral tradition that itself shapes the practice of *xiangtou,* who may justly be characterized as the ritual specialists of the cult of fox spirits. Although they are an important source of knowledge about foxes, *xiangtou* are also product of local tradition. Thus, despite the innovation of and diversity among individual practitioners, there are clear topical, theological, and practical tendencies that characterize the cult of fox worship. Returning to Yang's terminology, fox worship is a diffused institution.

To be fair to Yang's extremely useful analysis, he did not counterpose institutional and diffused religion in necessary opposition and did demonstrate the interplay of concepts and beliefs between the two. Nevertheless, we can better employ this framework if we remember that the degree to which any system of belief can be characterized as an institution is less a function of the religion itself than a subjective function of the devotee. A sincere devotee of even the most exclusive tradition is not simply an extension of the teaching of his or her sect. He or she will hold certain truths more dear and leave others as a matter of faith but in either case will selectively adapt the teaching to be a part of his or her personal religiosity. Similarly, even one coming from an overtly syncretic tradition will still recognize boundaries between religious influences and orient him or herself toward certain practices and votive traditions, even while professing other aspects of the sacred to be valid. When the subjectivity of the devotee is taken into account, we see how the same teaching, such as the Li Sect, can be an institutional religion for one, and diffused religiosity for another. External influences alone do not create a religious life; the vital question remains the degree and manner to which individual actively engages the sacred. Throughout all of the social, cultural, and theological changes that characterized this 150-year period, the religious lives of Cang County peasants remained first and foremost the purview of the individual and his or her religious proclivities, knowledge, and conscience.

Appendix A

A-1 Instances of Votive Construction and Repair in Cang and Qing Counties

Period	Number of Instances			
	Temple Construction	Temple Repair	Monastic Construction	Monastic Repair
1400–1449	4	3	4	2
1450–1499	15	8	5	4
1500–1549	10	14	6	7
1550–1599	16	14	2	4
1600–1649	10	9	1	3
1650–1699	8	10	1	2
1700–1749	10	16	1	8
1750–1799	10	21	0	10
1800–1849	17	27	1	4
1850–1899	18	74	0	15
1900–	4	42	0	1

Source: *Tianjin fu zhi,* 1899, *juan* 25, 15–41; *Cangxian zhi,* 1933, 287–335; *Qingxian zhi,* 1931, 224–262.

A-2 Temple Construction and Repair Led by Buddhist Monks, Cang and Qing Counties, by Year

Year	Name of Monk	Temple	Location	Act[a]
1379	Zhenjue	Shuiyue si	Lisanqiao Village, Qing	Fou
1430	Guangjin	Guanyin si	Qing County City	Rep
1435	Wujing	Xingguo si	Xingji Village, Qing	Fou
1436	Ze'an	Shuiyue si	Cang County suburban area	Reb
1471	Hongxiu	Zisheng si	She Family Camp, Qing	Rep
1478	Wenban	Guanyin si	Qing County City	Rep
1481	Wenban	Dizang si	Wangzhen dian, Qing	Rep
1603	Zhikui	Guandi miao	Dulin zhen, Qing[a]	Rep

continued

Year	Name of Monk	Temple	Location	Act
1522	Wuqing	Amitofo si	Tasi Village, Qing	Reb
1532	Lusi	Jishan si	Cang County suburban area	Rep
1538	Benhe	Omituofuo si	Tasi Village, Qing	Rep
1550	Benhe	Omituofuo si	Tasi Village, Qing	Rep
1588	Jinghe	Yaowang miao	Qing County City	Rep
1597 (approx.)	Xingde	Shuiyue si	Lisanqiao Village, Qing	Rep
1598	Quanxian	Huitang an	Dulin zhen, Qing[b]	Fou
1599	Hongquan	Zisheng si	She Family Camp, Qing	Rep
1650	Zhang (Daoist)	Dizang an	Dacheng Village, Qing	Rep
1481	Wenban	Dizang si	Wangzhen dian, Qing	Rep
1700	Zhedan	Dizang miao	Cang	Rep
1719	Hunyi	Shuiyue si	Cang County suburban area	Rep
1782	Fawang	Guandi miao	Dulin zhen, Qing[b]	Rep
1744	Fawang	Wangmu ge	Dulin zhen, Qing[b]	Rep
1780	Fawang	Huitang an	Dulin zhen, Qing[b]	Rep
1800	Yanhui	Tudi miao	Dulin zhen, Qing[b]	Rep
1797	Wuqing	Wofo si	Qing	Reb
1824	Benhe	Wofo si	Qing	Rep
1814	Yanhui	Dongyue miao	Dulin zhen, Qing[b]	Rep
1831	Ruli	Baiyi maio	Cangzhou City	Rep
1839	Hailin	Tianqi miao	Cangzhou City	Rep
1916	Benxin	Pangu miao	Dapangu Village, Qing[b]	Reb

Source: *Tianjin fu zhi,* 1899, *juan* 25, 15–41; *Cangxian zhi,* 1933, 287–335; *Qingxian zhi,* 1931, 224–262.

[a] Fou = founded; Rep = repaired; Reb = rebuilt.

[b] Reflects 1933 boundaries. Currently located within Cang County.

Appendix B

Votive Prayer from the *Precious Scripture of the Five Sages (Wusheng Baojuan)*

1. Incense Offering of the Hu Place

This prayer is the first of five, each offered to one of the Five Places. The scripture itself does not specify the speaker of the offering, although similar prayers are clearly intended to be recited by the member of the Five Places correspondent with that seat. Each of the Five Places has a similar set of rituals, using geographic and personal names appropriate for each Place, and incorporating minor changes in wording to provide some variety and maintain rhyme scheme. The following prayer is composed of seven-character couplets that would be easily chanted in a ritual setting.

[Your] Disciple bows to Mount Jiuhua	*Dizi dingli Jiuhua shan*
With the head bowed, one can see the Sagely Buddha in the heart	*Tou ding sheng fo zai xin jian*
Come to worship within Shuijian Cave	*Shuijian dong zhong lai canbai*
Blessed Buddha, guard my heart	*Nanmu tuofo hu xin bang*
Guanyin and Dizang in a carriage protected by a *yan*	*Dizang shengzong[1] yan hu jia*
Ancient Buddha on the Lotus Throne, bestow upon us the Law	*Gu fo lian tai ci fa yan*
Your disciples will do your work and spread the Way	*Dizi ti fo lai chuan dao*
Link together and open the districts and cities	*Lian huan zhenkai fu du cheng*
Bowing to the precious golden mark of the Buddha	*Tou ding fo bao jin pai yin*

[1] This is a reference to Guanyin (see Wang Hongkui, 1990, 186).

Wrap the body in a brilliant cloth soaked in the *li*   *Shen pi tou li shui jing sha*

Holding the prison lock in the hand, strike it with a pestle   *Shou tuo jian suo lian huan gan*

Break open the cycle of rebirth and release the nine senses   *Ba kai sheng si jiu ao fa*

Please come and accept our Worship

Appendix C

C-1   Materials Confiscated in Course of the Campaign against
the Way of Penetrating Unity, March 1951

	Cang County	Renqiu	Xian	Huanghua	Qing	Suning
Texts:						
Unnamed "Reactionary Spirit Writings"	75	12	2	3	11	8
Twenty-four *zhong* and eighteen *tiao*	...	...	2	...	...	...
Quanshi jing	358	425	4	600	...	402
Yiguan xuzhi	299	...	...	1	...	...
Mulun	8	...	2	...	...	...
Other	900	1,120	25	1	3	3
Total	1,640	1,557	35	605	14	413
Ritual objects:						
Donation charts	8	4	1	12	3	2
Votive objects[a]	58	46	...	...	311	31
Spirit-writing supplies	...	...	1	3	...	1
Total	66	50	2	15	314	34
Capital:						
Silver *yuan*	...	10	...	...	...	...
Copper *yuan*	...	...	...	...	...	...
Grain *(dan?)*	100	270	...	100	...	...
Tables and chairs	...	...	...	...	27	...
Blankets	...	...	...	...	6	...
Buildings	...	...	...	...	...	...
Other	15 *mou* of land	...	...	...	...	...

[a]Includes separate listings for statues, incense burners, lamps, and ritual plates.

Cang Township	Jiaohe	Jianguo	Botou Township	Henjian	Total
6	18	50	...	12	197
2	...	...	...	1	5
250	37	394	1,226	66	3,762
...	...	309	345	...	954
...	...	...	...	...	10
4	5	46	7	15	2,129
262	60	799	1,578	94	7,057
11	5	10	...	4	60
61	71	66	130	268	1,042
...	1	...	...	...	6
72	77	76	130	270	1,108
48	...	...	757	93	908
...	...	...	...	18	18
110	...	...	...	...	580
...	...	...	12	26	67
10	...	...	...	4	20
16	...	...	...	...	22
1,490,000 *yuan* and 1 cart	...	...	...	...	...

C-2 Punishments Accorded to Leaders and Members
of the Way of Penetrating Unity in Cangzhou, March 1951

	Daozhang	Dianchuanshi			Home tanzhu	Spirit Writers (sancai)
		Qianren		Tanzhu		
Total[b]	3/0	9/4	332/87	348/115	486/214	91/62
Arrested	1/0	4/0	136/38	41/8	15/4	2/1
Executed	1/0	4/0	62/6	10/0	4/0	…
Exiled	…	…	45/20	10/2	8/1	…
Released[b]	…	…	4/6	6/1	2/3	1/1
Detained for reeducation	…	…	59/22	169/46	168/75	41/19
Detained	…	…	30/5	19/0	4/0	…
Reeducated individually	…	…	24/10	27/13	30/72	21/8
Reeducated in group	…	…	0/1	49/13	54/31	20/11
Surveillance	…	…	5/6	74/20	50/22	…
Registered and released[c]	…	…	2/2	7/5	123/69	12/11
Employed in campaign	…	…	12/1	100/11	43/6	11/7
Escaped	2/0	5/4	147/18	36/14	38/3	19/13
Suicide	…	…	1/0	…	…	…
Other	…	…	10/13	114/56	132/63	29/15

Note: Data are presented as number of males/number of females.
[a]Including *jiangshi* (speakers), *bian dao yuan* (apologists), *yin bao ren* (guarantors), and scribes.
[b]Because of double counting, some totals differ from the sum of the itemized listings.
[c]Includes those placed under surveillance following release.

Lower-Order Specialists[a]	Total	Ordinary Members
145/93	1,936	39,499
11/3	263	…
3/0	90	…
1/0	89	…
1/3	30	…
16/7	643	33/3
0/1	59	…
…	305	12/8
12/3	194	19/1
4/4	185	2/0
31/15	275	…
7/0	198	…
…	320	…
…	…	…
15/18	505	…

C-3 Punishments Accorded to Leaders and Members of Other Sects, March, 1951

Punishment	Way of the Nine [illegible] (Jiu? Dao)	Buddhist Society (Fojiao hui)	Primal Chaos Sect (Hunyuan men)	Heaven and Earth Teaching	Way of the Sage Immortals (Shengxian dao)	Way of the Three Epochs (Sanjie dao)	Total	Other
Total								
Executed	1/0	...	...	...	...	...	...	1
Detained for reeducation	2/0	6/2	6/5	1/8	9/1	4/0	8/6	58
Reeducated individually	...	5/2	3/0	0/6	3/0	...	2/1	22
Reeducated in group	2/0	1/0	...	...	6/1	4/0	6/5	35
Surveillance	...	...	0/1	...	...	...	...	1

Note: Data are presented as number of males/number of females.

Appendix D
Scriptures of the Heaven and Earth Teaching

Although the scriptures of this teaching in Cang County are oral, other groups use written texts. Li Shiyu has kindly provided me with two *juan* of such scriptures, used by Heaven and Earth groups in Tianjin. Each of these contains about 100 pages of handwritten vertical text, consisting of numerous short pieces, ranging in length from a few lines to two pages. The individual sections are independently named as hymns, odes, scriptures, or incantations *(ji, zan, jing, zhou)* and present aspects of the history and teaching of the sect, as well as odes of praise for various deities. Like the oral scriptures of Cang County, these are meant to be recited in a ritual setting, both for the worship of the gods and the edification of the faithful.

1. Litany of Gods Invited to Heaven and Earth Festivals
From "A Hymn of Invitation to the Sages" (qing sheng qi)

The following excerpt outlines the gods invited to Heaven and Earth ceremonies. This compilation of gods includes some popular deities, but as many of the figures listed are austere, distant, and abstract. Notably absent from this compilation are any obviously unorthodox deities, roving spirits, or demonic figures.

> With incense, we invite the Buddhists: ancient Buddha and ancient Mother, the Eighteen Arhats, Maitreya and the Lamplighter Buddha [Dipamkara, Buddha of the former epoch];
> With incense, we invite the Daoists: the Three Pure Ones: the Limitless Ancestor, Fu Xi [inventor of writing], Shen Nong [inventor of agriculture] and Laozi.
> With incense, we invite the Confucians: the Primary Teacher, Confucius, the Seventy-Two Worthies, thinking of Mencius and desiring Zeng.

With incense, we invite the Heavenly Basin, the Golden Tower, each department of the 28 Constellations, and all of the stars.

With incense, we invite the Cloud Basin, Yuantong, the Four Great Bodhisattvas who rescue us from bitterness and suffering.

With incense, we invite the Human Basin, from ten thousand years of history, the brave and loyal who bring peace and order to the realm.

With incense, we invite the Earthly Basin, the dark and obscure Yan Buddha [king of the underworld, here called a Buddha], the Ten Courts obscured in darkness.

With incense, we invite the Sagely Basin, the great thinkers from the eight directions, of north and south, mountain and forest.

With incense, we invite from the West the Emperor who Assists Heaven, from the East, the North Star, Wenchang.

With incense, we invite from the North, the Northern Hegemon, Zhenwu, from the South, the fire bringer, Bing Ding.

With incense, we invite from the Center, the Empress of Heaven, the Sagely Mother, the King and Sage of Medicine, the Star who Delivers from Calamity.

With incense, we invite the Three Officials of Heaven, Earth and Water, the Dragon generals and soldiers from the Five Lakes and Four Seas.

The sun and moon, Father and Mother of the Big Dipper, Caishen, who increases wealth and longevity with ease.

Four great Heavenly Kings, Efficacious Official who Receives the Teaching, inspecting and touring the altars, protected on the right and left.

With twelve tour circuits and three worlds, speeding along reports, Duke Cao, who investigates the planes and visits the sages.

Lord of Walls and Moats of this prefecture and county, the Earth God of this place, Door Gods and Stove God of the six *jia* and six *ding*.

2. Heaven and Earth Scripture, Drawing in the Clear River (Qingjiang yin)

This scripture outlines the Five Kindnesses (*wu en*), which form the moral basis of the teaching and are chanted as the leader of the ritual lights five sticks of incense before the Heaven, Earth, Ruler, Parent, Teacher tablet.

With the first stick of true incense we show gratitude for the Kindness of Heaven. For the sun and moon, which illuminate the heavens and earth, for the propitious winds and rain that make the people peaceful and happy, today, we assemble this *hui* to show thanks for the Kindness of Heaven.

With the second stick of true incense we show gratitude for the Kindness of Earth. For the earth from which grow the Five Grains and feed the people, for the rich earth that supports luxuriant sprouts, today, we assemble this *hui* to show thanks for the Kindness of Earth.

With the third stick of true incense we show gratitude for the Kindness of our Ruler. Who spreads harmony over the people of ten thousand kingdoms for ten thousand springtimes, who dams up the lakes and illuminates all things, today, we assemble this *hui* to show thanks for the Kindness of our Ruler.

With the fourth stick of true incense we show gratitude for the Kindness of our Parents. For father and mother, with benevolence and love as deep as the ocean, who fed us at the breast, a labor of love that cannot be repaid, today, we assemble this *hui* to show thanks for the Kindness of our Parents.

With the fifth stick of true incense we show gratitude for the Kindness of our Teacher. The benevolence of our teacher, which has been passed down to this day, and the teaching which he spoke, of which, we have only recorded the bare essentials, today, we assemble this *hui* to show thanks for the Kindness of our Teacher.

Amithaba, we show gratitude for these Five Kindnesses.

In this passage, the "teacher" refers specifically to Dong Sihai. The transmission of the teaching is referred to as *chuan*, spreading the content of the teaching, and *dian*, passing of enlightenment from teacher to student, usually through physically touching the forehead of the initiate (see the *Tiandimen Scriptures, juan* 1).

Notes

Introduction

Archival documents are cited as "CA, document number, page." In the notes, gazetteers are cited in full in the first instance and subsequently as "Place, year, page" (e.g., *Qingxian*, 1931, 255). Also, the multivolume work edited by Niida Noboru, *Chōgoku nōson kankō chōsa* [An investigation of Chinese village customs] (1953–1958) is cited following the format "CN: volume, page."

1. Among the better-known studies of conflict between the state and religious militants are the studies of Susan Naquin, *Millenarian Rebellion in China: The Eight Trigrams Uprising of 1813* (New Haven, Conn.: Yale University Press, 1976) and *Shantung Rebellion: The Wang Lun Uprising of 1774* (New Haven, Conn.: Yale University Press, 1981). For an eloquent description of how state discourse of criminality shaped perception of the White Lotus tradition, see Barend ter Haar, *The White Lotus Teachings in Chinese Religious History* (Honolulu: University of Hawai'i Press, 1999).

2. Some gazetteers, particularly those from the Republican period, do contain significant information on local custom. Much of this information has been compiled in Ding Shiliang et al., eds., *Zhongguo difang zhi minsu ziliao huibian* [Collected materials on popular custom in Chinese local gazetteers] (Beijing: Beijing tushuguan chubanshe, 1989).

3. The most significant English language work on *baojuan* literature is Daniel Overmyer, *Precious Volumes: An Introduction to Chinese Sectarian Scriptures from the Sixteenth and Seventeenth Centuries* (Cambridge, Mass.: Harvard University Press and the Harvard University Asia Center, 1999).

4. The best-known work in this tradition is Pu Songling, *Strange Stories from a Chinese Studio*, trans. Herbert Giles (Shanghai: Kelly & Walsh, 1936). A similar source, the *Record of the Listener (Yijian zhi)*, has been used quite differently by Valerie Hansen, *Changing Gods in Medieval China, 1127–1276* (Princeton, N.J.: Princeton University Press, 1990), and more recently by Edward L. Davis, *Society and the Supernatural in Song China* (Honolulu: University of Hawai'i Press, 2001).

5. See for example, Meir Shahar, *Crazy Ji: Chinese Religion and Popular Literature* (Cambridge, Mass: Harvard University Press and the Harvard University Asia Center, 1998).

6. Recent scholarship has eloquently demonstrated the limited ability of

the elite strata to penetrate into popular religious organization and thought. For example, James Watson, "Standardizing the Gods: The Promotion of T'ien Hou ("Empress of Heaven") along the South China Coast, 960–1960," in *Popular Culture in Late Imperial China*, ed. David Johnson, Andrew J. Nathan, and Evelyn S. Rawski (Berkeley: University of California Press, 1985), 292–374; Meir Shahar and Robert P. Weller, eds., *Unruly Gods: Divinity and Society in China* (Honolulu: University of Hawai'i Press, 1996), xxiii; Michael Szonyi, "The Illusion of Standardizing the Gods: The Cult of the Five Emperors in Late Imperial China," *Journal of Asian Studies* 56 (February 1997): 113–135.

7. Paul R. Katz, *Images of the Immortal: The Cult of Lü Dongbin at the Palace of Eternal Joy* (Honolulu: University of Hawai'i Press, 1999); Carlo Ginzburg, *The Cheese and the Worms: The Cosmos of a Sixteenth-Century Miller*, trans. John and Anne Tedeschi (Baltimore: Johns Hopkins University Press, 1980), xxiii. See also the discussion of these issues in David Johnson, "Communication, Class, and Consciousness in Late Imperial China," in Johnson, Nathan, and Rawski, eds. (Berkeley: University of California Press, 1985), 34–72.

8. Philip C. C. Huang, *The Peasant Economy and Social Change in North China* (Stanford, Calif.: Stanford University Press, 1985); Prasenjit Duara, *Culture, Power and the State: Rural North China, 1900–1942* (Stanford, Calif.: Stanford University Press, 1988). A critical discussion of the Mantetsu materials and their limitations is given in Huang, 39–43.

9. Sasaki Mamoru and Lu Yao, eds., *Kindai Chūgoku no shakai to minshū bunka* [Society and mass culture in modern China] (Tokyo: Tōhō Shōten, 1992); Mitani Takashi et al., *Mura kara Chūgoku o yomu* (Tokyo: Aoki Shoten, 2000); Mitani Takashi et al., *Chūgoku nōson henkaku to kazoku, sonraku, kokka: Kahoku nōson chōsa no kiroku* (Tokyo: Kyuko Shōin, 1999).

10. On sectarianism, see Lu Yao, *Shandong minjian mimi jiaomen* [Secret popular sects in Shandong] (Beijing: Dangdai zhongguo chubanshe, 2000); on clan temples, see Jun Jing, *The Temple of Memories: History, Power, and Morality in a Chinese Village* (Stanford, Calif.: Stanford University Press, 1996). On the topic of local ritual and theatrical custom, there has been an explosion of ethnographic studies, published primarily in Chinese-language journals such as *Minsu quyi*.

11. See note 6.

12. The best examples of this work are the many collaborative volumes devoted or related to the topic of Chinese religion, such as Susan Naquin and Chün-fang Yü, eds. *Pilgrims and Sacred Sites in China* (Berkeley: University of California Press, 1992), and James Watson and Evelyn Rawski, eds., *Death Ritual in Late Imperial and Modern China* (Berkeley: University of California Press, 1988). Evelyn Rawski, "A Historian's Approach to Death Ritual," in Watson and Rawski, eds., 20–34, provides a particularly good overview of the potential benefits and biases of a disciplinary approach.

13. For different views of the role of religion in the indoctrination and cooptation of local elites, see Stephan Feutchwang, "School Temple and City God," in G. William Skinner, ed., *The City in Late Imperial China* (Stanford, Calif.: Stanford University Press, 1978), 581–608; Timothy Brook, *Praying for Power: Buddhism and the Formation of Gentry Society in Late-Ming China* (Cambridge, Mass.: Harvard University Press, 1993); and Hansen, *Changing Gods in Medieval China.* Quotation from Kung-chüan Hsiao, *Rural China: Imperial Control in the Nineteenth Century* (Seattle: University of Washington Press, 1960), 225.

14. Richard Von Glahn, "The Enchantment of Wealth: The God Wutong in the Social History of Jiangnan," *Harvard Journal of Asiatic Studies* 51, 2 (1991): 651–714; Kenneth Pomeranz, "Power, Gender, and Pluralism in the Cult of the Goddess of Taishan," in *Culture & State in Chinese History: Conventions, Accommodations, and Critiques,* ed. Theodore Huters, R. Bin Wong, and Pauline Yu (Stanford, Calif.: Stanford University Press, 1997), 182–204.

15. On the intellectual background of Republican attempts to reform religion, see Prasenjit Duara, "Knowledge and Power in the Discourse of Modernity: The Campaigns against Popular Religion in Early Twentieth-Century China," *Journal of Asian Studies,* 50, 1 (February 1991): 67–83. On the policies themselves, see Rebecca Nedostup, "Religion, Superstition and Governing Society in Nationalist China" (Ph.D. diss., Columbia University, 2001). On the Confucian "New Life Movement," see Arif Dirlik, "The Ideological Foundations of the New Life Movement: A Study in Counterrevolution," *Journal of Asian Studies,* 34, 4 (August 1975): 945–980.

16. Elizabeth Perry, *Challenging the Mandate of Heaven: Social Protest and State Power in China* (Armonk, N.Y.: M. E. Sharpe, 2002), "Introduction."

17. Another response is the transcendence of social division and formation of religious communities. In European history, such a change accompanied the Black Death. See A. N. Galpern, *The Religions of the People in Sixteenth-Century Champagne* (Cambridge, Mass.: Harvard University Press, 1976).

18. Although the early years of the People's Republic saw some debate on how the new state should treat religious organizations, it was implicitly assumed that religion would naturally wither and disappear under socialism. See Donald E. MacInnis, *Religious Policy and Practice in Communist China: A Documentary History* (New York: Macmillan, 1972), especially the chapters "Theoreticians Debate Religious Policy, Theory and Tactics," 35–89, and "Reforming Old Rites and Customs," 312–322. The imminent demise of religion in China was also predicted by observers in the West. See, for example, Wing-tsit Chan, *Religious Trends in Modern China* (New York: Columbia University Press, 1953).

19. The link between popular mentality and iconic representations of the sacred has been made most convincingly by scholars of Buddhism; for example, Chün-fang Yü has traced the feminization of statuary of Guanyin (Aval-

okiteśvara) to the rising domination of neo-Confucianism in Late Imperial China. Chün-fang Yü, *Kuan-yin, The Chinese Transformation of Avalokiteśvara* (New York: Columbia University Press, 2001).

20. See especially Stephen A. Sangren, *History and Power in a Chinese Community* (Stanford, Calif.: Stanford University Press, 1987).

21. This is a point made by Prasenjit Duara in his "cultural nexus" formulation. Duara, *Culture, Power, and the State*, 15–41.

22. The former type of authority is cited by Duara, *Culture, Power, and the State*, 139–147, and in greater detail by Hansen, *Changing Gods in Medieval China*. One commonly cited example of the domination of local religious institutions is the religious practice of Republican Shajing village, near Beijing, which divided villagers into grades of membership based on the amount of donations; however, those peasants who did not participate in the more elite functions of the village were anxious to add that such functions held no attraction for them, raising the question of just how "dominated" they were. Niida Noboru, ed., *Chōgoku nōson kankō chōsa* [An investigation of Chinese village customs] (Tokyo: Iwanami, 1953–1958) 1: 130–131, 135–136, 145, 173. See also chap. 2, n. 27, of the present volume. Shajing village is discussed in detail in Thomas DuBois, "The Sacred World of Cang County: Religious Belief, Organization, and Practice in Rural North China During the Late Nineteenth and Twentieth Centuries" (Ph.D. diss., University of California, Los Angeles, 2001), 365–381.

23. Maurice Freedman, "On the Sociological Study of Chinese Religion," in Arthur Wolf, ed., *Religion and Ritual in Chinese Society* (Stanford, Calif.: Stanford University Press, 1974): 19–41.

24. G. William Skinner, "Marketing and Social Structure in Rural China," *Journal of Asian Studies* 24, 1 (1964): 3–44; 24, 2 (1964): 195–228; 24, 3 (1964): 363–399. For an overview of recent scholarship and reassessment of the Skinnerian model, see Kären Wigen, "AHR Forum: Bringing Regionalism Back to History: Culture, Power, and Place: The New Landscapes of East Asian Regionalism," *American Historical Review*, 104, 4 (October 1999): 1183–1201.

25. This becomes important during periods when marketing structures are interrupted, such as during wartime or the heyday of Maoist rural policy. See G. William Skinner "Rural Marketing in China: Repression and Revival," *China Quarterly* 103 (September 1985): 393–413; Helen F. Siu, "Redefining the Market Town through Festivals in South China," in *Town and Country in China: Identity and Perception*, ed. David Faure and Tao Liu (Houndmills, Basingstoke, Hampshire: Palgrave, in association with St Antony's College, Oxford, 2002), 233–249.

26. John Lagerwey, "The Structure and Dynamics of Chinese Rural Society" in Hsu Cheng-kuang, ed., *Disijie guoji kejiaxue yantaohui lunwenji: Lishi yu shehui jingji* [Collected papers from the Fourth International Congress on Hakka Studies: history and social economy] (Taibei: Zhongyang yanjiuyuan minzuxue yanjiusuo, 2000), 1–43.

27. By far the most complete study of the geography of local religion are the surveys conducted by Willem Grootaers in the northern Hebei counties of Wanquan and Xuanhua, which trace the correspondence between the dispersal of local cults and that of dialect patterns. Willem A. Grootaers, "Temples and History of Wan-ch'üan (Chahar): The Geographical Method Applied to Folklore," *Monumenta Serica*, 13 (1948): 209–316, and "Rural Temples around Hsuan-hua (South Chahar): Their Iconography and Their History," *Folklore Studies* 10, 1 (1951): 1–115.

28. This dating of the *Diagram of Villages in Qing County* is based on Momose Hiro, *"Shinmatsu chokuri shō no sonzu sanshu ni tsuite"* [Three kinds of village diagrams in late Qing Zhili], in *Katō hakushi kanreki kinen tōyōshi shōsetsu kankōkai*, ed., *Katō hakushi kanreki kinen tōyōshi shōsetsu* [Collected essays in East Asian history in honor of Professor Kato's sixtieth birthday] (Tokyo: Fuzanbō, 1941).

Chapter 1: Background

1. Cui Shoulu et al., *Cangxian xianzhi* [Gazetteer of Cang County] (Beijing: Zhongguo heping chubanshe, 1995), 78–86, 559–561 (cited hereafter as *Cangxian*, 1995).

2. *Cangxian*, 1995, 17, 231, 242.

3. Quoted in *Cangxian*, 1995, 426.

4. According to a 1982 investigation, most of the 512 villages in Cang County were founded during the second year of the Yongle reign (1405). The few that date from the Qing period were settled primarily from other areas of Cang County itself. *Cangxian*, 1995, 426, 533–554.

5. In both Tianjin and Hejian, this trend continued unabated through the 1950s. Huang, 114–116, 323–324.

6. *Cangxian*, 1995, 16. A similar flood in 1964 literally leveled entire villages.

7. *Cangxian*, 1995, 122.

8. *Qingxian cuntu*, c. 1870–1875, *juan* 12.

9. *Cangxian*, 1995, 16.

10. *Cangxian*, 1995, 426–429; Arthur Peill, an eye surgeon and one of very few missionaries in late Qing Cangzhou, provides a detailed firsthand account of the Boxer siege. Arthur Peill, *The Beloved Physician of Tsang Chou Life-Work and Letters of Dr. Arthur D. Peill, F.R.C.S.E.*, ed. J. Peill (London: Headley, 1908).

11. Unless otherwise noted, the population figures given in this chapter refer to the rural areas exclusive of Cangzhou City. *Cangxian*, 1995, 49, 555.

12. Huang, 116–117.

13. Similar figures were quoted to me by informants in Ni-Yang Camp and Quan-Wang Village. Interview in Quan-Wang Village, October 5–6, 1997, and Ni-Yang Camp, Oct. 15, 1997. For a more complete discussion of taxation in rural North China, see Huang, 275–290; Duara, *Culture, Power, and the State,*

227–242; and Li Huaiyin, "Village Regulations at Work: Local Taxation in Huailu County, 1900–1936," *Modern China*, 26, 1 (2000): 79–100.

14. *Cangxian*, 1995, 555.

15. *Cangxian*, 1995, 431. Villagers recounted a less complete, but still extremely brutal, attack on the neighboring village of North White Pagoda. Interview in Quan-Wang Village, October 6, 1997. The Japanese occupation of North China, especially their difficulty in holding the rural areas, has been described in detail by numerous scholars, the classic work being Chalmers Johnson, *Peasant Nationalism and Communist Power: The Emergence of Revolutionary China* (Stanford, Calif.: Stanford University Press, 1962).

16. *Cangxian*, 1995, 555.

17. *Cangxian*, 1995, 565. This figure is an estimate based on an intake of 2,600 calories per day. Corn and wheat flour have similar caloric value—about 100 calories per thirty grams.

18. I speak primarily of the methodology of the late Republican ethnographers, such as the Mantetsu team and Sidney Gamble, who closely examined individual villages scattered throughout the North China Plain, as well as subsequent historiographic work that is based upon it. Data concerning religion in the Mantetsu materials is most complete for the Hebei village of Shajing, and much of the most valuable scholarship on religion in North China is based heavily on data from this and a handful of other villages. In view of the degree of variation even among adjacent communities, however, these data out of local context are of limited use. On local variation, see James L. Watson, "The Structure of Chinese Funerary Rite: Elementary Forms, Ritual Sequence and the Primacy of Performance," in *Death Ritual in Late Imperial and Modern China*, ed. James Watson and Evelyn Rawski (Berkeley: University of California Press, 1985): 3–19, and the discussion of village "individuation" in John Lagerwey, "The Structure and Dynamics of Chinese Rural Society."

19. *Cangxian*, 1995, 533–554.

20. *Qingxian cuntu, juan* 12.

21. According to Myron L. Cohen, lineage power in south central Hebei was almost completely independent of land or land use. Cohen, "Lineage Organization in North China," *Journal of Asian Studies* 49, 3 (1990): 509–534. This represents an important contrast to the classic image of lineage power in the Pearl River Delta as being based on corporate property, as presented in Maurice Freedman, *Lineage Organization in Southeast China* (London: Athlone Press, 1958), and refined by David Faure, *The Structure of Chinese Rural Society: Lineage and Village in the Eastern New Territories, Hong Kong* (Hong Kong: Oxford University Press, 1986), who revised this model to demonstrate that the power of the lineage derived from the power to restrict settlement and subsoil usage rights. Even in the South, however, the emphasis on economic concerns may be overstated. Work by Michael Szonyi in Fujian has demonstrated the inadequacy of portraying lineages solely in terms of normative cri-

teria, such as land ownership, characterizing them equally as rhetorical strategies of memory, organization and legitimation. Szonyi, *Practicing Kinship: Lineage and Descent in Late Imperial China* (Stanford, Calif.: Stanford University Press, 2002).

22. *Qingxian cuntu, juan* 12; *Jinmen baojia tushuo*. See also Willem Grootaers, "Temples and History of Wan-ch'üan" and "Rural Temples Around Hsuan-hua."

23. A few of the strongest families, such as the Wangs of Quan-Wang Village, maintained a regimen of ceremonies, particularly that of burning incense at family graves during Qingming (the "Clear and Bright" festival, during which the graves of ancestors are cleaned and restored), but this was the exception. On the basis of the contiguous residence of related households, as well as the custom (often legally enforced) of giving preferential treatment to lineage members in land sales, Duara forwards the idea that lineages were more important in North China than previously thought, particularly in villages distant from urban areas. He contrasts these "lineage communities" with "religious communities," in which the village, centered upon a common ritual life, was the more important unit of organization and identification. See Duara, *Culture, Power, and the State*, chap. 4, esp. 101–107.

24. The distribution of *shengyuan* was roughly proportionate to county population. Joseph Esherick, *The Origins of the Boxer Uprising* (Berkeley: University of California Press, 1987), 27–28.

25. *Qingxian cuntu, juan* 12.

26. Although this category is obviously subjective, I think that that the small number of peasants classified as "poor people" can at least be taken as evidence that the villagers were not overrun with beggars.

27. Ch'ü T'ung-tsu, *Local Government in China under the Ch'ing* (Cambridge, Mass.: Harvard University Press, 1962), 2.

28. *Qingxian cuntu, juan* 12.

29. This position, known in Huailu as "*xiangdi,*" rotated among villagers or between surname groups, as opposed to the gentry-based tax farming *(baolan)* seen in Jiangnan. Li Huaiyin, 79–83.

30. The *xiang* was the ambitious creation of the 1929 Rural Reorganization Act, which sought to combine small villages into administrative units of at least 100 households. The two tiers of administration went by many different names. See Duara, *Culture, Power, and the State*, 47–51, for other examples from Hebei and Shandong.

31. Interview in Quan-Wang Village, October 5, 1997.

32. After the Japanese occupation in 1937, Cang County was divided into 554 *bao* and 6,698 *jia*. The number of *jia* was frequently adjusted in order to make *bao* better conform to village boundaries. *Cangxian*, 1995, 383–384.

33. Before this time, many small, independent villages did pay taxes cooperatively. Often the tax burden was apportioned by ratio. Before the villages of

Ni Camp and Yang Camp combined into the modern Ni-Yang Camp, the former paid one-third and the latter two-thirds of their collective tax burden. Within each village, the tax burden was then apportioned according to land-holdings of each household. It was not until the Japanese occupation that the villages combined formally and the internal affairs of the community, such as tax payment, became subject to a single administrative system. The combination of nearby Quan Camp and Wang Village into Quan-Wang Village followed a similar chronology. Interviews in Quan-Wang Village, October 5–6, 1997, Ni-Yang Camp, October 15, 1997.

34. Duara, *Culture, Power, and the State*, 55–57, 217–243.

35. In September 1958, Cang County was divided into eleven People's Communes, East Wind numbers 1–5 and Red Flag numbers 1–6. In January 1959, East Wind 4 merged into Red Flag 1, bringing the total to ten. In 1961, East Wind 4 was ceded to Qing County, and the remaining nine were broken into twenty-nine smaller units that year. *Cangxian*, 1995, 70–71; Interview in Quan-Wang Village, December 15, 1997

36. Interviews in Quan-Wang Village, October 5–6, 1997, Ni-Yang Camp, October 15, 1997. Helen Siu (234–236) suggests that the decline of rural markets during the Maoist period may have further attenuated the cultural world of peasants into "cellularized" villages.

37. *Qingxian cuntu, juan* 12.

38. The self-sufficiency *(zi gei zi zu)* of local clusters of villages in the area of Shi Family Village is the subject of a short but interesting article, "*Shiji suo biaoxiande nongcun zigei zizu wenti*" [The problem of village self-sufficiency as revealed in periodic markets], by Yang Qingkun, *Dagong bao*, July 19, 1934. See also Nakamura Tetsuo, "*Shinmatsu kahoku ni okeru shijōken to shūkyo ken*" [Marketing spheres and religious spheres in late Qing North China], *Shakai Keizai Shigaku*, 40, 3 (1979): 1–26.

39. Ishida Hiroshi, "*Kyū Chugoku nōson ni okeru shijōken to tsūkon ken*" [Marketing spheres and marriage spheres in Old China], *Shirin* 63, 4 (1979): 113–124.

40. In contrast to the data presented by Ishida, quite a few Cang County marriages were contracted over a distance of greater than ten and less than thirty *li*. Although I cannot offer an explanation for this particular difference, the two key factors are population density and "friction of distance," or difficulty of transportation. Skinner's emphasis on the former in the distribution of markets ("Marketing and Social Structure," 1: 32–34) has been challenged by Yasutomi Ayumu, who demonstrated how the range of markets in Republican Manchuria varied by season, expanding dramatically in winter, when frozen roads were more easily traversed. "Rural Market System in Manchuria," paper delivered at the Japan Conference of the Association for Asian Studies, Sophia University, June 2001.

41. Interviews in Quan-Wang Village, October 5, 1997, November 29, 1997,

Ni-Yang Camp, October 15, 1997, October 24, 1997, and Hai Family Dock, December 1, 1997.

42. Ishida Hiroshi, "*Kyū Chugoku nōson*," Nakamura Tetsuro. See also the overview of Chinese and Japanese scholarship on "ritual spheres" *(jisi quan)* on pages 97–101 of Lin Mei-jung, "*You jisi quan dao xinyang quan: Taiwan minjian shehui de diyu goucheng yu fazhan*" [From ritual sphere to belief sphere: Territorial composition and development of Taiwan folk society], in *Zhongguo haiyang fazhan shi lunwen ji* [Collected essays on Chinese oceanic development], ed. Chang Yen-hsien (Taibei: Zhongyang yanjiuyuan sanmin zhuyi yanjiusuo, 1988).

43. One reason for this difference may be the proximity of villages to the market town. Those close to the town or the county seat would have access to a better transportation network, but would also have fewer reasons to venture into the hinterland. This was the case in the two villages mentioned by Duara, *Culture, Power, and the State*, 21–23, n. 22.

44. Skinner, "Marketing and Social Structure," 1: 38–39.

45. In one memorable example, my older respondents expressed disbelief that the earth could possibly be round or that daytime in China could be nighttime in the United States.

46. The many compilations of folk stories collected locally in China, such as that edited by Ke Hua in Cangzhou, show how certain tales and narrative themes have made their way to every corner of China. What is notable, however, is that these stories are often told within the context of local society. In the collection of stories from Cangzhou, the actors involved are generally said to hail from neighboring villages. Folklorists have noted the same phenomenon within "urban legends" of the United States, where an important trait is that the story is usually grounded in a slightly removed personal relationship (a "friend of a friend") to the teller. Ke Hua, ed., *Minjian wenxue jicheng Cangzhou diqu juan: gushi* [Compilation of Chinese popular literature, Cangzhou volume: Stories] (Nanpi County: n.p, 1988); Jan Harold Brunvald, *The Study of American Folklore: An Introduction* (New York: W. W. Norton, 1986).

47. *Qingxian cuntu, juan* 12.

48. This was the case with my informants, most of whom were illiterate. It should be emphasized, however, that those who do not rely on written texts often develop a phenomenal sophistication with the spoken word and rote memorization. This was the case with performers such as itinerant storytellers and operatic troupes, as well as religious specialists. The issue of specialized literacy in village society is taken up in James Hayes, "Specialists and Written Materials in the Village World," in *Popular Culture in Late Imperial China*, ed. David Johnson, Andrew J. Nathan, and Evelyn S. Rawski (Berkeley: University of California Press, 1985), 78–112.

49. Zhang Ping et al., *Cangxian zhi* [Gazetteer of Cang County] (1933; reprint Taibei: Cheng wen chu ban she, 1968), 421–458.

50. *Cangxian*, 1995, 352, 435–438.

51. The content of vows is very similar to those discussed in the second chapter of William Christian, *Local Religion in Sixteenth-Century Spain* (Princeton, N.J.: Princeton University Press, 1981).

52. Not all misfortunes are automatically assumed to be supernatural in origin, as chap. 3, on sickness and healing, will discuss. In general, the immediacy of the event or some sort of ironic justice mark it as such. Concerning the peasant who cursed Caishen, peasants recounting the story remarked, "He had made Caishen's face (in the sense of reputation) unattractive, so Caishen gave him the same treatment." Similarly, in the following story, abuse of a ceremony to ward off hail was very appropriately repaid by a series of hailstorms localized in that village. Interview in Quan-Wang Village, October 6, 1997, Ni-Yang Camp, October 27, 1997.

53. In contrast to more readily accessible acts of devotion, curses and maledictory rituals represent a specialized tradition, and few of my informants knew any details other than the fact that such rituals exist. Access to such knowledge was itself often a mark of dangerous marginality among groups such as late Imperial stone masons. See Klaas Ruitenbeek, *Carpentry and Building in Late Imperial China: A Study of the Fifteenth-Century Carpenter's Manual* Lu Ban jing (Leiden: E. J. Brill , 1993). For a discussion of the liminality of hatred in village society, see David Warren Sabean, *Power in the Blood: Popular Culture and Village Discourse in Early Modern Germany* (New York: Cambridge University Press, 1990).

54. For an introduction to these issues, see Meir Shahar and Robert Weller, "Introduction: Gods and Society in China," in Shahar and Weller, eds., 1–37, esp. 23–30.

55. Wolfram Eberhardt, "Temple-Building Activities in Medieval and Modern China: An Experimental Study," *Monumenta Serica*, 23 (1964): 279. Thirty-three of forty-three of the districts studied were in Guangdong and Fujian. Other data came from Hubei, Anhui, and Zhejiang.

56. Interview in Quan-Wang Village, December 13, 1997.

57. The call to "destroy temples and build schools" *(huimiao xingxue)* was first raised during the late Qing Hundred Days of Reform and was again taken up during the Republic. In certain areas of Hebei, such as Ding County, particularly zealous local officials embarked on a crusade against popular temples. See Li Jinghan, *Ding xian shehui diaocha gaikuang* [A summary of the investigation of the society of Ding County] (Beijing: Beijing University, 1933), 417–430. In Cang County, the campaign was carried out with less enthusiasm. Here, the greatest destruction of temples came during the warfare of the 1930s as temples, often the strongest structures in a village, were requisitioned by advancing troops and destroyed by retreating ones.

58. Interview in Dulin Town and Ni-Yang Camp, October 15, 1997.

59. The appropriateness of this term is subject to debate, descending as it

does from earlier pejorative use in the original sources; however, because the English does not necessarily carry such connotations and remains the standard in most secondary literature, I will continue to use it in this text.

60. See ter Haar, 1999. A similar phenomenon occurred in early modern Europe, where the rising doctrinal authority of the Catholic Church over local society increasingly cast indigenous pagan cults and practices as satanic. See Giovanni Levi, *Inheriting Power: The Story of an Exorcist*, translated by Lydia G. Cochrane (Chicago: University of Chicago Press, 1988), and Carlo Ginzburg, *The Night Battles: Witchcraft & Agrarian Cults in the Sixteenth & Seventeenth Centuries* (Baltimore: Johns Hopkins University Press, 1983).

61. C. K. Yang, *Religion in Chinese Society: A Study of Contemporary Social Functions of Religion and Some of Their Historical Factors* (Berkeley: University of California Press, 1961), 204–205.

62. Ming dynasty teachings hailing from Shandong include the Luo Sect *(Luo jiao)* and the Li Sect *(Zaili jiao)*. Those from northern Hebei include the East and West Great Vehicle Teachings *(Dong, Xi Dacheng jiao)*, the Way of Yellow Heaven *(Huangtian dao)*, and Red Yang Teaching (*Hongyang jiao*, also known as "the Teaching of Primordial Chaos," *Hunyuan jiao*).

63. On religious belief and the breakdown of social order, see Philip Kuhn, *Rebellion and Its Enemies in Late Imperial China: Militarization and Social Structure, 1796–1864* (Cambridge, Mass.: Harvard University Press, 1970). For more specific treatment of sectarian rebellion, see Naquin, *Millenarian Rebellion in China* and *Shantung Rebellion*; see also Blaine Gaustad, "Prophets and Pretenders: Intersect Competition in Qianlong China," *Late Imperial China* 21, 1 (2000): 1–40.

64. Sawada Mizuho, *Kōchū haja shōben* [Research into precious scrolls] (Tokyo: Dōkyō kankō kai, 1972), 52–56. For an expert introduction to the origins and content of a number of sectarian scriptures, see Overmyer, *Precious Volumes*, 300–369. For a remarkably detailed recreation of scriptural and sectarian networks during the late Ming, see Richard Hon-chun Shek, "Religion and Society in the Late Ming: Sectarianism and Popular Thought in Sixteenth- and Seventeenth-Century China" (Ph.D. diss., University of California, Berkeley, 1980).

65. Interviews in Yangliuqing, March 15, 1998, and June 9, 1998; Huanghua County, Hebei, April 11, 1998; and Dong Family Village, Shandong, April 29, 1998.

66. "Chinese religion," being neither essentially "Chinese," nor a unified "religion," is a double misnomer that I will, nonetheless, use throughout this study. The juxtaposition is not to suggest that Islam or Christianity is any less "Chinese" than Buddhism (another "foreign religion").

67. *Cangxian*, 1933, 146

68. The remainder of the population is nearly all Han (97 percent), plus a small number of Manchus (0.3 percent). *Cangxian*, 1995, 559.

69. *Qingxian cuntu, juan 12.* Interviews in Dulin Town, June 30, 2002, Ni-Yang Camp, October 27, 1997.

70. *Hebei sheng zhi: zongjiao juan* [Hebei provincial gazetteer, religion] (Beijing: Zhongguo shuji chubanshe, 1991), 294, 289–302, 428–429. For a detailed account of the Boxer period in Cangzhou city, as well as of the small Christian presence, see the collected letters of Arthur Peill (chap. 1., n. 10).

71. Peill notes a case in which marketgoers in Cangzhou city, intrigued by the reputation of the Boxers, went to see a display of spirit possession. In this case, the spirit was Zhu Bazhen, "Pigsy" from the *Journey to the West.* Once these men, all from outside the area, had been taken by the spirit of Zhu, they began to snort and root around in the mud like pigs, a display onlookers apparently found less than inspiring (Peill, 48).

72. Peter Vandergeest and Nancy Lee Peluso discuss this sociological tendency to emphasize central places and networks of coercion over abstract conceptions of territory in light of Weberian definitions of state power. See "Territorialization and State Power in Thailand," *Theory and Society* 24 (June 1995): 385–426.

Chapter 2: Religious Life and the Village Community

1. See Introduction, note 24.

2. The classic work on this question is Hatada Takashi, *Chūgoku sonraku to kyōdōtai riron* [Chinese villages and the theory of village community] (Tokyo: Iwanami Shoten, 1973). Such questions are increasingly taken up by Chinese scholars of village society; see for example, Mao Dan, *Yige cunluo gongtongtai de bianqian: guanyu jianshan xiacun de danweihua de guancha yu chanshi* [Changes in the communal nature of a village: Investigation and explanation of Lower Village, Jian mountain] (Shanghai: Xuelin chubanshe, 2000).

3. Donald DeGlopper, "Religion and Ritual in Lukang," in *Religion and Ritual in Chinese Society,* ed. Arthur Wolf (Stanford, Calif.: Stanford University Press, 1974), 43–69.

4. Sangren, 62–69.

5. Sangren, 93–95.

6. Willem Grootaers emphasized the importance of artisanal tradition in propagating standard forms of temple iconography. Local painters, who generally resided in larger villages, were an important influence on local religiosity through their art. "The patterns they learned from their master (in most cases, their father) are applied by [the artists] with a minimum of interference from the part of villagers who entrusted them with the decoration of the temple." As such, not only decorative motifs but also the representation of certain deities became common throughout an extended area. See Grootaers, "Rural Temples around Hsuan-hua," 13, 55.

7. Interviews in Little Terrace Village, December 1, 1997.

8. The process was also seen in the eclipse of saint cults by the worship of Christ and Mary in early modern Spain. See Christian, *Local Religion in Sixteenth-Century Spain*, 181–208.

9. This particular case deserves special mention because of the story surrounding the statue itself. The statue, a crudely carved wooden image of an old man, is typical of the iconography of the Earth God cult and dates back before the memory of any of the villagers present, although all agreed that it was certainly "very old." It is remarkable for its tenacity, a sure sign of divine power; repeated attempts to destroy or dispose of the statue have all failed. The original temple was destroyed during the Republican period, and the statue was picked out of the rubble but was again lost. During the early 1950s, it was discovered buried in a field and secreted to the home of a faithful old woman, where it waited out the Cultural Revolution. During the late 1970s, a neighbor child found the statue and, frightened by its appearance, threw it into a nearby river. It was picked up downstream and appeared again the village in the wares of a traveling peddler. The common consensus is thus that the god had a strong affection for the village and wanted to stay. In addition, there are numerous subsidiary tales concerning the statue healing the sick, granting wishes, and the like. Interviews in Duliu Town, October 20, 1997.

10. David Johnson, ed. *Ritual Opera, Operatic Ritual: "Mu-lien Rescues His Mother."* In *Chinese Popular Culture: Papers from the International Workshop on the Mu-lien Operas, with an Additional Contribution on the Woman Huang Legend by Beata Grant* (Berkeley: University of California Press, 1989). Esherick (1987) and Shahar (1998) eloquently make the latter point.

11. Sangren, 68.

12. See, for example, Lin Mei-jung, especially pages 94–101.

13. Faure, 3–4.

14. Sangren, 55–72, 93–96.

15. David Johnson, "Temple Festivals in Southeastern Shanxi: The *Sai* of Nan-she Village and Big West Gate," *Minsu Quyi* 91 (1994): 91.

16. See Huang Zhusan and Wang Fucai, *Shanxi sheng, Quwo xian, Renzhuang cun 'shangu shenpu' diaocha baogao* [Investigation and report of the "Flat Drum Roster of the Gods" in Renzhuang Village, Quwo County, Shanxi]. *Minsu quyi congshu* (Taibei: Caituan fa ren Shi Hezheng minsu wenhua jijin hui, 1994).

17. Duara, *Culture, Power, and the State*, 124–128, 132–137. It also speaks for the interest some might have in representing the community as only those with the right to participate in village ritual. See Faure, 7–8.

18. This is particularly true concerning those rituals which surround Qingming. See Cohen, 521–528. On lineage ritual and its enforcement, see Szonyi, chap. 5.

19. This would not necessarily take place in the context of communal rituals. David Sabean discusses how receiving Holy Communion, seemingly a

matter of individual piety, was mandatory in the villages of seventeenth-century Württemberg. Refusal to take the sacrament was a public declaration of such a lingering grudge that not only demonstrated a rift within the village, but also left the individual vulnerable to demonic influence, presenting a tangible threat to the community as a whole. Such cases were serious enough that when they could not be settled inside the village, they were brought before secular or Church authorities.

20. CN I: 104, 220; IV: 31–32, 38, 60, 89, 356, 433, 436; V: 28, 440.

21. Sasaki and Lu, 52, 94, 274.

22. Christian, 55–59.

23. Charles Litzinger, "Temple Community and Village Cultural Integration in North China: Evidence from 'Sectarian Cases' *(Chiao-an)* in Chih-li, 1860–1895" (Ph.D. diss., University of California, Davis, 1983), 160.

24. In villages with no ritual specialists, the *huishou* might be responsible for the simple ceremony of burning incense on behalf of the community. This could have religious implications, as well, as in the Mantetsu village of Sibeichai, where villagers vied to be chosen as *huishou* because of the belief that this individual would receive special protection from the Buddha. See CN: 3, 43.

25. In Shajing, participation in the activities of the Five Festivals Society *(Banwuhui)* was a very public mark of elite status in the village. Although the society assembled on each of the five major village festivals, the required donation of thirty-five *yuan* precluded most villagers from participating. See CN I: 130–131, 135–136, 145, 173.

26. Interviews in Quan-Wang Village, October 5, 1997, Ni-Yang Camp, October 16, 1997.

27. Sidney Gamble, *North China Villages: Social, Political, and Economic Activities before 1933* (Berkeley: University of California Press, 1963), 119; Grootaers, "Temples and History of Wan-ch'üan," 217, and "Rural Temples around Hsuan-hua," 9.

28. Li Jinghan, 418–419.

29. *Qingxian cuntu, juan* 12; *Jinmen baojia tushuo* (n.p., 1842).

30. Sasaki and Lu, 51.

31. Interviews in Quan-Wang Village, October 5–6, 1997.

32. In the Daoist rituals of Putian, Fujian, each household is expected to make a financial contribution. In Putian, however, each family is expected to send a male representative to participate, and families cast lots to determine who will act as *huishou*. See Kenneth Dean, *Taoist Ritual and Popular Cults of Southeast China* (Princeton, N.J.: Princeton University Press, 1993), 50–53.

33. Interviews in White Yang Bridge, November 14–15, 1997, and Rear Camp, November 15–16, 1997. A slightly different situation existed in the highly commercialized Tianjin suburb of Duliu, where sectarian activities were supported by donations from merchant houses. See Sasaki and Lu, 296.

34. The term *"hui"* can refer either to a meeting or the group that organizes it. Thus, *"miao hui"* can be either a temple festival or the temple committee, depending upon the context.

35. The crossover between administrative and natural social boundaries has been addressed by Mingming Wang, "Place, Administration and Territorial Cults in Late Imperial China: A Case Study from South Fujian," *Late Imperial China* 16 (1995): 33–79. In his discussion of the subjective religious meaning of administrative units of late Imperial urban Quanzhou, Wang shows that these were not antithetical, but, rather, that "a spatial institution could be invented, utilized to govern society, and equally importantly . . . the same institution could be remolded into an alternative spatial institution and altered in terms of its function and meaning" (34).

36. This village was founded by members of the surname Hai and was formerly known as Hai Family Dock.

37. Here celebrated on February 19 and October 15, respectively.

38. Interviews in Hai Dock, November 29–30, 1997, and July 7, 1998.

39. This is common practice in villages such as Ni-Yang Camp and White Yang Bridge.

40. One story from Ni-Yang Camp demonstrates the importance of sincerity over amount of the donation. During a sectarian festival in the early 1990s, one well-off villager made a donation of only five *fen* (one-half *yuan*, a very small amount of money) and then proceeded to gorge himself on the banquet that followed, commenting loudly on what a bargain it was to eat so well for so little money. That night, he became violently ill and for one week was unable to eat without vomiting immediately thereafter. Those who related this story explained that he had been punished "by the Buddha," not for the amount of his donation, but the lack of sincerity with which it was given. Interview in Ni-Yang Camp, October 16, 1997.

41. The informality of this affiliation is particularly evident in the vague answers leaders and villagers alike gave to questions concerning sectarian "membership." In contrast to their precise knowledge of sectarian leaders and networks, my informants shrugged off the question "How many villagers are in the teaching?" *(You duoshao cunmin zai hui?)* with such answers as "All of them" or "None of them." It was only when the question was made more specific—such as "how many people attended the last public ritual *(hui)?*" or "How many families have a Dong Sihai altar in their home?" that responses again became more concrete. A similar case is seen in the Mantetsu surveys of Shajing village, concerning affiliation with the "Five Festivals Society" *(Banwuhui).* See CN: I, 130–131.

42. Interviews in Quan-Wang Village, October 5, 1997

43. The latter is most likely a reference to Guanyin, although even villagers who remembered the shrine were unclear on the identity of the deity.

44. Again, there are many ways to perform this ceremony. Sectarians chant

their own scriptures and perform a ritual not unlike that seen at the New Year festival. Villages without a sectarian group might just as easily perform their own ritual, but this, too, requires some religious knowledge and initiative. With two sects in immediate proximity, this village has had little impetus to relearn lost ritual techniques.

45. Interviews in Ni-Yang Camp, October 16, 1997, Little Terrace Village, November 30–December 1, 1997.

46. Huang, 219–274; Duara, *Culture, Power, and the State*, 118–157.

47. Huang, 267–268.

48. Duara, *Culture, Power, and the State*, 148

49. Sangren, 55–72, 93–96.

50. For a detailed examination of lineages as rhetorical and practical structures, see Szonyi, 2002.

Chapter 3: Spirits, Sectarians, and Xiangtou

1. In this area, the most common medical care consists of a small clinic run by a villager who has studied the essentials of Chinese and Western medicine for one or two years in nearby Cangzhou City. Such clinics are usually one room in the house of the villager and are stocked with a basic array of pain relievers, antibiotics, and Chinese traditional medicines.

2. The term *"xiangtou"* literally translates as "head of the incense." A more common name for such healers is *wupo shenhan*, which has a distinctly derogatory tone, translating roughly as "witches and sorcerers." The term *"xiangtou"* may have derived from monastic Buddhism. In modern Taiwan, for example, the *xiangtou* is the monk who cares for a burning stick of incense while his fellows sit in meditation. It can also refer to the leader of a pilgrimage group *(xiang ke)*. Regardless of its origin, the term appears elsewhere in the vocabulary of popular religion. In other areas of Hebei, *xiangtou* refers simply to village religious leaders, apparently with no specific reference to healing. CN, I: 130, 145, 173–176; Gamble, 344.

3. Fei Xiaotong, *Peasant Life in China: A Field Study in the Country Life of the Yangtze Valley* (New York: E. P. Dutton, 1939), 165–169.

4. The terms *shi* and *xu*, which are most commonly translated as "true" and "false," are somewhat misleading at first glance. A *xu* condition is as real as a *shi* disease, the difference being that former has not yet manifested itself with specific physical symptoms. These names are likely taken from traditional Chinese medicine, which designates conditions of *xu* or *shi* to mean a deficiency or excess of *qi*, the life force that flows through the body.

5. The most obvious manifestation of this is in scriptures such as the *Great Treatise on Response and Retribution (Tai shang ganying bian)*, in which different sorts of crimes are punished by a shortening of lifespan.

6. The Five Pecks of Rice Teaching is another name given to the early Celes-

tial Masters *(Tian shi)* school, which formed in Sichuan in the second half of the second century A.D. Their initial success was based largely on healing, in which confession was an integral part. See Barbara Hendrichke, "Early Daoist Movements," in *Daoism Handbook,* ed. Livia Kohn (Leiden: E. J. Brill, 2000), 139–141 and 153–155. See also the discussion of healing in Judith Berling, *The Syncretic Religion of Lin Chao-en* (New York: Columbia University Press, 1980), 71–73 and 137–144.

7. Lu Yao has provided a general discussion of the healing practices of this sect under its alternate name as the "Single Incense Teaching" *(yizhu xiang jiao).* Of course, the healing practices of even a single teaching are subject to significant local variation. As discussed later in this chapter, the blending of such practices is a hallmark of local religious life. Lu Yao, 59–62.

8. Other manifestations of the Heaven and Earth Teaching demonstrate a more literal understanding of the causality between the health of the "heart" (in the spiritual or physical sense) and the body, one evocative of the relationships of correlative cosmology. In Huimin County, Shandong, the origin and spiritual center of the teaching, Lu Yao recorded set sayings relating the heart to the six organs of perception—the eyes, ears, mouth, nose, hands, and feet. In others, the heart was the chief of the five internal organs. Lu Yao, 59–61.

9. Poo Mu-chou, *In Search of Personal Welfare: A View of Ancient Chinese Religion* (Albany: SUNY Press, 1988), 137–141.

10. Davis, especially 45–53.

11. "Miao Su," quoted in Hu Pu'an, *Zhonghua quanguo fengsu zhi* [A gazetteer of customs in China] (Shanghai: Shanghai shudian, 1988; reprint of 1923 original), vol. 1: 197.

12. "Shuanghuai Sui Chao," quoted in Hu Pu'an, 1: 291.

13. "Heilongjiang Fengsu Suoji," quoted in Hu Pu'an, 2: 84. See also note 23 below for a second description of healing practices in Manchuria. On the thaumaturgical value of scripture recitation, see John Kieschnick, *The Eminent Monk: Buddhist Ideals in Medieval Chinese Hagiography* (Honolulu: University of Hawai'i Press, 1997), 90–92.

14. Shan Min, *Huli xinyang zhi mi* [The riddle of belief in foxes] (Beijing: Renmin Chubanshe, 1994), 201.

15. For a detailed introduction to classical literature on fox spirits, see Shan Min or Xiaofei Kang, "The Fox and the Barbarian," *Journal of Chinese Religions* 27 (1999): 35–68. See also Pu Songling.

16. See, for example, Pu Songling, tales 13, 15, 19, 22, 23, 35, and 62.

17. *Cangxian,* 1933, 1275–1276.

18. In Minnan dialect, *tongzi* is pronounced as *dangki,* the subject of numerous studies of shamanism in Taiwan.

19. Shan Min, 32.

20. Davis, 63.

21. Li Jinghan, 398–401.

22. One particularly characteristic illustration of the belief in local spirits *(dixian)* is the "Fox Hall" *(huxian tang)* in Jilin, in which altars to various incarnations of fox spirits were joined by those of numerous other spirits. The most basic function of this temple was healing by witches and sorcerers *(wuxi)* who "burn and read incense, *ketou* and read sutras" as well as others with a closer tie to Manchurian shamanism, who entered trances and spoke for the spirits. Ōtani Kohō, "*Shūkyō chōsa hōkoku shū*" [Collected reports on an investigation of religion] (1937), translated into the Chinese by Teng Mingyu and reprinted in *Changchun wenshi ziliao* 4 (1988): 41–43.

23. This is a reference to traditional Chinese medicine, in which taking the pulse is a fundamental diagnostic technique. Most peasants know that, when one visits the doctor, one has one's pulse taken. Thus, although the practice employed by Wu has nothing to do with Chinese medicine, it is implicitly accepted by most of my informants as valid.

24. The blurring of practical boundaries between the staid Heaven and Earth Teaching and those of local healers strikes me as a close parallel to the interaction between twelfth-century Daoist ritual masters and local spirit medium cults. See Davis, 45–66.

25. This method is often associated with sectarian practice. The depositions of members of Red Yang teaching *(Hongyang jiao)* specialists refer repeatedly to the reading of incantations and scriptures. See Zhongguo di yi lishi dang'an guan, ed., "*Jiaqing nianjian Hongyangjiao dang'an*," *Lishi dang'an* 1 (2000): 21–41.

26. This story is very well known locally and was recounted to me by a number of peasants as an example of the "superstitious" (as opposed to scientific) activities of *xiangtou*. Two practicing *xiangtou* cited this story as an example of a fraud within their profession. This technique of exorcism is mentioned obliquely in Pu Songling, story 126.

27. "Tianjin shi xiao'er tiaoqiang zhi fengsu," quoted in Hu Pu'an, 2: 51.

28. The name used for a sect usually ends in "teaching" *(jiao)* or, more commonly, "gate" *(men)*. Thus, another common phrase used for entering a sect is literally to "enter the doorway" *(ru men)*.

29. Shan Min, 29, 209.

30. Xiaofei Kang, 35–67.

31. Again, this speaks only for one particular area. As near as Ding County, the worship of fox spirits was quite common. See Li Jinghan, 399.

32. This same method was used by healers in the Red Yang Teaching, two centuries earlier. See "*Jiaqing nianjian Hongyangjiao dang'an*," 26.

33. It should be noted that the shamanistic tradition mentioned previously is similarly absent in the actual healing. Although the *xiangtou* is a tool of the spirit, actual possession, particularly the highly ecstatic sort reported by Li Jinghan, is rarely seen. The same peasants who could name twenty *xiangtou* with neighboring villages only knew of one, the aforementioned Ms. Wu, who

made any appearance of possession. Similarly, none knew of such a technique having been used in the past.

34. The subject of healing and *qi* circulation *(yunqi gonfu)* is discussed in detail in chapter 7.

Chapter 4: Monastic Buddhism

1. Keith Robbins, 1975, "Institutions and Illusions: The Dilemma of the Modern Ecclesiastical Historian," in *The Materials, Methods and Sources of Ecclesiastical History: Papers Read at the Twelfth Summer Meeting and Thirteenth Winter Meeting of the Ecclesiastical Historical Society,* ed. Derek Baker (New York: Barnes and Noble Books, 1975), 355–367.

2. A selection of this criticism can be seen in Donald S. Lopez, ed., *Curators of the Buddha: The Study of Buddhism under Colonialism* (Chicago: University of Chicago Press, 1995). Quotation from Stephen Teiser, *The Ghost Festival in Medieval China* (Princeton, N.J.: Princeton University Press, 1988), 20–25.

3. Another interesting example is the reformulation of the "Buddhist" tradition in response to the religious persecutions of Meiji Japan. See James Edward Ketelaar, *Of Heretics and Martyrs in Meiji Japan: Buddhism and Its Persecution* (Princeton, N.J.: Princeton University Press, 1990).

4. This is the driving problematic of the great histories of Chinese Buddhism, such as Kenneth Ch'en, *Buddhism in China: A Historical Survey* (Princeton, N.J.: Princeton University Press, 1964).

5. Philip Kuhn, *Soulstealers: The Chinese Sorcery Scare of 1768* (Cambridge, Mass.: Harvard University Press, 1990), 107–113.

6. Vincent Goosaert, "Counting the Monks: The 1736–1739 Census of the Chinese Clergy," *Late Imperial China* 21, 2 (2000): 40–85, especially 60–61.

7. This period is described in Holmes Welch, *The Practice of Chinese Buddhism* (Cambridge, Mass.: Harvard University Press, 1967). The estimated number of monks per province during the 1930s is from appendix 1 of that work.

8. Goossaert, "Counting the Monks," 60; Welch, *The Practice of Chinese Buddhism,* appendix 1.

9. Welch, *The Practice of Chinese Buddhism,* 246.

10. Huang Pengnian, *Jifu fancha zhi* [Gazetteer of Buddhist monasteries in Jifu (Hebei)], 1910, *juan* 178–182 in *Jifu tongzhi* [Complete gazetteer of Jifu (Hebei)] (Shijiazhuang: Hebei renmin chubanshe, 1985).

11. To avoid confusion between popular temples and specifically Buddhist ones, I will refer to the latter as "monasteries," regardless of the actual occupation of these buildings by monks.

12. *Si,* twenty-seven total, thirteen in Tianjin; *Tang,* eleven total, three in Tianjin; *An,* fifty-three total, thirty-eight in Tianjin. The five mosques in the area were omitted from the data. *Jinmen baojia tushuo,* 1842.

13. *Qingxian cuntu, juan* 12.

14. Timothy Brook, "From Late-Imperial to Modern: Buddhism in the Chinese Constitution." Paper presented at the "From Late Imperial to Modern Chinese History: Views from the Eighteenth Century" conference, University of California, Los Angles, 1998. See also the large compilations of temple gazetteers, such as Bai Huawen et al., ed., *Zhongguo fosi zhi* (Yangzhou: Jiangsu guangling guji chubanshe, 1996).

15. Brook, "Late-Imperial to Modern," 1998.

16. The writer alluded to was Lu Longqi, the magistrate of Lingshou County in Zhili and editor of its local history, published in 1685. The decision to omit Buddhist and Daoist temples altogether was debated by local Zhili literati over the next century. Most lauded the anti-Buddhist sentiment of Lu Longqi, but few followed his example in their own writings. See Brook, "Late-Imperial to Modern."

17. The information from this section is drawn primarily from *Cangxian*, 1933, 286–335; Zheng Qinghuan et al., *Qingxian zhi* [Gazetteer of Qing County] (1933; reprint Taibei: Cheng wen chubanshe, 1968), 224–262; and Xu Zongliang et al., *Tianjin fu zhi* [Gazetteer of Tianjin Prefecture] (1899; reprint Taibei: Taiwan xue sheng shu ju, 1968), 2076–2127. Each of these presents what appears to be a relatively complete list of temples. Naturally, the most attention is given to the Confucian cult in the county seat, but overall the picture is quite close to the state of temple construction given in ethnographic sources such as Grootaers and Li Jinghan. In particular, these gazetteers appear far more complete than those from neighboring Xian and Nanpi Counties, demonstrating that the compilation of such information was not always subject to formulaic misrepresentation.

18. Timothy Brook, *Praying for Power*, 89–126, 325–330; quotation from page 113.

19. Ch'en, 1964, 434–454; Welch, *The Practice of Chinese Buddhism*, 217, quotes *Daqing luli xinzeng tongcuan qizheng* 8:23 as the source for a very similar proscription.

20. Welch, *The Practice of Chinese Buddhism*, 134.

21. Willem Grootaers noted that (former) monasteries were less prevalent in areas of recent settlement. Relying especially on the date of artifacts found inside temples, he comes to the conclusion that the majority were originally founded before the Yuan and rebuilt during the early Ming dynasty. Grootaers, "Temples and History of Wan-ch'üan," 257; "Rural Temples around Hsuan-hua," 74–77.

22. Brook, *Praying for Power*, 162–165.

23. *Qingxian cuntu, juan* 12, Qingxian, 1931, 252.

24. Goossaert, 40; Ch'en, 452.

25. Goossaert, 45–51.

26. The *Jinmen baojia tushuo* contains separate categories for various occupations, such as scholars, merchants, and boatmen, as well as Buddhist monks

and Daoist priests, which are listed together under the heading *sengdao.* See Ch'ü T'ung-tsu, 150–154, for the limitations of *baojia* records.

27. Li fa yuan [Legislative Yuan], *Zhonghua minguo fagui huibian* [Compiled laws and regulations of the Republic of China], vol. 3: *Neizheng* [Internal administration] (Shanghai: Zhonghua shu ju, 1933), 4, 815.

28. See Nedostup.

29. Welch, *The Practice of Chinese Buddhism,* 411. See also the recent analysis of Taixu and his legacy by Don Pittman, *Toward a Modern Chinese Buddhism: Taixu's Reforms* (Honolulu: University of Hawai'i Press, 2001).

30. *Jinmen baojia tushuo,* 1842.

31. In contrast, roughly twenty times that number were reported in Anhui. Quoted in Welch, *The Practice of Chinese Buddhism,* appendix 1.

32. *Cangxian,* 1933, 1623.

33. Liu Shuxin et al., *Nanpi xian zhi* [Gazetteer of Nanpi County] (1932; reprint Taibei: Cheng wen chubanshe, 1968), 124–125, 503.

34. *Cangxian,* 1995, 598.

35. Grootaers, "Temples and History of Wan-ch'üan," 257–258; "Rural Temples around Hsuan-hua," 74.

36. Li Jinghan, 150, 420. In view of the information in the chapters 3 and 7 of this study, I would likely disagree with Li's definition of "religious specialist" but suspect that it is based on religious services being a primary source of income.

37. Sasaki and Lu, 264; CN I, 171–174, 190.

38. Esherick, 277; Sasaki and Lu, 35.

39. Peill, 57. For an account of the Boxers in Cangzhou, see Peill, 40–68.

40. Interviews in Dulin Town, June 30, 2002, Ni-Yang Camp, October 27, 1997.

41. Interviews in Rear Camp and Zhifangtou, November 15, 1997.

42. Kuhn, *Soulstealers,* 112.

43. *Zhonghua minguo fagui huibian: neizheng,* 815.

44. The term *youpo* is a degendered transliteration of the Sanskrit *upāsaka, upāssikā* (layman, laywoman). The more general term for such lay faithful is *jushi. Cangxian,* 1933, 1623.

45. "*Keneng shi daoshi de fomen, haishi foshide daomen, hai keneng dou shi.*" Interviews in Hai Dock, November 30, 1997.

46. See the description of this ceremony in the previous chapter. Similar "taking a teacher" *(ren shifu)* and "crossing the threshold" *(guo men kang)* ceremonies are performed by sectarians. Interviews in Ni-Yang Camp, October 16 and 27, 1997.

47. In 1941, the monastery had two residents, an older monk and his disciple. *Hebei sheng zongjiao yanjiu hui bian, "Bohai dao zongjiao tuanti diaocha biao" in Hebei difang zongjiao tuanti diaocha biao.*

48. The apparent contradiction of a technically atheistic state taking a cen-

tral role in local Buddhist revival is not without significant historical prece-
dent. The role of the state as both protector and arbiter of religion often forces
it to develop a multiplicity of identities, as when the Orthodox tsarist Russia
took on responsibility for policing Islam in its Central Asian domains. See
Robert Crews, "Empire and the Confessional State: Islam and Religious Politics in Nineteenth-Century Russia" *American Historical Review* 108, 1 (February 2003): 50–83.

49. Interviews in Water Moon Monastery, Cangzhou City, June 30, 2002.

Chapter 5: Pseudomonastic Sectarians

1. The name itself refers to the Confucian principle of *li*, variously translated as "reason" or "principle." A literal translation of the name would be
"the teaching in or with *li*." Other variations of this name include *Limen* (also
the Li Sect) and *Qingli* (Pure Li). The term *li* was often used to signify the sect
itself or the essence of its teaching. A member of the sect, for example, could
be said to "have *li*" *(you li)*. This teaching has no relation to the similarly
named "Domestic *Li*" *(Zaijiali)* teaching.

2. J. J. M. de Groot, *Sectarianism and Religious Persecution in China: A Page
in the History of Religion* (Amsterdam: Johannes Muller, 1903).

3. The dharma name Rulai (sanskrit *tat'agata*, meaning "thus appearing")
is a rather grandiose allusion to the enlightened Buddha. Zhao Dongshu, *Lijiao huibian* [Compiled materials on the Li Sect] (Taibei: Zhonghua lijiao qing
xin tang gongsuo,1953), 213; Yü, 451.

4. *The Five Buddhas Deliver Our Teacher*, quoted in Sasaki and Lu, 333–335;
Zhao Dongshu (115) introduces a number of instances in which Guanyin appears to Yang as an old man and dictates the scriptures to him.

5. Zhao Dongshu, 34, 115–116, 119–120, 159; *Precious Scripture of the Five
Sages*, 258.

6. The Five Proscriptions (*wu jie*, also translated as the "five vows") of
Buddhism prohibit taking life, stealing, licentiousness, deceit, and consump-
tion of meat or alcohol. The Way of Former Heaven *(Xiantian dao)* and
Dragon Flower Teaching *(Longhua jiao)* each kept five, the foremost of which
was the Buddhist admonition against taking life. Cheng Xiao, *Wanqing xiangtu yishi* [Rural consciousness in the late Qing] (Beijing: Renmin Chunab-
she, 1990), 204; de Groot, 190–191, 209–211.

7. The essence of this Confucian morality was later written into a short
poem that, unfortunately, loses the rhythm when translated into English
(Sasaki and Lu, 296, also quoted in Cheng Xiao, 205):

The Li Sect is a good sect,	*Zaili shi hao dao,*
With four seasons and four filial pieties,	*si jie yu si xiao,*
Learn benevolence, righteousness,	*xue ren xue yi xue zhongdao,*
loyalty and the way,	

Give up your tobacco, alcohol, bullying and stealing.	*jie yan jie jiu jie qiandao.*
Today, you learn *li* from your teacher	*Jinri dequ shifu li,*
Then, go home and serve your father and mother.	*Huijiaqu ba fumu xiao.*

8. Zhao Dongshu, 264–266.

9. Li Shiyu, "Tianjin Zailijiao Diaocha Yanjiu," reprinted in *Minjian zong-jiao* 2 (1996), 170–176.

10. This is the opinion expressed in articles by Bi Wenzhen and Wang Hongkui, two former leaders of the teaching in the suburbs of Tianjin. Bi Wenzhen et al., "*Jiu Tianjin de limen*" [The Li Sect in old Tianjin], *Tianjin wenshi ziliao xuanji* 52 (1990): 184–192; Wang Hongkui. "*Lijiao de qiyuan yu fazhan*" [The origins and development of Zailijiao], *Tianjin wenshi ziliao xuanji* 52 (1990): 173–183.

11. Bi Wenzhen, 185; Li Jiexian, "*Lijiao chuanru Tianjin yu xilao gongsuo*" [The spread of Zailijiao to Tianjin and the Old West Common House], *Tianjin wenshi ziliao xuanji* 24 (1983): 189–205, 191.

12. Wang Hongkui, 173.

13. See also note 4. Li Shiyu, "Tianjin Zailijiao," 180. For a masterful discussion of the worship of Guanyin by sectarian groups, see chapter 11 of Chün-fang Yü, 2001.

14. The ten primary disciples of Patriarch Yang came from all corners of the North China Plain, demonstrating the size of the physical area through which people, ideas, and organizations freely interacted during the early Qing. Of the ten disciples, two were from Shandong, two from Tianjin, one from Beijing, one from Henan, and four from throughout Hebei. See Zhao Dongshu, 165–166; Wang Hongkui, 174–177.

15. Wang Hongkui, 178–179, lists the village in which Yin Ruo was raised as Kezong, rather than Keniu. See Zhao Dongshu, 165–177, 215.

16. Wang Hongkui, 177–178. I have chosen to render the term *gongsuo* in English translation to distinguish it from other scholarship on a secular institution with the same name. Although "common house" is not a precisely literal translation (such as "public place") of *gongsuo*, it captures the practical use of the Chinese term by the Li Sect. The term "*gongsuo*" has had many uses in Qing and Republican China. It referred to a village green or village offices, particularly during the Republican period, when such offices were created by administrative fiat. It could also generally signify an organization; the 1933 Cang County gazetteer mentions three "fire rescue *Gongsuo*" (*jiu huo gongsuo*), *Cangxian*, 1933, 293–295.

17. Li Shiyu, "Tianjin Zailijiao," 177.

18. This is similar to the division between *dangjia* and *huishou* discussed in chapter 2.

19. Li Shiyu, "Tianjin Zailijiao," 178. The term *dangjia* literally means

"household manager" and appears in Buddhist and secular usage. Peasants in Kang Family Camp and Shajing Village, near Beijing, used the term to signify a household head. CN I: 51, 270, 293. Holmes Welch also mentions the use of the term in monastic life. See Welch, *The Practice of Chinese Buddhism*, 130, 133–137, 200, 469, 485.

20. Bi Wenzhen, 189.

21. Li Shiyu, "Tianjin Zailijiao," 179, raises this point.

22. Sasaki and Lu, 320. The idea that a life of personal cultivation and purity will protect the body from decay was also common in Buddhism. Monks of particularly high repute were often spared cremation for a number of years to verify that their bodies had been preserved. See Welch, *The Practice of Chinese Buddhism*, 342–345.

23. Bi Wenzhen, 188–189; Sasaki and Lu, 329–333.

24. Zhao Dongshu, 199–200; Wang Hongkui, 179–180. De Groot also mentions Yi Chang'a, 158.

25. Zhao Dongshu, 200; Wang Hongkui, 180.

26. Zhao Dongshu, 201–203. It is highly unlikely that the Li Sect could have commanded such a large portion of the population as active members. Particularly considering that the sect required complete abstention as its primary requirement and that there was a clear process and ceremony of induction into the sect, one cannot count the large circle of passive or episodic patrons that one might see in other teachings.

27. Shao Yong, *Zhongguo huidaomen* [Chinese sectarians] (Shanghai: Shanghai renmin chubanshe, 1997), 115–116.

28. Ibid., 115–120, 165–167.

29. Zhao Dongshu, 255–260.

30. Shao Yong, 299.

31. Zhao Dongshu, 242–243.

32. Ibid., 226–229.

33. Li Shiyu, "Tianjin Zailijiao," 176–177.

34. Ibid., 169; Shao Yong, 115.

35. Zhao Dongshu, 214.

36. Li Jiexian, 198–200.

37. Yi Zhe, "'*Limen gongsuo*' de nei mu" [The inner curtain of the "*Zailijiao gongsuo*"], *Tianjin shi hedong qu wenshi ziliao*, 3 (1990): 114–126. This attitude reflects earlier antisectarian polemics, such as the *Detailed Refutation of Heterodox Teachings*. Li Sect devotion did employ Buddhist scriptures, most commonly the Universal Gateway chapter *(pu men pin)* from the *Lotus Sutra*, in addition to Confucian-based morality tracts, such as the *Classic of Filial Piety* (*xiao jing*) and *Classic of Loyalty (zhong jing)*. See Zhao Dongshu, 157. For the appropriation of Guanyin scriptures by sectarian groups, see Yü, chapter 11.

38. Li Jiexian, 201; Zhao Dongshu, 157; Sasaki and Lu, 333; Li Shiyu, "Tianjin Zailijiao," 171. Other cities, such as Beijing and Shanghai, also produced their own publications. See Li Shiyu, "*Tianjin Zailijiao*," 188.

39. This scripture is also known as the *Precious Scripture of the Five Mountains (wu shan baojuan)*. It is mentioned in Li Shiyu, *"Tianjin Zailijiao,"* 203–204, and in Sawada Mizuho, *Hōkan no kenkyu*, 150, in the latter as the *Precious Scripture of the Five Sages (Wushengzong baojuan)*. It also appears in Zhang Xishun et al., eds., *Baojuan* (Shanxi: Shanxi renmin chubanshe), vol. 24.

40. Five Phases cosmology is discussed in Joseph Needham, *Science and Civilisation in China.*, vol. 2 (Cambridge: Cambridge University Press, 1956), 232–268. The table of classifications included on pages 268–269 is similar to that which appears in the scripture.

41. Members were cautioned, "Above, do not pass it to your father or mother; below, do not pass it to your wife or children" *(shang bu chuan fumu, xia bu chuan qi zi)*. See Li Shiyu, "Tianjin Zailijiao," 184.

42. This is a commonly seen method of sectarian induction, employed also by the Way of Penetrating Unity. For a description of the Li Sect ceremony, see Li Shiyu, "Tianjin Zailijiao," 176, 205–207.

43. Tianjin shi zhi bianxuan chu, *Tianjin shi gaiyao* [An overview of Tianjin] (Tianjin: Tianjin shi zhengfu, 1934). Also in Li Shiyu, "Tianjin Zailijiao," 169.

44. The dates of the *zhaikou* were largely a function of the individual common house, but the most common case seems to have been to hold the ceremony three times each year, on 2/18 and 9/18, commemorating the birth and death of Guanyin, and on 12/8 *(laba)*. Other dates often corresponded to important days in the popular religious calendar, such as the birthday of the Sakyamuni Buddha. Li Jiexian, 198.

45. The entire festival lasted from 3/16 to 3/23. See Xu Zhaoqiong, *Tianjin huanghui kao* [A record of the Empress of Heaven Festival in Tianjin]. Reprint vol. 6, *Tianjin fengtu congshu* (Tianjin: Tianjin guji chubanshe, 1988). See also Li Shiyu, "Tianjin Zailijiao," 181.

46. *Zhonghua minguo 21 nian 6 yue 19 ri, quanguo chao luojia puto shan* (n.p., n.d.).

47. Sasaki and Lu, 292–294, Chiang Chu-shan, *"1930 niandai tianjin Duliu zhen shangren de zongjiao yu shehui huodong canyu—yi 'zailijiao' wei li"* [Participation of merchants in religious and social activities in the 1930s Duliu, Tianjin—the example of Zailijiao] in *Mingqing yi lai minjian zongjiao de tansuo* [An inquiry into popular religion since the Ming-Qing], ed. Wang Chienchuan and Chiang Chu-shan (Taibei: Shangding wenhua chubanshe, 1996), 266–291.

48. Sasaki and Lu, 328.

49. Merchants would occasionally travel to Tianjin for temple fairs or to watch opera. See Sasaki and Lu, 319, 293, 323.

50. Ibid., 330.

51. Ibid., 333–336, 345, 346.

52. Ibid., 296, 317, 332, 336.

53. Ibid., 317, 329, 341 (emphasis added).

54. Ibid., 141, 154, 302, 331, 345.

55. Ibid., 296, 330, 343.

56. The Green Gang was a secret brotherhood that was often associated with underworld activity. Ibid., 355.

57. Chiang Chu-shan, 275–276.

58. These brigades had 500 people each and were at least as significant as a realm of public social interaction as they were actual fire-fighting teams. These brigades also had *zhaikou* that, like those of the Li Sect, were primarily large vegetarian dinners with an attendant social and ritual function. See Sasaki and Lu, 296, 325, 356–357; Chiang Chu-shan, 276–277.

59. Sasaki and Lu, 356–357.

60. Particularly since many neighboring communities did not have the teaching. See Sasaki and Lu, 302.

61. Concerning the residence of teachers in Lanshui Cave, see Wang Hong-kui, 177–178, and Zhao Dongshu, 226–229. The writers of the Cang County gazetteer were overtly sympathetic to the teaching and presented it in an extremely favorable light. *Cangxian*, 1933, 1630. Interviews in Cangzhou City, June 29–30, 1999.

62. *Cangxian zhi*, 1933, 1630–1632 (emphasis added). The 1994 gazetteer from Cang County is even less helpful, giving only a perfunctory list of urban Common Houses, and ignoring the existence of the teaching in the country-side altogether. See *Cangxian*, 1995, 598, 602.

63. In Ding county, located in southern Hebei, Li Jinghan counted ninety members, living in sixteen villages. See Li Jinghan, 444.

64. Li Shiyu, "Tianjin Zailijiao," 178; interviews in Yang Camp, March 15–16, 1998; Little Terrace, April 29, 1998; and Tianjin, July 5–7, 1999.

65. Barend Ter Haar, *White Lotus*, on "label" and "autonym," chapter 6.

66. CN VI, 226–227.

67. Li Jinghan, 445–446.

68. Ōtani Kohō, 41–43.

Chapter 6: Apocalyptic Sectarians

1. The name "Way of Penetrating Unity" refers to a quote from the *Lunyu* (*Analects*, 4:15) in which Confucius tells his disciple, "My Way is penetrated by a single unity" (*wu dao yi yi guan zhi*). This sect is often rendered in English as the "Unity Sect," a formulation that I have chosen to alter slightly, to emphasize the idea that the transmission of the sect has continued unbroken since the beginning of time. The Way of Penetrating Unity has evolved con-siderably since it was established in Taiwan in 1949 and particularly since 1987, when it was finally recognized by the government of the Republic of China. For this reason, I have chosen to limit references to the numerous outstanding

studies of the Way of Penetrating Unity in modern Taiwan, such as Sung Kuang-yü, *Tiandao Gouchen* (Taibei: Yuanyou chubanshe, 1984); David Jordan and Daniel Overmyer, *The Flying Phoenix: Aspects of Chinese Sectarianism in Taiwan* (Princeton, N.J.: Princeton University Press, 1986); and Philip Clart, "The Ritual Content of Morality Books: A Case Study of a Taiwanese Spirit-Writing Cult." (Ph.D diss., University of British Columbia, 1996).

2. As had the Li Sect, the Way of Penetrating Unity emerged from a pre-existing sectarian tradition, which complicates the question of its precise origins. Li Shiyu has claimed that the pedigree of the teaching reaches back to the White Lotus Teaching *(Bailian jiao)* of the Song dynasty, while Ma Xisha and Han Bingfang ground the teaching in the mid-Qing Green Lotus *(Qinglian)* and late Ming Great Vehicle *(Dacheng)* teachings. Li Shiyu, *Xiandai Huabei Mimi Zongjiao* [Secret religions in modern North China] (Shanghai: Shanghai wenyi chubanshe, 1948), 33–35; Ma Xisha and Han Bingfang. *Zhongguo minjian zongjiao shi* (Beijing: Renmin chubanshe, 1992), chap. 18.

3. Sung Kuang-yü, 102, 117.

4. Instead, Lu Yao credits Wang Jueyi with the "Singular One Following the End" Teaching *(Mo hou yi zhu jiao)*, which he considers to be an ancestor of the Way of Penetrating Unity. Lu Yao, 372, 379–383, 386–387.

5. Lu Yao, 387–391; Shao Yong, 1997, p. 200.

6. Shao Yong, 295; Song Guangyu, 122–123.

7. Lu Yao, 424–429; Shao Yong, 200, 295–296.

8. Sung Kuang-yü, 123–124. Similarly, many *tan* were established in existing temples.

9. See Daniel Overmyer, *Precious Volumes,* for a discussion of the development of this theme in sectarian scripture. Within the Way of Penetrating Unity, the Eternal Venerable Mother is usually referred to as the "Venerable Mother of the Great Void" *(wuji laomu),* often with the character for mother turned sideways. I will use the name Eternal Venerable Mother because it is the older and more general of the two.

10. In this respect, the Way of Penetrating Unity is nothing if not complete. From its beginnings with Pangu, the teaching traces its line to the ancient sage kings and then to Confucius and Mencius. It then moves west to India, to include the Buddha, returning to China with Bodhidharma, afterward remaining within the sectarian tradition, including such figures as Luo Weiqun (an early Qing disciple of the Great Vehicle Teaching—counted as the eighth generation of the final era) and Huang Dehui (disciple of Great Vehicle Teaching and founder of the Way of the Golden Elixir *[Jindan dao]*—the ninth generation). A similar genealogy is claimed by the Way of Yellow Heaven *(Huangtian dao).* See Li Shiyu, 50–54, 59–62; Pu Wenqi, *Minjian mimi zongjiao cidian* [Dictionary of secret popular religion] (Chengdu: Sichuan ci shu chubanshe, 1996), 186, 310, 375. Alternately, Wang Jueyi is counted as the fifteenth patriarch of the era after the teaching was returned to China by Bodhidharma. Zhang is

counted as the eighteenth (Song Guangyu, 102). Li Shiyu, *Xiandai Huabei*, 52–55, and Lu Yao, 371–379, each explain the line of teachers in great detail.

11. Lu Yao, 371.

12. For a general introduction to recent scholarship on the millenarianism in China, see David Ownby, "Chinese Millennial Traditions: The Formative Age," *American Historical Review* 104, 5 (December 1999): 1513–1530.

13. Li Shiyu, *Xiandai Huabei*, 38–45; Kubo Noritada, *"Ikkandō hokō: 'Yiguandao shi shenma dongxi' no shōkai"* [An introduction to the supplement in Yiguandao: "what is Yiguandao"?], *Tōyō Bunka Kenkyūjo kiyō* 11 (1956): 183–185, 191.

14. Her son, Chen Huaqing, who would later become a local official during the Japanese occupation, continued to spread his own branch of the Way of Penetrating Unity, but it never gained influence outside of the Jining area. Shao Yong, 366.

15. See Lu Yao, 431–437, for the degree of variation within Shandong. This method of spreading the teaching is especially evident during the Japanese occupation. See CA, 13.

16. During the earliest days of the sect, new members were admitted only by Zhang Guangbi himself, who traveled twice to Tianjin in order to induct new members. As the sect spread further, the surrogate *dianchuanshi* was introduced. Song Guangyu, 124. For a full account of the initiation rite itself, see Jordan and Overmyer, 222–236.

17. For a brief history of spirit-writing cults, see Clart, chap. 1.

18. Li Shiyu, *Xiandai Huabei,* 63–66.

19. Lu Yao, 388–389.

20. Li Shiyu, *Xiandai Huabei,* 63–65. Song Guangyu, 126.

21. Lu Yao, 391.

22. Song Guangyu, 125.

23. The texts of spirit writing were later edited into "Morality Books" *(shan shu)*, and the Republican period saw a literal explosion of such texts. In modern Taiwan, halls that specialize in spirit-writing cults often keep a magazine or otherwise regularly publish the writings of the gods. For the social and ritual base of spirit writing in modern Taiwan, see Clart.

24. Shao Yong, 296–298; Kubo Noritada, *"Ikkandō fukō,"* 189.

25. Stephen D. O'Leary, "When Prophecy Fails and When It Succeeds: Apocalyptic Prediction and the Reentry into Ordinary Time," in *Apocalyptic Time,* vol. 86, *Studies in the History of Religions,* ed. Albert I. Baumgarten (Leiden: Brill, 2000), 343.

26. Shao Yong, 298.

27. Shao Yong, 364–373, 467, 472. In 1951, Tianjin had an urban population of at least 4.2 million, meaning that more than 3 percent of the entire city came to forward register as members of the Way of Penetrating Unity during this campaign. See Han Junxing et al., *Tianjin shi renkou tongji ziliao huibian,*

1949–1983 [Collected statistics on the population of Tianjin City, 1949–1983] (Tianjin: Nankai daxue chubanshe, 1986).

28. Li Shiyu, *Xiandai Huabei,* 34. Long earlobes and hands are marks of a Buddha, and a full beard at birth is an obvious sign of wisdom commonly associated with Laozi, the founder of Daoism. Red birthmarks are considered a sign of spiritual protection. To have all of these signs in abundance is clearly the mark of a celestial being. The Southern Dipper is a constellation of six stars located in Sagittarius, the first of seven constellations associated with the Daoist Dark Warrior *(Xuanwu).* See Hu Fuchen et al., *Zhonghua daojiao cidian* [Dictionary of Chinese Daoism] (Beijing: Zhongguo shehui kexueyuan chubanshe, 1995), 794.

29. Li Shiyu, *Xiandai Huabei,* 34–35. Many of the specifics of the millenarianism espoused by the Way of Penetrating Unity are taken directly from and allude to the Complete Enlightenment *(Yuandun)* Teaching, an influential branch of Eastern Great Vehicle Teaching *(Dong dacheng jiao)* of the Ming dynasty. The founder of this teaching, also christened the True Heavenly Buddha, was surnamed Zhang, and is known to history alternatively as "Gong Chang" and Tianranzi, both also being pen names *(zi)* taken by Zhang Guangbi. This was more than mere admiration on the part of Zhang Guangbi. The sacred texts of the Complete Enlightenment Teaching and the deification of Gong Chang as the True Heavenly Buddha remained long after the sect had fallen into decline. In the early nineteenth century, Huang Yübian used extant texts to outline the place of Gong Chang in the eschatology of the Eternal Venerable Mother and lamented that the worship of Gong Chang remained strong. See Sawada Mizuho, *Kōchū haja shōben* [An annotated "detailed refutation of heresies"] (Tokyo: Kokusho Kankokai, 1972), 21–62. A detailed analysis of the life histories of Gong Chang and Piaogao is given in Richard Shek, "Religion and Society."

30. For a example of the charges, see *Xin Sheng Wanbao,* 8/31 April 1951; *Renmin Ribao,* 6/26, 6/28, 7/6, 7/7, 7/19, 1951.

31. Shao Yong, 364, 366, 368, 370, 437–444; Kubo Noritada, *"Ikkandō fukō,"* 194–195, 201–204; Lu Yao, 437.

32. Mistrust of the young organization was evident as early as March 1935, when Guomindang police detained Zhang Guangbi and two of his disciples upon their arrival in Nanjing. See Lu Yao, 431; Song Guangyu, 39. Li Shiyu, personal conversation, July, 1998.

33. Lu Yao, 2000, 428–432.

34. Ibid., 440.

35. Lu Yao, 431; Shao Yong, 437.

36. *Xin Sheng Wanbao,* April 7, 8, 9, 10, 15, 16, 18, 1951. Shao Yong also mentions the attraction of sectarian healing in Tianjin, bringing up a case in which leaders of the Way of Penetrating Unity allegedly used this as a method to rape more than seventy women. Shao Yong, 365. Note also the similarity between these techniques of religious healing and those discussed in chapter 3.

37. Esherick, 54–58.

38. *Xin Sheng Wanbao,* April 10, 11, 24, 1951.

39. CA, 13.

40. The Cangzhou Special Region was the creation of the early People's Republic, to make the twelve counties of Cangzhou administratively independent from Tianjin. CA, 8, 14.

41. Unfortunately, I have not been able to locate a copy of this text or any detailed information on it.

42. CA, 9; CA, 14 concurs that the political activities of the Way of Penetrating Unity were becoming "increasingly extreme."

43. *Renmin Ribao,* February 22, 1951. For a brief chronology of national level policies, see Cai Shaoqing, *Zhongguo mimi shehui* [Chinese secret societies]. Vol. 4, *Zhonguo shehui jingjishi congshu* (Taibei: Nantian Press, 1996), 365–368.

44. For broader view of this campaign, see Kenneth Lieberthal, "The Suppression of Secret Societies in Post-Liberation Tianjin," *China Quarterly* 54 (1973). The place of the move against the Way of Penetrating Unity (rendered as *I kuan-tao*) is addressed briefly on 243–244.

45. CA, 1; CA, 6; CA, 7; CA, 3; CA, 4; CA, 8; CA, 10.

46. CA, 3.

47. CA, 1; CA, 2; CA, 7; CA, 10.

48. CA, 4; CA, 13.

49. CA, 4.

50. CA, 13, 4. Of the 156 mentioned, 48 were party cadres, 25 were party members, 47 were mass cadres, 27 were base cadres, and 7 were members of the Communist Youth League *(tuanyuan).*

51. CA, 7; CA, 10; CA, 13.

52. CA, 2; CA, 9; CA, 11; CA, 12; CA, 13; CA, 14.

53. CA, 2; CA, 4; CA, 13; CA, 14.

54. CA, 7.

55. CA, 13; CA, appended table.

56. *Shanxi Provincial Committee Report of Experiences during the Eradication of the Way of Penetrating Unity,* quoted in Shao Yong, 443.

57. CA, 1; CA, 9.

58. For more background on healing, see chapter 3, particularly the discussion of taking a teacher *(ren shifu).*

59. CA, 7.

60. Cang Township was treated as an independent administrative unit within Cang County in these documents. CA, 3.

61. CA, 12.

62. CA, 16.

63. CA, 13.

64. Cangxian, 1995, 600.

65. Yue Daiyun and Carolyn Wakeman, *To the Storm: The Odyssey of a Revolutionary Chinese Woman* (Berkeley: University of California Press, 1985), 139–142.

66. Lu Yao, 447–448.

67. I have taken some liberty in translating *"huidaomen"* as "cult." My reason for doing so is that the term *"huidaomen"* is itself an invention of post-1949 historiography and is used widely in propaganda, usually with a distinctly pejorative tone. It is not part of the ordinary vocabulary of most peasants, who would only refer to sectarians as *huidaomen* in a political setting.

68. The assumption that a millenarian ideology will necessarily lead to rebellious activity is effectively discredited in Richard Shek, "Millenarianism without Rebellion: The Huangtiao Dao in North China." *Modern China* 8, 3 (July 1982): 305–336.

69. Albert I. Baumgarten, "Introduction," in *Apocalyptic Time*, ix–xiii.

70. Jane Dawson, "Apocalyptic Thinking of the Marian Exiles," in *Prophecy and Eschatology,* ed. Michael Wilkes (Oxford: Blackwell, for the Ecclesiastical History Society, 1994).

71. Baumgarten, ix–xiii.

72. See the discussion of Leon Festiger's theories of prophecy and cognitive dissonance in O'Leary, 341–344.

Chapter 7: Village Sectarians

1. Each of these teachings appears under different names. The latter, in particular, is also known as the "As-You-Wish" sect *(ruyi men)* and the "Single Stick of Incense Teaching" *(Yizhuxiang jiao)*, among others. It should not be confused with the better known, but unrelated, Heaven and Earth Society *(tiandi hui)*.

2. J. J. M. de Groot sees the importance of sectarian groups in mainstream religious life to have been a direct result of the decline of institutional Buddhism. As discussed in chapter 4, this situation was more likely to have been the case in Fujian, where de Groot worked, than in Cang County. See de Groot, 133–136, 156.

3. The Teaching of the Most Supreme is mentioned in an ethnographic study of Duliu, a suburb of Tianjin, although this source gives no indication of their activities or organization. See Sasaki and Lu, 302, 345, as well as in the 1995 gazetteer of nearby Xian County. Qin Huanze et al., *Xian xianzhi* [Gazetteer of Xian County] (Beijing: Zhongguo heping chubanshe, 1995), 63. In addition, I have encountered such groups in the city of Tianjin.

4. In "Religion and Society," Shek discusses this in terms of the White Yang Teaching (301–306).

5. Livia Kohn, *God of the Dao, Lord Lao in History and Myth* (Ann Arbor: Center for Chinese Studies, University of Michigan, 1998), 53–54, 313.

6. Ma Xisha and Han Bingfang, *Zhongguo minjian zongjiao shi* [History of Chinese popular religion] (Beijing: Renmin chubanshe, 1992), 1258–1261; Sawada, *Hōkan no kenkyū*, 49. This distinction between the Primordial Chaos Teaching and the scriptural tradition of the same name points to important discrepancies between the two. The most significant is the identification of the "Patriarch of Primordial Chaos" in the scriptural tradition, not as the transcendent form of Laozi, but rather as the Amithaba Buddha or as the Ming sectarian figure, Piaogao. See Shek, "Religion and Society," 167–172, 276–287.

7. The term "Imperial Ultimate" *(Huangji)* is a third component to the neo-Confucian dyad of the "Ultimate Void" *(Wuji)* and "Supreme Ultimate" *(Taiji)*. In sectarian scriptures, these three were occasionally correlated to the tripartite division of time into three *kalpas*. See Sawada, 1972, 109–110; Ma and Han, 1261–1263; Shao Yong, 60.

8. "*Shouyuan jiao, li famen, du xia er nu; shouyuan zu, ling shanren, longhua xiangfeng.*" Ma Xisha, "*Ming, Qing shidai de shouyuan jiao, hunyuan jiao yuanliu*" [Origins of Ming-Qing Return to the Origin and Primal Chaos teachings], in *Mingqing yi lai minjian zongjiao de tansuo*, ed. Wang Chien-ch'uan and Chiang Chu-shan (Taibei: Shangding wenhua chubanshe, 1996), 81–110. Quotation from 84–85.

9. Feng Tso-che and Li Fu-hua, *Zhongguo min jian zong jiao shi* (Taibei: Wenjin chubanshe, 1994), 262–266, locate the common ancestor of the two in the Ming dynasty Vast Yang Teaching, whereas Chuang Chi-fa, "*Jiao luan yu min bian*," in *Zhongguo jindai xiandai shi lunji*, vol. 2 (Taibei: Taiwan shang wu yin shu guan, 1985), 325–330; Suzuki Chūsei, "Shinchō Chūki ni okeru minkan shūkyō kessha to sonno sennen ōkoku undo e no keisha" [Popular religious societies in the mid-Qing and their tendency toward millenarianism], in *Sonno sennen ōkoku teki minshu undō no kenkyū* [Studies on millenarian popular movements], ed. Suzuki (Tokyo: Tokyo Daigaku Shuppankai, 1982), 297–298; and Shek, "Religion and Society," 276, equate the two with the Primordial Chaos or Primordial Chaos Red Epoch teachings. The relation between the homophonous Vast Yang and Red Epoch teachings complicates matters even further. Ma and Han (1054), Shek, "Religion and Society," 276, Suzuki, 297–298, and Shao Yong, 19, hold that these are simply two of many alternate terms for the same teaching. According to Daniel Overmyer, *Precious Volumes*, 322, however, there is little direct documentary evidence to support this claim. Others agree that that the Ming history of the Primordial Chaos Teaching was deeply intertwined with that of many others, in particular with the Vast Yang Teaching, but stop short of equating the two. See Asai Motoi, "Minmatsu Shinsho no daijōen dokyō" [The Great Vehicle and Instantaneous Enlightenment teachings of the late Ming and early Qing], *Tōkai daigaku kiyō*, 73 (2000): 19–56, especially 31–35; Ma Xisha, 81–85; Ma and Han, 1258, 1264, 1302; Gaustad, "Prophets and Pretenders," 3–4.

10. Ma Xisha, 85–95.

11. It has been noted, for example, that each trigram of the Eight Trigrams Teaching came to operate with relative autonomy, often acting as independent teachings. See Ma and Han, 968; Ma Xisha, 85–90; Suzuki, 212–213.

12. In "Religion and Society," 252–287, this how Shek characterizes the Way of Yellow Heaven and Red Yang Teachings.

13. Gaustad, "Prophets and Pretenders," 9–10; Ma Xisha, 91–95.

14. *Zhongguo di yi lishi dang'an guan.* This theme runs consistently through the reports.

15. Sawada, *Kōchū haja shōben*, 62. Ma Xisha notes that the Vast Yang scriptural tradition was also that of the Primordial Chaos Teaching through the Ming dynasty but that the latter also developed its independent scriptures during the Qing (83).

16. Hu Fuchen et al. go as far as to equate the two terms, 1448.

17. Ma and Han, 924.

18. Li Shiyu, *"Tianjin Hongyangjiao Diaocha Yanjiu"* [Investigation and research into the teaching of the Red Epoch in Tianjin], *Minjian zongjiao* 2 (1996): 124–126. For a discussion of the mid-Qing campaign against these sects, particularly the Primordial Chaos Teaching, see Gaustad, "Religious Sectarianism and the State in Mid-Qing China" (Ph.D. diss., University of California, Berkeley, 1994), 140–166.

19. These include such texts as the *Hunyuan hongyang linfan Piaogao jing* [Red Epoch scripture of the descent of Piaogao into the world] and *Hunyuan hongyang wudao mingxin jing* [Red Epoch scripture to awaken to the Dao and brighten the heart], both of which are listed in the *Detailed Argument against Heterodox Teachings*. Although they had never heard of these scriptures, it should be noted that members of the Teaching of the Most Supreme with whom I spoke were sufficiently intrigued to ask where they might obtain a copy.

20. This is mentioned very briefly in the dictionary entry for the Teaching of the Most Supreme given in Pu Wenqi, *Minjian mimi zongjiao cidian.*

21. I am grateful to Li Shiyu, who has done extensive work with organizations of the Teaching of the Most Supreme in and around Tianjin, for confirming the uniqueness of the Cang County variant. Personal conversation, June 25, 1999.

22. The greatest difference between the two groups appears to be the music that accompanies the chanting of scripture. As noted further on, a ritual group consists of at least seven musicians (*wuchang*, literally, "martial group"), who play wind and percussion instruments to accompany the chanting. Mastering the proper music, which is played without written scores, is certainly as difficult as the texts of the scriptures themselves. A second difference concerns costume. In both North and South Chest groups, the leader of the ritual group *(dangjia)* wears a round hat, similar to those worn by Buddhist monks. Atop this hat is a small wire hook, which in the costume of the

North Chest points to the front and in that of the South Chest faces the rear. Nobody seemed to know the purpose or significance of the hook, but all insisted that the difference between the two costumes was certainly important.

23. Pu Wenqi, who has done fieldwork in this area, comes to this conclusion. See *Minjian mimi zongjiao cidian*, 286–287. Information about the practice and organization of the sect during this period is based on a series of interviews with Teaching of the Most Supreme sectarians in Quan-Wang Village and Yang Camp and former specialists in Hai Dock and Shi Family Camp, as well as Heaven and Earth specialists in Yang Camp.

24. This festival is briefly mentioned in *Qingxian*, 1931, 81, although the sectarian contribution is omitted.

25. Pu Wenqi, *"Tiandimen diaocha yu yanjiu"* [Investigation and research into the Heaven and Earth Sect], *Minjian Zongjiao* 2 (1996): 211–259; Lu Yao, 42–89.

26. For the stylized nature of such accounts in the histories of secret societies, see Dian Murray with Qin Baoqi, *The Origins of the Tiandihui: Chinese Triads in Legend and History* (Stanford, Calif.: Stanford University Press, 1994). As with many such teachings, exactly where the Heaven and Earth Sect fits into the larger genealogy of sectarian evolution remains a subject of some debate. Following the lead of Li Shiyu, Pu Wenqi and Wang Erh-min also agree that the Heaven and Earth Sect is a branch of the White Lotus. In contrast, Chuang Chi-fa holds the teaching to be derived from the Primordial Chaos/Red Epoch tradition mentioned in the introduction to the Teaching of the Most Supreme. I cannot contribute much to this debate, although my own experience with Heaven and Earth scriptures has revealed very little emphasis on the Ancestor of Primordial Chaos. Wang Erh-min, *"Mimi zongjiao yu mimi shehui zhi shengtai huanjing ji shehui gongneng"* [The operating environment and social functions of secret religions and secret societies], *Zhongguo jin-daishi lunji*, vol. 2 (Taibei: Taiwan shang wu yin shu guan, 1985), 63–66; Chuang Chi-fa, 327–330; Pu Wenqi, *"Tiandimen,"* 225–226.

27. Both Lu Yao and Ma and Han include chapters on the teaching under the name "Single Stick of Incense Teaching" *(Yizhu xiang jiao)*. These discussions each provide far more detail on other branches of the sect, as well as on its tradition of personal practice and healing than are included in this study.

28. *"Dao Jie,"* Heaven and Earth Scripture, *juan* 1.

29. For another example of the place of "inviting the spirits" in popular liturgy, see Huang Zhusan and Wang Fucai.

30. "Short Eulogy for Approaching the Great Ancestor" *(Chao lao zu xiao zan)*, Heaven and Earth Scripture, *juan* 1. The text in Chinese is more compact: *yi bao tian en, er bao di en, san bao huang wang shui tu en, si bao yang you en, wu bao shi en. He hui zhong tu bao wu en.* The teacher is a reference to Dong Sihai.

31. Division into branches based on the Eight Trigrams is a common fea-

ture of sectarian organization. See, for example, Naquin, *Millenarian Rebellion*, 90–92, 205–206, 217–218.

32. Heaven and Earth members in Cang County and Tianjin still refer to themselves as belonging to the *kan* trigram, which also includes Tianjin, Beijing, and Manchuria. For a complete list of the eight trigrams and the spread of the teaching throughout China, see Lu Yao, 45–47.

33. Pu Wenqi, *"Tiandimen,"* 217.

34. *"Jiaqing 18 nian chayue Zhili Qingxian, Cangzhou ruyi liguajiao yihemen an"* (Jiaqing eighteenth year: Investigation of the As-You-Wish, Li Gua Teaching, Righteous-Harmonious Sect of Zhili, Qing County, Cangzhou), quoted in Lu Yao, 76. See also Ma and Han, 924.

35. The history of the sect is recorded in its scriptures, which include a genealogy of leaders from Dong Sihai to the present leader, Tu. Many of these scriptures are also quoted in Pu Wenqi, *"Tiandimen,"* 215–219.

36. This was identified by my informants *first* as the festival of Ksitigarbha *(Dizang Pusa)* and *second* as the Lower Primordial *(xia yuan)*.

37. Lu Yao, 75–82.

38. Pu Wenqi, *"Tiandimen,"* 240. It should be emphasized that this reliance on oral scriptures is not necessarily the case in other areas. Branches of the Heaven and Earth Teaching in Tianjin, for example, have written copies of the same texts used by the teaching in Cang County. Naturally, the circulation of these texts is limited to those in the teaching, and, over the years, members commit most of their content to memory. This remains, however, very different from a consciously oral tradition. I am grateful to Li Shiyu for allowing me to make photocopies of the Heaven and Earth scriptures in his collection. These texts are introduced in Appendix D.

39. *Cangxian*, 1933, 1701–1702.

40. This was one strategy of the national campaign, as well, in which notable Buddhist and Daoist figures were mobilized to take a public stand against the Way of Penetrating Unity. The same tactics were also employed against the Catholic Church during the early 1950s.

41. Lu Yao, 83–85, notes that in these cases, the teaching had allegedly begun to speak of the coming *kalpa*.

42. This new formulation rendered the tablet *"tian, di, min, qin, shi"* and lasted until the onset of the Cultural Revolution.

43. Like other sectarian functions in this area, this is a highly public ceremony, involving hours or even days of scripture recitation, as well as a formal procession by the sectarians around the village, complete with musicians and banners.

44. I have translated this literally, as the choice of terminology in establishing the degree of unacceptability is of vital importance in determining the appropriate response. Calling an activity "not revolutionary" implies that it is disagreeable and should be stopped, as opposed to "counterrevolutionary"

(*fan geming*), which represents a threat. The implicit contrast is between "village superstition" and criminalized sects such as the Way of Penetrating Unity.

45. This is made very clear in the account of Yue Daiyun, who recalls the reticence of peasants in Xiaohongmen to share information with Red Guards. Yue and Wakeman, 125–150.

46. At first hearing, such claims may sound rather like an idealized revision of village history. This same story, however, was repeatedly confirmed by both ordinary peasants and sectarian specialists in Heaven and Earth and Most Supreme villages alike. In light of the extraordinarily emotional accounts that these same peasants gave of other aspects of life during this period, I find no reason to doubt their veracity.

47. After the end of the Cultural Revolution, many of these bodies were reinterred in the traditional moundlike graves of North China. Where the actual body was irrecoverable, it was reburied symbolically, using a wooden tablet or piece of paper to represent the remains of the deceased. This ritual was performed primarily by sectarians.

48. The life of the teaching is evident in the miracle tales that have already begun to form around the deceased *dangjia*.

49. This last statement may or may not be exaggerated, but it is typical of how the sectarians of one village often speak disparagingly of their neighbors, who are invariably portrayed as deficient in morals or ritual knowledge.

50. Roughly seventy-five U.S. dollars in 1999 or, to put it into local context, three weeks' salary for peasant construction workers employed in Cangzhou or Tianjin.

Conclusion: Cang County and Chinese Religion

1. In his classic *Islam Observed*, Geertz discusses the degree of divergence that can develop in a highly doctrinaire religion such as Islam as the religion becomes part of local (and later, personal) identity. See Geertz, *Islam Observed: Religious Development in Morocco and Indonesia* (New Haven, Conn.: Yale University Press, 1968).

2. Hampton C. DuBose, *The Dragon, Image and Demon or the Three Religions of China, Confucianism, Buddhism and Taoism* (London: Partridge, 1886), 244–255, 255.

3. C. K. Yang, 297.

Character Glossary

ahong　阿訇
an　庵
An Daben　安大本

ba jie　八戒
Bagua jiao　八卦教
bai yang　白陽
Bailian jiao　白蓮教
Baiyi miao　白衣廟
Balang　八郎
Banwu hui　辦五會
bao　保
bao miao　報廟
Baohu wenwu ju　保護文物局
baojuan　寶卷
baolan　包攬
baozhang　保長
beigui　北櫃
Benxin　本心
Benxuan　本玄
bi nan　避難
bi xie　避邪
Botou (Township)　泊頭
bu geming　不革命
bu shao xiang, bu dian la　不烧香，不点蜡
buwu　卜巫

Cai Yucun　菜雨村

Caishen　财神
Cang (County)　滄
Cangmenkou　仓門口
Cangzhou　滄州
Cao (Village)　曹
chanhui ban　忏悔办
chao xi di　朝西地
cheng huang　城皇
chengbanren　承辦人
chong jian　重建
chu jia　出家
cun dang zhi shuji　村黨之書籍
cun dong　村董
cun gui　村規
cun hui　村會
cunzhang　村長

da jing　大經
da ming shizi fo jing　大明十字佛經
da nan　大難
Dacheng jiao　大乘教
Dachu (Village)　大褚
Dai (County)　代
daifu　大夫
Dai-Qi Camp　代齊營
dangjia　當家
dao ren　道人
Daode jing　道德經

247

daomen　道門

daoqin bu ke bu du　道親不可
　不讀

daoshi　道士

daoshou　道首

daoye　道爺

daoyou　道友

daozhang　道長

Daxing (County)　大興

di cai　地才

di xian　地仙

dian (rent)　佃

dian (transmit through touch)　點

dianchuanshi　點傳師

ding daxian de furen　丁大仙的
　夫人

Ding Fanlong　丁樊龍

Dizang　地藏

Dong Jisheng　董吉升

Dong Sihai　董四海

Dongjia lin　董家林

Dongyue miao　東嶽廟

dudie　度牒

Dule si　独樂寺

Dulin (Township)　杜林

Duliu　獨流

duozai taonan　躲災逃難

fa　法

Falungong　法輪功

fan geming　反革命

fandong　反動

fandong huidaomen　反動會道門

fanqing fuming　反清復明

Feng Jinjing　馮進京

fojiao hui　佛教會

fomen　佛門

foshuo huangji jieguo baojuan　佛说
　皇极结果宝卷

fu　符

fuluan　扶鸞

Gangzili (Village)　榿子李

genben jing　根本經

gong-chang shichuan　弓長師傅

gongde fei　公德費

gongsuo　公所

guan shi yin pusa　觀世音菩薩

Guandi　关帝

Guanyin　觀音

Guanyin jing　觀音經

Guanyin tang　觀音堂

guanyu zhenya fangeming huodong
　de zhishi　關於鎮壓反革命活動
　的知識

gufo tianzhen kaozheng longhua
　baojing　古佛天真考证龙华宝经

gui　櫃

guiling　鬼靈

guitou　櫃頭

guo menkang　过門閌

Guo-Bu Village　郭布村

Hai (Family) Dock　海(家)碼頭

Haichaoyin　海潮音

Hao mai　號脈

Hebei bangzi　河北棒子

Hejian　河間

Henan (Village)　河南

Hongqi er she　紅旗二社

hongyang　紅陽，弘陽，洪陽，
　宏陽，洪洋

hongyang wubu jing　紅陽五部經

Hongyangji　紅陽記

Hongyangjiao (Red Epoch)　紅陽教

Hongyangjiao (Vast Yang)　弘陽教

Houtian dao　後天到

Houxiazhai (Village)　後夏寨

Hu　胡

Hu (County)　戶

Hu Er Yinjin　胡二引进

Huailu (County)　获鹿

huan tongzi　換童子

huan yuan　还愿

huang shulang　黃鼠狼

Huanghua (County)　黃骅

Huangtian dao　黃天道

huanyuan　換願

huashen　化身

huazi　化子

hui　會

hui miao xing xue　毀廟行學

hui tang an　慧堂庵

Huichu (Village)　回褚

Huimin (County)　惠民

huishou　會首

huitou　會頭

huli　狐狸

Hunyuan hongyang jiao　混元紅
　陽教

Hunyuan jiao　混元教

hunyuan laojun　混元老君

hunyuan laozu　混元老祖

Hunyuan men　混元門

huoguan　火罐

ji　集

jia　甲

jian manren jiu sha　見滿人就殺

jiangshi　講師

Jianguo (County)　建國

Jiaohe (County)　交河

jiaomen　教門

jiaoquan　教勸

jiaxian　家仙

jiazhang　甲長

jie　劫

jie yan jiu jiao　戒煙酒教

Jigong huofo　濟公活佛

Jimo (County)　即墨

Ji'nan　濟南

Jindan dao　金丹道

jing　經

jinggui　經櫃

Jining (County)　濟寧

Julu (County)　鉅鹿

jushi　居士

kai huang　開荒

Kaishi daohua shiyi　開示道話
　實義

kan　坎

Keniu　柯牛

Kezhong　柯中

kuaiban　快板

kyōdōtai　共同體

Lanshui (Cave)　瀾水

Lengshuigou (Village)　冷水沟

Li duo　理鐸

Li Hongzhang　李鴻章

Li Longjiang　李龍江

Li Zhongxiang　李忠祥

Liaoyuan jing　了愿經

Ligua jiao　离卦教

Ligua laojun jiao　离卦老君教

Lijiao jiuzhenlu　理教究真錄

Limen xu zhi　理門須知

ling　靈

Liu Lisan　劉力三

Liu Qingxu　劉清虛

Liu Wenguang　劉文光

Longhua jiao　龍華教

Longwang　龍王

Lu Longqi　陆隴其

Lu Zhongjie　路中節

Lu Zhongyi　路中一

Lu zu tianji zhi mi　呂祖天極指迷

luan xing　亂性

luanshou　鸞手

luo jiao　羅教

Luo Weiqun　羅蔚群

Ma Kaishan　馬開山

meipo　媒婆

men　門

Meng (Village)　孟

miao hui　廟會

mie qing fu da ming　滅清輔大明

Mile fo　彌勒佛

ming xiang　命香

Mingde tang　明德堂

mingshan tang　明善堂

minjian wenhua　民間文化

mixin　迷信

Mohou yizhu jiao　末後一著教

mowang　魔王

nangui　南櫃

Nanhai gu fo　南海古佛

Nanpi (County)　南皮

neidan　内丹

Ni Camp　倪屯

nian jing　念經

Niangniang shen　娘娘神

Ni-Yang Camp　倪杨屯

paiwei　牌位

Pan (Mountain)　盤山

Pangu　盤古

pianfang　偏方

Piaogao　飄高

po si jiu　破四舊

Pu'an tang　普安堂

Qian-Hai Village　钱海庄

Qianren　前人

qilao　耆老

Qing (County)　青

qing bang　青幫

qing li　清理

qing shen　請神

qing sheng zhi　請聖偈

Qing shilu　清實录

Qingming　清明

Qingshui jiao　清水教

qingzhen beida si　清真北大寺

Qingzhou　青州

qiong bu zai li fu bu zai bang
　　窮不在理，富不在幫

qiongmin　窮民

qiu yu　求雨

Quan Family Village　權家庄

Quanshi jing　權世經

Quan-Wang Village　權王庄

Quanzhen　全真

Rear Camp　候營

Ren cai　人才

ren cuowu　認錯誤

ren shifu　認師父

renwu　人物

rujiao bijie　入教避劫
Rulai　如来
ruyi men　如意門

sai　賽
san cai　三才
san guang　三光
Sanguan　三官
Sanjie dao　三劫道
sanyuan　三元
sha li　傻理
Shajing (Village)　沙井
shan shu　善書
shangyuan　上元
Shanhu (Village)　山呼
Shanggulin　上沽林
she　社
Shen Ruchao　沈如潮
shen shi　神師
shen xiang　神香
shen yi　神姨
shengchan dui　生產隊
Shengxian dao　圣仙道
shengyuan　生員
Shengzong　聖宗
shi　實
Shi Family Camp　施家屯
shibing　實病
Shifo si　石佛寺
shifu　師夫
shizun　師尊
shou yuan　受元，收元，收圓
shouyuan hui　收元會
Shouyuan jiao　收元教
shui hui　水毀
Shuiyue si　水月寺
simiao dengji lü　寺廟登記律

song shen　送神
Songbo　松柏

Taiji laomu　太极老母
taishang laojun　太上老君
taishang laojun hunyuan shangde
　huangdi　太上老君混元上德
　皇帝
Taishang men　太上門
Taixu　太虛
tan　壇
tang　堂
tanzhu　壇主
Tian cai　天才
tian di jun qin shi　天地君親師
Tian hou　天后
Tian Jintai　田金台
Tiandi men　天地門
Tianli jiao　天理教
Tianqi miao　天齊廟
tianzhen fo　天真佛
tiao qiang　跳牆
tongzi　童子
tongzi li　童子理
Tu Family Camp　涂家營
tu gun　土棍
Tu Pinyi　涂品一
tuanyuan　團員
tudi (disciple)　徒弟
Tudi (Tutelary deity)　土地
tui dao　退道
tun　屯

Wang Jingwei　汪精衛
Wang Jueyi　王覺一
Wang Languang　王蘭廣
Wang Shutian　王書田

Wangmu ge   王母阁

wanjiao gui yi   萬教歸一

wenchang   文場

wu   巫

wu bu jing   五部經

wu da xian   五大仙

wu dao lu   悟道錄

wu dao yi yi guan zhi   吾道一以
　貫之

wu en   五恩

wu xing   五行

wu zuo   五坐

wuchang   武場

Wudao   五道

Wudou mi   五斗米

wufo baojuan   五佛寶卷

wufo du zu   五佛渡祖

Wuji laomu   無極老母

wupo shenhan   巫婆神漢

wusheng baojuan   五聖寶卷

wusheng laomu   無生老母

wushu   巫术

Wutai (County)   五台

Wuwei jiao   無為教

wuxi (witches and sorcerers)   巫覡

Wuxi (City)   无锡

wuzi jing   无字经

wuzi zhenyan   五字真言

Xi dacheng jiao   西大乘教

xia fa   下法

xia yuan   下元

Xian (County)   献

xian fo yanjiu ban   仙佛研究班

xian zuzhi fa   縣組織法

xiang   鄉

xiang ke   香客

xiangtou   香頭

xiangzan   香贊

xianling   縣令

xiangdi   鄉地

Xiantian dao   先天道

Xiao (Village)   肖

xiao jing   孝經

xiaoban   小辦

xiaofu   孝服

Xiaoli (Village)   小李

xie jiao   邪教

Xilao gongsuo   西老公所

Xiliucheng (village)   西流城

xin fo   信佛

xin jing   心經

xin sheng wanbao   新生晚報

xinba bao'en   新八保恩

Xingguo si   興國寺

Xinkailu (Village)   新開路

xiu lian   修練

xu   虛

Xu Gongfu   徐公甫

yan   狿

yan gu   掩骨

Yang Camp   楊屯

Yang Chengqing   羊澄清

Yang Hongbin   楊洪斌 (?)

Yang Rulai   羊如來

Yang Zai   羊宰

Yangliuqing   杨柳青

Yao Hetian   姚鶴天

Yao wang   藥王

yao yan   妖言

Yi Chang'a   伊昌阿

yi xin bao da ming   一心保大明

yi xue   義學

yi zhu xiang jiao   一柱香教

Yiguan dao   一貫道

Yiguan daomai tujie   一貫道脉
　　图解

Yiguan hairen dao   一貫害人道

Yin Laifeng   尹來風

yin qin du qin, yin you du you
　　因親渡親因友渡友

Yin Ruo   尹若

Yin Zhongshan   尹重山

yinbao ren   引保人

ying shen   迎神

you li   有理

you qiu bi ying   有求必應

you seng   游僧

youpo   優婆

Yuandunjiao   圓頓教

Yühuang jing   玉皇經

yun you   云游

yunqi gonfu   運气功夫

zai xiang   災香

Zaijiali   在家理

Zailijiao   在理教

zan   贊

zhaikou   齋口

Zhang Guangbi   張光璧

Zhang Jindou   張進斗

Zhang Ren   張仁

Zhang Tianran   張天然

Zhang Wushan   張吾山

Zhang-Xing Village   張幸庄

Zhao Family Camp   趙家营

Zhao-Guan Camp   趙官营

zhen   鎮

zhenkong jiaxiang   真空家鄉

zhenya fan geming   鎮壓反革命

Zhifangtou   紙房頭

zhong jing   忠經

Zhongguo renmin fojiao xiehui
　　中國人民佛教協會

Zhonghua lianhe zaijiao hui   中華
　　聯合在理教會

zhong-ri qinshan   中日親善

zhongyuan   中元

zhouyu   咒語

zishou suoguo   自首所過

zongdu   總督

zonghui   總會

Zongli   總理

zupu   族谱

Bibliography

Only those works of direct interest to the text are reproduced in the bibliography. The publication data for works of more peripheral significance are included within the text of the notes.

Primary Documents

Cui Shoulu 崔守禄 et al. *Cangxian xianzhi* 滄縣縣志 [Gazetteer of Cang County]. Beijing: Zhongguo heping chubanshe, 1995.

Hebei difang zongjiao tuanti diaocha biao 河北地方宗教團體調查表 [Investigation into local religious organizations in Hebei], n.p., n.d.

Hebei sheng zhi, zongjiao juan 河北省志，宗教卷 [Hebei provincial gazetteer, religion], vol. 68. Beijing: Zhongguo shu ji chubanshe, 1991.

Huang Pengnian 黃彭年. *Jifu fancha zhi* 畿辅梵刹志 [Gazetteer of Buddhist monasteries in Jifu (Hebei)], 1910, *juan* 178–182 of *Jifu tongzhi* 畿辅通志 [Complete gazetteer of Jifu (Hebei)]. Shijiazhuang: Hebei renmin chubanshe, 1985.

Jinmen baojia tushuo 津門保甲圖 [Diagram of household registration in Tianjin], n.p., 1842.

Li fa yuan 立法院 [Legislative Yuan]. *Zhonghua minguo fagui huibian* 中華民國法規彙編 [Compiled laws and regulations of the Republic of China]. Vol. 3, *Neizheng* 內政 [Internal administration]. Shanghai: Zhonghua shu ju 1933.

Lijiao yuanliu 理教原流 [The origins of Zailijiao]. Hand copied, n.p., n.d. [Inscription identifies text as being from Republican-era Jinghai county, Hebei.]

Liu Shuxin et al. *Nanpi xian zhi* 南皮縣志 [Gazetteer of Nanpi County]. 1932; reprint Taibei: Cheng wen chubanshe, 1968.

Niida Noboru 仁井田陞, ed. *Chūgoku nōson kankō chōsa* 中國農村慣行調查 [An investigation of Chinese village customs]. 6 vols. Tokyo: Iwanami Shoten, 1953–1958.

Ōtani Kohō 大谷湖峰. "Shūkyō chōsa hōkoku shū" 宗教調查報告集 [Collected reports on an investigation of religion]. 1937. Chinese translation by Teng Mingyu 滕铭予. Reprinted in *Changchun Wenshi zliao* 長春文史資料 4 (1988): 1–168.

Qin Huanze 秦焕泽 et al. *Xian xianzhi* 献县志 [Gazetteer of Xian County]. Beijing: Zhongguo heping chubanshe, 1995.

Qingxian cuntu 青縣村圖 [Diagram of villages in Qing County], n.p., n.d.

Sasaki Mamoru 佐々木衛 and Lu Yao 路遙. *Kindai chūgoku no shakai to minshū bunka* 近代中國の社會と民眾文化 [Society and mass culture in modern China]. Tokyo: Tōhō Shoten, 1992.

Tiandimen jiao 天地門教. *Tiandimen baojuan* 天地門寶卷 [Heaven and Earth Sect scriptures], 2 *juan*. Hand copied, n.p., n.d.

Tianjin shi zhi bianxuan chu 天津市志編纂處. *Tianjin shi gaiyao* 天津市概要 [An overview of Tianjin]. Tianjin: Tianjin shi zhengfu, 1934.

Wusheng Baozhuan 五聖寶卷 [Precious scripture of the Five Sages], in *Baojuan* 寶卷, Zhang Xishun 張希舜 et al., eds. Vol. 24: 142–337. Shanxi: Shanxi Renmin chubanshe, 1994.

Xingya zongjiao xiehui 興亞宗教協會 [Rising Asia religion society]. *Huabei zongjiao nianjian* 華北宗教年鑒 [Yearbook of religion in North China]. Beiping: Xingya zongjiao xiehui, 1941.

Xu Zhaoqiong 徐肇琼. *Tianjin huanghui kao* 天津皇會考記 [A record of the Empress of Heaven Festival in Tianjin]. Reprint vol. 6, *Tianjin fengtu congshu*. Tianjin: Tianjin guji chubanshe, 1988.

Xu Zongliang 徐宗亮 et al. *Tianjin fu zhi* 天津府志 [Gazetteer of Tianjin prefecture]. 1899. Reprint Taibei: Taiwan xue sheng shu ju, 1968.

Zhang Ping 張坪 et al. *Cangxian zhi* 滄縣志 [Gazetteer of Cang County]. 1933. Reprint Taibei: Cheng wen chubanshe, 1968.

Zheng Qinghuan 郑清寰 et al. *Qingxian zhi* 青县志 [Gazetteer of Qing County]. 1931. Reprint Taibei: Cheng wen chubanshe, 1968.

Zhongguo di yi lishi dang'an guan 中国第一史档案馆. "Jiaqing nianjian Hongyangjiao dang'an" 嘉庆年间红阳教档案 [Record of the Red Yang Teaching incident during the Jianqing Reign], *Lishi Dang'an* 史档案 [Historical archives] 1 (2000): 21–41.

Zhongguo di yi lishi dang'an guan 中国第一史档案馆, ed. *"Qingdai longhuahui shiliao xuanbian"* [Selected historical materials from the Qing Dragon Flower Assembly], *Lishi Dang'an* 历史档案 [Historical archives] 3 (2000): 40–59.

Zhonghua minguo 21 nian 6 yue 19 ri, quanguo chao puto shan 中華民國21年6月19日全國朝普陀山 [Journey to Puto Mountain on June 19, 1932]. Presented to Han Tingbai et al. at the Lanshui Cave, Ji Mountain. Hand copied, n.p., n.d.

Archival Documents

1. Chinese Communist Hebei Provincial Committee 中共河北省委. *"Guanyu qudi huidaomen de zhishi"* 關於取締會道門的指示 [Concerning orders for the eradication of sectarians], January 6, 1951.

2. Xian County Local Committee 獻縣地委. *"Guanyu qudi gongzuo, xiang diwei baogao"* 關於取締工作向地位報告 [Report concerning eradication work], January 13, 1951.

3. Cangzhen Township Committee 滄鎮鎮委. *"Guanyu qudi huidaomen de jihua"* 關於取締會道門的計劃 [Concerning plans for the eradication of sectarians], January 14, 1951.

4. Botou Township Government 泊頭鎮鎮委. *"Guanyu juti shixing sheng, diwei de qudi huidaomen zhishi de jueding"* 關於具體實行省，地位的取締會道門知識的決定 [Decisions concerning the specific implementation of the provincial and local orders for the eradication of Huidaomen], January 23, 1951.

5. Cang County Local Committee 滄縣地委. *"Guanyu juti shixing shengwei diwei de qudi huidaomen zhishi de zhishi"* 關於具體實行省位，地位的取締會道門知識的知識 [Concerning orders for the specific implementation of the provincial and local orders for the eradication of Huidaomen], January 24, 1951.

6. Chinese Communist Hebei Provincial Committee 中共河北省委. *"Zai qudi fandong huidaomen gongzuo zhong dui dangyuan, tuanyuan, ganbu ji minbing canjia huidaomen wenti de chuli banfa"* 在取締反動會道門工作中對黨員，團員，幹部及民兵參加會道門的處理辦法 [How to handle the problem of party and Youth League members, cadres, and People's soldiers who participate in reactionary sectarian groups during the movement to ban these groups], January 27, 1951.

7. Cang County Local Committee 滄縣地委. *"Guanyu zhixing 'shengwei qudi huidaomen gongzuo zhishi' de zhishi"* 關於執行'省委取締會道門工作指示'的指示 [Concerning directives for the implementation of "Provincial Directives for the Eradication of Sectarians"], January 28, 1951.

8. Cang County Local Committee 滄縣地委. *"Guanyu juti shixing sheng, diwei qudi huidaomen zhishi zaici zhishi"* 關於具體實行省，地位的取締會道門知識再次知識 [Another directive concerning the specific implementation of provincial and local orders for the eradication of sectarians], February 2, 1951.

9. Jianguo County Government 建國縣委. *"Jianguoxian zheduan qudi gongzuo zhengge qingkuang xiang diwei de baogao"* 建國縣這段取締工作整個情況向地位的報告 [A complete summary of the state of the current round of eradication work in Jianguo County: Report for the Cangzhou Committee] February 9, 1951.

10. Cang County Local Committee 滄縣地委. *"Guanyu qudi gongzuo buchong zhishi"* 關於取締工作補充知識 [Supplement to eradication orders], February 18, 1951.

11. Jiaohe County Local Committee 交河縣地委. *"Guanyu jin yi bu jinxing chedi quanmian qudi gongzuo zhaokai quanxiang you yiguandao cunzhuang ganbu daotu huiyi xiang diwei de baogao"* 關於進一步進行徹底

全面取締工作召開全鄉有一貫道村莊幹部道徒會議向地位的報告 [A report to Cangzhou on the meeting of cadres, village heads, and sectarians in villages with Yiguandao in order to eradicate (the sect) completely in the county], February 20, 1951.

12. Huanghua County Local Committee 黃驊縣委. "*Guanyu qudi yiguandao gongzuo zongjie baogao*" 關於取締一貫道工作總結報告 [Summary of work to eradicate Yiguandao], March 5, 1951.

13. Cang County Local Committee 滄縣地委. "*Guanyu qudi huidaomen gongzuo zongjie baogao*" 關於取締會道門工作總結報告 [Summary of work to eradicate sectarians], March 6, 1951.

14. Jianguo County Government 建國縣委. "*Baowei weiyuanhui de qudi gongzuo zonghe baogao*" 包圍委員會的取締工作綜合報告 [A summary of the eradication work completed by the Defense Committee], March 14, 1951.

Secondary Materials

Asai Motoi 浅井纪. "*Minmatsu Shinsho no daijōen dokyō*" 明末清初の大乘円頓教 [The Great Vehicle and Instantaneous Enlightenment teachings of the late Ming and early Qing]. *Tōkai daigaku kiyō* 東海大學紀要 73 (2000): 19–56.

AvRuskin, Tara L. "Neurophysiology and the Curative Possession Trance: The Chinese Case." *Medical Anthropology Quarterly*, new series, 2, 3, "Health and Industry" (September 1986): 286–302.

Baumgarten, Albert I. "Introduction." In *Apocalyptic Time*, Albert I. Baumgarten, ed. Vol. 86: *Studies in the History of Religions*, vii–xv. Leiden: Brill, 2000.

Berling, Judith. *The Syncretic Religion of Lin Chao-en.* New York: Columbia University Press, 1980.

Bi Wenzhen 畢文槙 et al. "Jiu Tianjin de limen" 舊天津的理門 [The Li Sect in Old Tianjin] *Tianjin wenshi ziliao xuanji* 天津文史資料輯 52 (1990): 184–192.

Brook, Timothy. *Praying for Power: Buddhism and the Formation of Gentry Society in Late-Ming China.* Cambridge, Mass.: Harvard University Press, 1993.

———. "From Late-Imperial to Modern: Buddhism in the Chinese Constitution." Paper presented at the conference "From Late Imperial to Modern Chinese History: Views from the Eighteenth Century," University of California, Los Angeles, November 14, 1998.

Brunvald, Jan Harold. *The Study of American Folklore: An Introduction.* 3d ed. New York: Norton, 1986.

Cai Shaoqing 菜少卿. *Zhongguo mimi shehui* 中國秘密社會 [Chinese secret societies]. Vol. 4: *Zhonguo shehui jingjishi congshu* [Collected works on Chinese social and economic history]. Taibei: Nantian Press, 1996.

Chan, Wing-tsit. *Religious Trends in Modern China.* New York: Columbia University Press, 1953.

Ch'en, Kenneth. *Buddhism in China: A Historical Survey.* Princeton, N.J.: Princeton University Press, 1964.

Cheng Xiao 程蕭. *Wanqing xiangtu yishi* 晚清鄉土意識 [Rural consciousness in the late Qing], *Qingshi yanjiu congshu* [Collected research on Qing History]. Beijing: Renmin Chubanshe, 1990.

Chiang Chu-shan 蔣竹山. *"1930 niandai Tianjin Duliu zhen shangren de zongjiao yu shehui huodong canyu—yi 'zailijiao' wei li"* 1930年代天津獨流鎮商人的宗教與社會活動參與—以'在理教'為例 [Participation of merchants in religious and social activities in 1930s Duliu, Tianjin: The example of Zailijiao]. In *Mingqing yi lai minjian zongjiao de tansuo* 明清以來民間宗教的探索 [An inquiry into popular religion since the Ming-Qing], Wang Chien-ch'uan 王見川 and Chiang Chu-shan 蔣竹山, eds., 266–291. Taibei: Shangding wenhua chubanshe, 1996.

Chien-ch'uan and Han Bingfang 韓秉芳. *Zhongguo minjian zongjiao shi* 中國民間宗教史 [History of Chinese popular religion]. Beijing: Renmin Chubanshe, 1992.

Christian, William A., Jr. *Local Religion in Sixteenth-Century Spain.* Princeton, N.J.: Princeton University Press, 1981.

Ch'ü T'ung-tsu. *Local Government in China under the Ch'ing.* Cambridge, Mass.: Harvard University Press, 1962.

Chuang Chi-fa 莊吉發. *"Jiao luan yu min bian"* 教亂與民變 [Religious unrest and popular change] in *Zhongguo jindai xiandai shi lunji* 中國近代現代史論集 [Essays on modern and contemporary Chinese history]. Vol. 2. Taibei: Taiwan shang wu yin shu guan, 1985.

Clart, Philip. "The Ritual Content of Morality Books: A Case Study of a Taiwanese Spirit-Writing Cult." Ph.D. diss., University of British Columbia, 1996.

Cohen, Myron S. "Lineage Organization in North China," *Journal of Asian Studies* 3 (1990): 509–534.

Cong Hanxiang 從韓香, ed. *Jindai ji lu yu xiangcun* 近代冀魯豫鄉村 [Villages of modern Hebei, Shandong, and Shanxi]. Beijing: Zhongguo she hui ke xue chu ban she, 1995.

Davis, Edward L. *Society and the Supernatural in Song China.* Honolulu: University of Hawai'i Press, 2001.

Dawson, Jane. "Apocalyptic Thinking of the Marian Exiles." In *Prophecy and Eschatology,* Michael Wilkes, ed., 75–91. Oxford: Blackwell, for the Ecclesiastical History Society, 1994.

Day, Clarence Burton. *Chinese Peasant Cults: Being a Study of Chinese Paper Gods.* Shanghai: Kelly & Walsh, 1940.

Dean, Kenneth. *Taoist Ritual and Popular Cults of Southeast China.* Princeton, N.J.: Princeton University Press, 1993.

DeGlopper, Donald. "Religion and Ritual in Lukang." In *Religion and Ritual in Chinese Society*, Arthur Wolf, ed., 43–69. Stanford, Calif.: Stanford University Press, 1974.

de Groot, J. J. M. *Sectarianism and Religious Persecution in China: A Page in the History of Religion*. Amsterdam: Johannes Muller, 1903.

Ding Shiliang 丁世良 et al., eds. *Zhongguo difang zhi minsu ziliao huibian* 中国地方志民俗汇编 [Collected materials on popular custom in Chinese local gazetteers]. Beijing: Beijing tushuguan chubanshe, 1989.

Dirlik, Arif. "The Ideological Foundations of the New Life Movement: A Study in Counterrevolution." *Journal of Asian Studies* 34, 4 (August 1975): 945–980.

Dong Jiqun 董季群. *Tianjin Tianhou gong* 天津天后宫 [The Empress of Heaven Temple in Tianjin]. Tianjin: Cangzhou Daily Press, 1993.

Duara, Prasenjit. *Culture, Power, and the State: Rural North China, 1900–1942*. Stanford, Calif.: Stanford University Press, 1988.

———. "Knowledge and Power in the Discourse of Modernity: The Campaigns against Popular Religion in Early Twentieth-Century China." *Journal of Asian Studies* 50, 1 (February 1991): 67–83.

DuBois, Thomas. "The Sacred World of Cang County: Religious Belief, Organization, and Practice in Rural North China during the Late Nineteenth and Twentieth Centuries." Ph.D. diss., University of California, Los Angeles, 2001.

DuBose, Hampton C. *The Dragon, Image and Demon or the Three Religions of China, Confucianism, Buddhism, and Taoism*. London: Partridge and Co., 1886.

Eberhardt, Wolfram. "Temple-Building Activities in Medieval and Modern China: An Experimental Study." *Monumenta Serica* 23 (1964): 264–318.

Esherick, Joseph. *The Origins of the Boxer Uprising*. Berkeley: University of California Press, 1987.

Faure, David. *The Structure of Chinese Rural Society: Lineage and Village in the Eastern New Territories, Hong Kong*. Hong Kong: Oxford University Press, 1986.

Fei Xiaotong. *Peasant Life in China: A Field Study in the Country Life of the Yangtze Valley*. New York: E. P. Dutton, 1939.

Feutchwang, Stephan. "School Temple and City God." In *The City in Late Imperial China*, G. William Skinner, ed., 581–608. Stanford, Calif.: Stanford University Press, 1978.

Freedman, Maurice. "On the Sociological Study of Chinese Religion." In *Religion and Ritual in Chinese Society*, Arthur Wolf, ed., 19–41. Stanford, Calif.: Stanford University Press, 1974.

———. *Lineage Organization in Southeast China*. London: Athlone Press, 1958.

Galpern, A. N. *The Religions of the People in Sixteenth-Century Champagne.* Cambridge, Mass.: Harvard University Press, 1976.

Gamble, Sidney. *North China Villages: Social, Political, and Economic Activities before 1933.* Berkeley: University of California Press, 1963.

Gaustad, Blaine. "Religious Sectarianism and the State in Mid-Qing China." Ph.D. diss., University of California, Berkeley, 1994.

———. "Prophets and Pretenders: Inter-Sect Competition in Qianlong China," *Late Imperial China* 21, 1 (2000): 1–40.

Ginzburg, Carlo. *The Cheese and the Worms: The Cosmos of a Sixteenth-Century Miller,* translated by John and Anne Tedeschi. Baltimore: Johns Hopkins University Press, 1980.

———. *The Night Battles: Witchcraft & Agrarian Cults in the Sixteenth & Seventeenth Centuries.* Baltimore: Johns Hopkins University Press, 1983.

Goosaert, Vincent. "Counting the Monks: The 1736–1739 Census of the Chinese Clergy." *Late Imperial China* 21, 2 (2000): 40–85.

Grootaers, Willem A. "Temples and History of Wan-ch'üan (Chahar): The Geographical Method Applied to Folklore," *Monumenta Serica* 13 (1948): 209–316.

———. "Rural Temples around Hsuan-hua (South Chahar): Their Iconography and Their History." *Folklore Studies* 10, 1 (1951): 1–115.

Grootaers, Willem A., Li Shiyu, and Wang Fushi. *The Sanctuaries in a North Chinese City: A Complete Survey of the Cultic Buildings in the City of Hsüan-hua* (Chahar). Brussels: Institut Belges de Hautes Études Chinoises, 1995.

Gu Xijia 顧希佳. *"Taihu liuyu minjian xinyang zhong de shenling tixi"* 太湖流域民間信仰中的神靈體系 [The spirit system in the popular belief of the Taihu Basin]. *Shijie zongjiao yanjiu* 世界宗教研究 [Research on world religions] 42 (1990): 123–133.

Han Bo 韓薄. *Huidaomen yu zongjiao de qufen* 會道門與宗教的區分 [The difference between sectarians and religion]. Beijing: Qunzhong Chubanshe, 1984.

Han Junxing 韓俊興 et al. *Tianjin shi renkou tongji ziliao huibian, 1949–1983* 天津市人口統計資料彙編, 1949–1983 [Collected statistics on the population of Tianjin City, 1949–1983]. Tianjin: Nankai University Press, 1986.

Hansen, Valerie. *Changing Gods in Medieval China, 1127–1276.* Princeton, N.J.: Princeton University Press, 1990.

Hatada Takashi 旗田巍. *Chūgoku sonraku to kyōdōtai riron* 中国村落と共同体理論 [Chinese villages and the theory of village community]. Tokyo: Iwanami Shoten, 1973.

Hayes, James. "Specialists and Written Materials in the Village World." In *Popular Culture in Late Imperial China,* David Johnson, Andrew J.

Nathan, and Evelyn S. Rawski, eds., 78–112. Berkeley: University of California Press, 1985.

Hendrichke, Barbara. "Early Daoist Movements." In *Daoism Handbook*, Livia Kohn, ed., 134–164. Leiden: Brill, 2000.

Hsiao, Kung-chüan. *Rural China: Imperial Control in the Nineteenth Century*. Seattle: University of Washington Press, 1960.

Hu Pu'an 胡樸安. *Zhonghua quanguo fengsu zhi* 中華全國風俗志 [A gazetteer of customs in China]. 1923; reprint Shanghai: Shanghai shudian, 1988.

Hu Fuchen 胡孚琛 et al. *Zhonghua daojiao da cidian* 中华道教大辞典 [Dictionary of Chinese Daoism]. Beijing: Zhongguo Shehui kexueyuan chubanshe, 1995.

Huang, Philip C. C. *The Peasant Economy and Social Change in North China*. Stanford, Calif.: Stanford University Press, 1985.

Huang Zhusan 黃竹三 and Wang Fucai 王福才. *Shanxi sheng, quwo xian, renzhuang cun "shangu shenpu" diaocha baogao* 山西省曲沃縣任莊村 "扇鼓神譜"調查報告 [Investigation and report of the "Flat Drum Roster of the Gods" in Renzhuang Village, Quwo County, Shanxi]. *Minsu Quyi Congshu* 民俗曲藝叢書 [Collected works on popular drama]. Taibei: Caituan fa ren Shi Hezheng minsu wenhua jijin hui, 1994.

Ishida Hiroshi 石田浩. *"Kyū Chūgoku nōson ni okeru shijōken to tsūkon ken"* 旧中國農村における市場圈と通婚圈 [Marketing spheres and marriage spheres in Old China]. *Shirin* 63, 5 (1979): 102–126.

———. *"Kaihōzen no kahoku nōson shakai no ichiseikaku: Tokuni sonraku to byō no kanren ni oite"* 解放前の華北農村社会の一性格：特に村落と廟の関聯において [Characteristics of preliberation North Chinese village society: Especially regarding relations between village and temple]. *Kansai daigaku (keizai ronshū)* 関西大学（経済論集）[Kansai University (economic essays)] 32, 2 (1982): 95–135; 32, 3 (1982): 211–269.

Jing, Jun. *The Temple of Memories: History, Power, and Morality in a Chinese Village*. Stanford, Calif.: Stanford University Press, 1996.

Johnson, Chalmers. *Peasant Nationalism and Communist Power: The Emergence of Revolutionary China, 1937–1945*. Stanford, Calif.: Stanford University Press, 1962.

Johnson, David. "Communication, Class and Consciousness in Late Imperial China." In *Popular Culture in Late Imperial China*, David Johnson, Andrew J. Nathan, and Evelyn S. Rawski, eds., 34–72. Berkeley: University of California Press, 1985.

———. "Temple Festivals in Southeastern Shanxi: The *Sai* of Nan-she Village and Big West Gate." *Minsu quyi* 民俗曲藝 91 (1994).

Johnson, David, ed. *Ritual Opera, Operatic Ritual: "Mu-lien Rescues His Mother" in Chinese Popular Culture/Papers from the International*

Workshop on the Mu-lien Operas; with an Additional Contribution on the Woman Huang Legend by Beata Grant. Berkeley: University of California Press, 1989.

Jordan, David K., and Daniel L. Overmyer. *The Flying Phoenix: Aspects of Chinese Sectarianism in Taiwan.* Princeton, N.J.: Princeton University Press, 1986.

Kang Xiaofei. "The Fox *(hu)* and the Barbarian *(hu)*: Unraveling Representations of the Other in Late Tang Tales." *Journal of Chinese Religions* 27 (1999): 35–67.

Katz, Paul R. *Images of the Immortal: The Cult of Lü Dongbin at the Palace of Eternal Joy.* Honolulu: University of Hawai'i Press, 1999.

Ke Hua, ed. 可華 *Zhongguo minjian wenxue jicheng Cangzhou diqu juan: gushi* 中國民間文學集成滄州地區卷：故事 [Compilation of Chinese popular literature, Cangzhou volume: stories]. N.p., Nanpi County, 1988.

Kieschnick, John. *The Eminent Monk: Buddhist Ideals in Medieval Chinese Hagiography.* Honolulu: University of Hawai'i Press, 1997.

Kohn, Livia. *God of the Dao, Lord Lao in History and Myth.* Ann Arbor: University of Michigan Center for the Chinese Studies, 1998.

Kubo Noritada 窪德忠. *"Ikkandō ni tsuite"* 一貫道に対て [Concerning Yiguandao]. *Tōyō Bunka Kenkyūjo kiyō* 東洋文化研究所紀要 4 (1953): 173–249.

———. *"Ikkandō hokō: 'Yiguandao shi shenma dongxi' no shōkai"* 一貫道補考「一貫道是什麼東西」の紹介 [An introduction to the supplement in Yiguandao "what is Yiguandao?"]. *Tōyō Bunka kenkyūjo kiyō* 東洋文化研究所紀要 11 (1956): 179–212.

Kuhn, Philip. *Rebellion and Its Enemies in Late Imperial China: Militarization and Social Structure, 1796–1864.* Cambridge, Mass.: Harvard University Press, 1970.

———. *Soulstealers: The Chinese Sorcery Scare of 1768.* Cambridge, Mass.: Harvard University Press, 1990.

Lagerwey, John. "The Structure and Dynamics of Chinese Rural Society." In Hsu Cheng-kuang 徐正光, ed., *Disijie guoji kejiaxue yantaohui lunwenji: Lishi yu shehui jingji* 第四屆国际客家学研讨会论文集/历史与社会经济 [Collected papers from the Fourth International Congress on Hakka Studies: history and social economy], 1–43. Taibei: Zhongyang yanjiuyuan minzuxue yanjiusuo, 2000.

———. *Taoist Ritual in Chinese History and Society.* New York: MacMillan, 1987.

Le Roy Ladurie, Emmanuel. *The Peasants of Languedoc,* trans. with an introduction by John Day. Urbana: University of Illinois Press, 1976.

Levi, Giovanni. *Inheriting Power: The Story of an Exorcist,* translated by Lydia G. Cochrane. Chicago: University of Chicago Press, 1988.

Li Fuhua 李富華 and Feng Tso-che 馮佐哲. *Zhongguo min jian zong jiao shi*

中国民间宗教史 [History of Chinese popular religion]. Taibei: Wenjin chubanshe, 1994.

Li Huaiyin, "Village Regulations at Work: Local Taxation in Huailu County, 1900–1936." *Modern China* 26, 1 (2000): 79–100.

Li Jiexian 李洁賢. *"Lijiao chuanru Tianjin yu xilao gongsuo"* 理教傳入天津與西老共所 [The spread of Zailijiao to Tianjin and the Xilao Gongsuo]. *Tianjin wenshi ziliao xuanji* 天津文史資料輯 24 (1983): 189–205.

Li Jinghan 李景漢. *Ding xian shehui diaocha gaikuang* 定縣社會調查概況 [A summary of the investigation of the society of Ding County]. Beijing: Beijing University, 1933.

Li Shiyu 李世瑜. *Xiandai Huabei Mimi Zongjiao* 現代華北秘密宗教 [Secret religions in modern North China]. Shanghai: Shanghai wen yi chubanshe, 1948.

———. *"Tianjin Hongyangjiao Diaocha Yanjiu"* 天津紅陽教調查研究 [Investigation and research into the teaching of the Red Epoch in Tianjin]. *Minjian zongjiao* 民間宗教 2 (1996): 121–169.

———. *"Tianjin Zailijiao Diaocha Yanjiu"* 天津在理教調查研究 [Investigation and research into the Li Sect in Tianjin]. *Minjian zongjiao* 民間宗教 2 (1996): 169–210.

Li Wei-tsu. "On the Cult of the Four Sacred Animals (Szu Ta Men) in the Neighborhood of Peking." *Folklore Studies* 7 (1948): 1–94.

Lieberthal, Kenneth. "The Suppression of Secret Societies in Post-Liberation Tianjin." *China Quarterly* 54 (1973): 242–266.

Lin Mei-jung 林美容. *"You jisi quan dao xinyang quan: Taiwan minjian shehui de diyu goucheng yu fazhan"* 由祭祀圈到信仰圈：台灣民間社會的地域構成與發展 [From ritual sphere to belief sphere: territorial composition and development of Taiwan folk society]. In *Zhongguo haiyang fazhan shi lunwen ji* 中國海洋發展史論文集 [Collected essays on Chinese oceanic development], 3, Chang Yen-hsien 張炎憲, ed., 95–125. Taibei: Zhong yang yan jiu yuan san min zhu yi yan jiu suo, 1988.

Lin Pen-hsuan 林本炫. *"Yiguandao yu zhengfu zhi guanxi"* 一貫道與政府之關係 [Government relations with Yiguandao] in *Zongjiao yu wenhua* 宗教與文化 [Religion and culture], Cheng Chih-ming, ed., 315–362. Taibei: Taiwan xuesheng shuju, 1990.

Litzinger, Charles A. "Temple Community and Village Cultural Integration in North China: Evidence from 'Sectarian Cases' (Chiao-an) in Chih-li, 1860–1895." Ph.D. diss., University of California, Davis, 1983.

Lu Yao 路遙. *Shandong minjian mimi jiaomen* 山東民間秘密教門 [Secret popular sects in Shandong]. Beijing: Dangdai zhongguo chubanshe, 2000.

Ma Xisha 馬西沙. *"Ming, Qing shidai de shouyuan jiao, hunyuan jiao yuanliu"* 明清时代的收元教，混元教源流 [Origins of Ming-Qing Return to the Origin and Primal Chaos teachings]. In *Mingqing yi lai minjian zongjiao de tansuo* 明清以來民間宗教的探索 [An inquiry into popular religion since the Ming-Qing], Wang Chien-ch'uan 王見川 and Chiang Chu-shan 蔣竹山, eds., 81–110. Taibei: Shangding wenhua chubanshe, 1996.

MacInnis, Donald E., *Religious Policy and Practice in Communist China: A Documentary History*. New York: Macmillan/London: Hodder and Stoughton, 1972.

Mitani Takashi 三谷孝 et al. *Mura kara Chūgoku o yomu* 村から中国を読む [Reading China from the village]. Tokyo: Aoki Shoten, 2000.

Momose Hiro 百瀬弘. *"Shinmatsu chokuri shō no sonzu sanshu ni tsuite"* 清末直隷省の村図三種について [Three kinds of village diagrams in late Qing Zhili]. In *Katō hakushi kanreki kinen tōyōshi shūsetsu* 加藤博士還暦記念東洋史集說 [Collected essays in East Asian history in honor of Professor Kato's sixtieth birthday], *Katō hakushi kanreki kinen tōyōshi shūsetsu kankōkai*, ed., 841–860. Tokyo: Fuzanbō, 1941.

Nakamura Tetsuo 中村哲夫. *"Shinmatsu kahoku ni okeru shijōken to shūkyo ken"* 清末華北における市場圏と宗教圏 [Marketing spheres and religious spheres in late Qing North China]. *Shakai Keizai Shigaku* 40 (1974/1975): 1–26.

Naquin, Susan. *Millenarian Rebellion in China: The Eight Trigrams Uprising of 1813*. New Haven, Conn.: Yale University Press, 1976.

———. *Shantung Rebellion: The Wang Lun Uprising of 1774*. New Haven, Conn.: Yale University Press, 1981.

———. "The Transmission of White Lotus Sectarianism in Late Imperial China," In *Popular Culture in Late Imperial China*, David Johnson, Andrew J. Nathan, and Evelyn S. Rawski, eds., 255–291. Berkeley: University of California Press, 1985.

Naquin, Susan, and Yü Chün-fang, eds. *Pilgrims and Sacred Sites in China*. Berkeley: University of California Press, 1992.

Nedostup, Rebecca. "Religion, Superstition, and Governing Society in Nationalist China." Ph.D. diss., Columbia University, 2001.

Needham, Joseph. *Science and Civilisation in China*. Vol. 2. Cambridge: Cambridge University Press, 1956.

Noguchi Testuro 野口鐵郎. *"Zhenkong jiao de xipu"* 真空教的系譜 [Genealogy of the True Emptiness Teaching], translated by Liu T'ien-hsiang 劉天祥. In *Mingqing yi lai minjian zongjiao de tansuo* 明清以來民間宗教的探索 [An inquiry into popular religion since the Ming-Qing], Wang Chien-ch'uan 王見川 and Chiang Chu-shan 蔣竹山, eds., 174–205. Taibei: Shangding wenhua chubanshe, 1996.

O'Leary, Stephen D. "When Prophecy Fails and When It Succeeds: Apocalyptic Prediction and the Reentry into Ordinary Time." In *Apocalyptic Time*, Albert I. Baumgarten, ed. Vol. 86: *Studies in the History of Religions*, 341–362. Leiden: Brill, 2000.

Overmyer, Daniel. *Folk Buddhist Religion: Dissenting Sects in Late Traditional China.* Cambridge, Mass.: Harvard University Press, 1976.

———. "Values in Ming and Ch'ing *Pao-chüan.*" In *Popular Culture in Late Imperial China,* David Johnson, Andrew J. Nathan, and Evelyn S. Rawski, eds., 219–256. Berkeley: University of California Press, 1985.

———. *Precious Volumes: An Introduction to Chinese Sectarian Scriptures from the Sixteenth and Seventeenth Centuries.* Cambridge, Mass.: Harvard University Asia Center/Harvard University Press, 1999.

Ownby, David. "Chinese Millennial Traditions: The Formative Age." *American Historical Review* 104, 5 (December 1999): 1513–1530.

Peill, Arthur D. *The Beloved Physician of Tsang Chou: Life-Work and Letters of Dr. Arthur D. Peill, F.R.C.S.E.* Edited by J. Peill. London: Headley, 1908.

Perry, Elizabeth J. *Rebels and Revolutionaries in North China, 1845–1945.* Stanford, Calif.: Stanford University Press, 1980.

———. *Challenging the Mandate of Heaven: Social Protest and State Power in China.* Armonk, N.Y.: M. E. Sharpe, 2002.

Pittman, Don. *Toward a Modern Chinese Buddhism: Taixu's Reforms.* Honolulu: University of Hawai'i Press, 2001.

Pomerantz, Kenneth. "Power, Gender, and Pluralism in the Cult of the Goddess of Taishan." In *Culture & State in Chinese History: Conventions, Accommodations, and Critiques,* Theodore Huters, R. Bin Wong, and Pauline Yu, eds., 182–204. Stanford, Calif.: Stanford University Press, 1997.

Poo Mu-chou. *In Search of Personal Welfare: A View of Ancient Chinese Religion.* Albany: SUNY Press, 1988.

Prip-Møller, J. *Chinese Buddhist Monasteries: Their Plan and Its Function as a Setting for Buddhist Monastic Life.* Copenhagen: G.E.C. Gad, 1937.

Pu Songling, *Strange Stories from a Chinese Studio,* translated by Herbert Giles. Shanghai: Kelly & Walsh, 1936.

Pu Wenqi 濮文起. *Minjian mimi zongjiao cidian* 民間秘密宗教辭典 [Dictionary of secret popular religion]. Chengdu: Sichuan ci shu chubanshe, 1996.

———. "*Tiandimen diaocha yu yanjiu*" 天地門調查于研究 [Investigation and research into the Heaven and Earth Sect]. *Minjian Zongjiao* 民間宗教 2 (1996): 211–259.

Rawski, Evelyn. "A Historian's Approach to Death Ritual." In *Death Ritual in Late Imperial and Modern China,* James Watson and Evelyn Rawski, eds., 20–34. Berkeley: University of California Press, 1988.

Robbins, Keith, "Institutions and Illusions: The Dilemma of the Modern Ecclesiastical Historian." In *The Materials, Methods and Sources of Ecclesiastical History: Papers Read at the Twelfth Summer Meeting and*

Thirteenth Winter Meeting of the Ecclesiastical Historical Society, Derek Baker, ed., 355–367. New York: Barnes and Noble Books, 1975.

Ruitenbeek, Klaas. *Carpentry and Building in Late Imperial China: A Study of the Fifteenth-Century Carpenter's Manual Lu Ban jing.* Leiden: Brill, 1993.

Sabean, David Warren. *Power in the Blood: Popular Culture and Village Discourse in Early Modern Germany.* New York: Cambridge University Press, 1987.

Sangren, Stephen A. *History and Power in a Chinese Community.* Stanford, Calif.: Stanford University Press, 1987.

Sawada Mizuho 澤田瑞穗. *Kōchū haja shōben* 校注破邪詳辯 [An annotated "Detailed Refutation of Heresies"]. Tokyo: Kokusho Kankokai, 1972.

————. *Hōkan no kenkyū* 寶卷の研究 [Research into precious scrolls]. Tokyo: Kokusho Kankōkai, 1975.

Seiwert, Hubert. "Popular Religious Sects in South-east China: Sect Connections and the Problem of the Luo Jiao/Bailian Jiao Dichotomy." *Journal of Chinese Religions* 20: 33–60.

Shahar, Meir. *Crazy Ji: Chinese Religion and Popular Literature.* Cambridge, Mass.: Harvard University Press and the Harvard University Asia Center, 1998.

Shahar, Meir, and Robert Weller, eds. *Unruly Gods: Society and Divinity in China.* Honolulu: University of Hawai'i Press, 1996.

Shan Min 山民. *Huli xinyang zhi mi* 狐狸信仰之密 [The riddle of belief in foxes]. Beijing: Beijing Renmin chubanshe, 1994.

Shao Yong 紹雍. *Zhongguo huidaomen* 中國會道門 [Chinese sectarians]. Shanghai: Shanghai Renmin chubanshe, 1997.

Shek, Richard Hon-chun. "Religion and Society in the Late Ming: Sectarianism and Popular Thought in Sixteenth- and Seventeenth-Century China." Ph.D. diss., University of California, Berkeley, 1980.

————. "The Revolt of the Zaili, Jindan Sects in Rehe (Jehol), 1891." *Modern China* 6, 2 (April 1980): 161–196.

————. "Millenarianism without Rebellion: The Huangtiao Dao in North China." *Modern China* 8, 3 (July 1982): 305–336.

Siu, Helen F. "Redefining the Market Town through Festivals in South China." In *Town and Country in China: Identity and Perception,* David Faure and Tao Tao Liu eds., 233–249. Houndmills, Basingstoke, Hampshire: Palgrave, in association with St Antony's College, Oxford, 2002.

Skinner, G. William. "Marketing and Social Structure in Rural China." *Journal of Asian Studies* 24, 1 (1964): 3–44; 24, 2 (1965): 195–228; 24, 3 (1965): 363–399.

————. "Rural Marketing in China: Repression and Revival." *China Quarterly* 103 (September 1985): 393–413.

Sung Kuang-yü 宋光宇 *Tiandao Gouchen* 天道鉤沉 [Raising up the heavenly way]. Taibei: Yuanyou chubanshe, 1984.

Suzuki Chūsei 鈴木中正. *"Shinchō chūki ni okeru minkan shūkyō kessha to sono sennen ōkoku undō e no keisha"* 清朝中期に於ける民間宗教結社とその千年王国運動への傾斜 [Popular religious societies in the Mid-Qing and their tendency toward millenarianism]. In *Sonno sennen ōkoku teki minshū undō no kenkyū* [Studies on millenarian popular movements], Suzuki Chūsei, ed., 151–350. Tokyo: Tokyo Daigaku Shuppankai, 1982.

Szonyi, Michael. "The Illusion of Standardizing the Gods: The Cult of the Five Emperors in Late Imperial China," *Journal of Asian Studies* 56 (February 1997): 113–135.

———. *The Ghost Festival in Medieval China.* Princeton, N.J.: Princeton University Press, 1988.

———. *Practicing Kinship: Lineage and Descent in Late Imperial China.* Stanford, Calif.: Stanford University Press, 2002.

Teiser, Stephen F. "Popular Religion." *Journal of Asian Studies* 54, 2 (1995): 378–395.

ter Haar, Barend. *The White Lotus Teaching in Chinese Religious History.* Honolulu: University of Hawai'i Press, 1999.

Vandergeest, Peter, and Nancy Lee Peluso. "Territorialization and State Power in Thailand." *Theory and Society* 24 (June 1995): 385–426.

Von Glahn, Richard. "The Enchantment of Wealth: The God Wutong in the Social History of Jiangnan." *Harvard Journal of Asiatic Studies* 51, 2 (1991): 651–714.

Wang Erh-min 王爾敏. *"Mimi zongjiao yu mimi shehui zhi shengtai huanjing ji shehui gongneng"* 秘密宗教與秘密社會之生態環境及社會功能 [The operating environment and social functions of secret religions and secret societies], *Zhongguo jindai xiandai shi lunji* 中國近代現代史論集. Vol. 2: 59–68. Taibei: Taiwan shang wu yin shu guan, 1985.

Wang Hongkui 王鴻逵. *"Lijiao de qiyuan yu fazhan"* 理教的起源與發展 [The origins and development of Zailijiao], *Tianjin wenshi ziliao xuanji* 天津文史資料輯 52 (1990): 173–183.

Wang Mingming, "Place, Administration and Territorial Cults in Late Imperial China: A Case Study from South Fujian," *Late Imperial China* 16 (1995): 33–79.

Watson, James. "Standardizing the Gods: The Promotion of T'ien Hou ("Empress of Heaven") along the South China Coast, 960–1960." In *Popular Culture in Late Imperial China*, David Johnson, Andrew J. Nathan, and Evelyn S. Rawski, eds., 292–374. Berkeley: University of California Press, 1985.

———. "The Structure of Chinese Funerary Rite: Elementary Forms, Ritual Sequence and the Primacy of Performance." In *Death Ritual in Late*

Imperial and Modern China, James Watson and Evelyn Rawski, eds., 3–19. Berkeley: University of California Press, 1988.

Watson, James, and Evelyn Rawski, eds. *Death Ritual in Late Imperial and Modern China.* Berkeley, University of California Press, 1988.

Welch, Holmes. *The Practice of Chinese Buddhism.* Cambridge, Mass.: Harvard University Press, 1967.

———. *Buddhism under Mao.* Cambridge, Mass.: Harvard University Press, 1972.

Wigen, Kären. "AHR Forum: Bringing Regionalism Back to History: Culture, Power, and Place: The New Landscapes of East Asian Regionalism," *American Historical Review* 104, 4 (October 1999): 1183–1201.

Yang, C. K. *Religion in Chinese Society: A Study of Contemporary Social Functions of Religion and Some of Their Historical Factors.* Berkeley: University of California Press, 1961.

Yang, Martin. *A Chinese Village: Taitou, Shantung Province.* New York: Columbia University Press, 1945.

Yang Qingkun. *"Shiji suo biaoxiande nongcun zigei zizu wenti"* [The problem of village self-sufficiency as revealed in periodic markets]. *Dagong bao,* July 19, 1934.

Yasutomi Ayumu. "Rural Market System in Manchuria." Paper delivered at the Japan Conference of the Association for Asian Studies, Sophia University, Tokyo, June 2001.

Yi Zhe 衣者. *"'Limen gonsuo' de nei mu"* '理門公所'的內幕 [The inner curtain of the *"Zailijiao gongsuo"*]. *Tianjin shi hedong qu wenshi ziliao* 天津市河東區文史資料 3 (1990): 114–126.

Yü, Chün-fang. *Kuan-yin: The Chinese Transformation of Avalokiteśvara.* New York: Columbia University Press, 2001.

Yue Daiyun and Carolyn Wakeman. *To the Storm: The Odyssey of a Revolutionary Chinese Woman.* Berkeley: University of California Press, 1985.

Zhao Dongshu 趙東書. *Lijiao huibian* 礼教汇编 [Compiled materials on the Li Sect]. Taibei: Zhonghua lijiao qingxin tang gongsuo, 1953.

Zhonghua renmin gonghe guo gong'anbu 中华人民共和国公安部 [Department of Public Security of the People's Republic of China. *Fandong Huidaomen Jieshao* 反動會道門介紹 [An introduction to reactionary sects]. Beijing: Qunzhong chubanshe, 1985.

Zhu Wentong 朱文通. "*Guanyu Mingqing shiqi minjian mimi zongjiao de jige wenti*" 關於明清時期民間秘密宗教的幾個問題 [Concerning a few questions about secret popular religion during the Ming and Qing], *Hebei Xuekan* 河北學刊 6 (1992): 99–103.

Index